UNPARENTED

UNPARENTED

Healing from Narcissistic and Borderline Family Systems

Dr. Ashley Quiroz, Psy.D.

Copyright © 2025 by Dr. Ashley Quiroz, Psy.D.

All rights reserved. No part of this publication may be reproduced, distributed, or transmitted in any form or by any electronic or mechanical means, including information storage and retrieval systems, without a prior written permission from the publisher, except by reviewers, who may quote brief passages in a review, and certain other noncommercial uses permitted by the copyright law.

ISBN: 979-8-89228-810-1 (Paperback)
ISBN: 979-8-89228-811-8 (Hardcover)
ISBN: 979-8-89228-812-5 (eBook)

Printed in the United States of America

CONTENTS

PROLOGUE..xiii

PART 1   The Memoir 1

CHAPTER 1: "Don't Deck the Halls" 3
CHAPTER 2: "Watch for Geese"..8
CHAPTER 3: "You're Getting It" 14
CHAPTER 4: "Elevator Romance".....................................19
CHAPTER 5: "My Father's Many Daughters" 23
CHAPTER 6: "The Poison"..26
CHAPTER 7: "Marble Rye"..29
CHAPTER 8: "The Painted Horses" 34
CHAPTER 9: "Drugs or Religion"......................................37
CHAPTER 10: "The Motherland" 40
CHAPTER 11: "Red like a lobster" 45
CHAPTER 12: "I don't know what to tell you" 50
CHAPTER 13: "The Green" 55
CHAPTER 14: "Butter" 60
CHAPTER 15: "A Special Kind of Freedom" 65
CHAPTER 16: "Witch Trials and Chowder" 71

CHAPTER 17: "A Different Kind of Sickness" 75

CHAPTER 18: "Hawaii is Where Honeymooners Go" 79

CHAPTER 19: "A Female Role Model" 83

CHAPTER 20: "Don't Call Me Doctor" 88

CHAPTER 21: "The Facebook Reunion" 94

CHAPTER 22: "The Transformation" 102

CHAPTER 23: "Not Even The Ocean" 106

CHAPTER 24: "Holiday Tension" 110

CHAPTER 25: "The Rebuilding" 113

CHAPTER 26: "What House?" 118

CHAPTER 27: "Being the Parent" 123

CHAPTER 28: "Congratulations" 126

CHAPTER 29: "The Dress" 130

CHAPTER 30: "Just Take a Nap" 133

CHAPTER 31: "The Birthday" 136

CHAPTER 32: "The Confirmation" 141

CHAPTER 33: "The Reflection" 144

CHAPTER 34: "It All Started to Make Sense" 147

PART 2   Concepts and Research 149

Understanding Narcissism 151

    Subtypes of Narcissistic Personality Disorder 154

        Grandiose/Overt Narcissists 154

        Vulnerable/Covert Narcissists 154

        High-Functioning/Exhibitionistic Narcissists 155

Defining Cluster B 156

Recognizing Borderline Personality Disorder (BPD) 158

- Subtypes of Borderline Personality Disorder 161
  - Petulant Type 161
  - Self-Destructive Type 162
  - Discouraged Type 162
  - Impulsive Type 163
- **The Romantic Attraction Between Narcissists and Borderlines** .. 164
  - Assortative Mating 164
  - Emotional Immaturity 168
  - Imbalance of Power 170
- **The Four Types of Narcissistic Relationships** 171
  - The Pairings 172
    - The Toxic Relationship 172
    - The Manipulative Relationship 172
    - The Perfect Match 172
    - The Rescue Relationship 173
  - Subtle Toxicity 174
  - Superficiality of Relations 176
- **The Narcissistic Cycle of Abuse** 177
  - The Stages 178
    - Idealization & Love Bombing 178
    - Devaluation 178
    - Breadcrumbing & Hoovering 179
    - Discard 180
    - The Cycle Repeats 180
  - Why These Relationships Perpetuate 181
  - Codependency Manifesting 182

Gaslighting: Understanding Its Forms and How It Silences You 183
    Forms of Gaslighting 184
        Withholding 184
        Countering 184
        Blocking 185
        Trivializing 185
    The Cumulative Effect of Gaslighting 186
Other Manipulation Tactics Within Romantic Relationships .. 188
    DARVO 188
    Traumatic Invalidation 189
The Narcissist as a Parent 192
    Subtypes of the Narcissistic Parent 193
        Cerebral Narcissistic Parent 193
        Malignant Narcissistic Parent 194
        Antagonistic or Competitive Narcissistic Parent 194
    Key Parenting Dynamics 194
        Competition 194
        Smear Campaigns and Family Denial 195
        Disregard for Feelings 196
        Manipulation and Self-Doubt 198
        Scapegoating 199
        Triangulation and Parentification 200
        Playing the Victim 201
        Acting Out 202
    Types of Neglect 203
The Narcissistic Family Tree 204
    Key Roles 204

- The Orbiting Spouse 204
- The Golden Child and The Scapegoat 204
- The Flying Monkeys 204
- Family Tree Dynamics 205
  - Preferential Treatment 205
  - Setup to Fail 206
  - Betrayal Blindness 206
  - Trauma Bonding 207
  - Poor Coping Skills 207
  - Conditional Love 208
- The Influence on the Offspring: Romantic Relationships 209
- The Challenge of Healthy Connection 210
- Workaholism as Avoidance 211
- An Obsession with Justice 211
- Anxiety as Adaptation 212
- Emotional Stunting 212

The Aftermath of Trauma 213
- Loss of Voice: Invisibility as a Survival Strategy 213
- Isolation and the Strain of Social Interpretation 214
- Attachment Styles as Related to Traumatic Experience 215
  - Disorganized Attachment: The Fear of Safety 216
  - Anxious Attachment: The Clingy and Uncertain 218
  - Avoidant Attachment: The Distant and Self-Protective 219
- Rupture and Repair 221
- The Lasting Scars of Eggshell Parenting: Trauma, Dissociation, and Emotional Confusion 223
- Narcissistic Trauma's Impact on the Growing Brain 226

    Oxidative Stress..227
    Interpreting and Relating to our Environment after Trauma ...228

Introspective Questions 230

PART 3   Finding Wellness..231

    The Silent Epidemic: Understanding the
        Rise of Estrangement 234

    The Gray Rock Method: A Tool for
        Managing Narcissistic Abuse...238

    Dual Awareness: Reconnecting Mind and Body 239

    Grounding: Reconnecting with the Present Moment..........241

    Self-Care: Nourishing the Soul...242

    Examining Ambition and Burnout 244

    Breath Work: Regulating Our Nervous System...................245

    Meditative Moments: Cultivating Stillness.........................247

    Choosing Our Responses: Empowerment
        Through Awareness..248

    Development of Self-Awareness:
        The Art of Conscious Living..249

    Learning as a Tool: The Power of Curiosity........................ 251

    Spirituality: A Journey of Self-Discovery
        Through Astrology...253

    Non-Attachment: Embracing Freedom
        Through Letting Go...255

    Finding Your Voice: From Silence to Empowerment 256

    The Gift of Living: Healing Through
        Simplicity and Self-Compassion.......................................258

Bibliography..263

Legal Disclaimer

This memoir contains the author's personal memories, perceptions, and subjective impressions. It is a work of personal recollection, and, as such, certain events are described as the author remembers them; memory is inherently fallible and may be incomplete, inaccurate, or affected by the passage of time. For purposes of privacy, confidentiality, and narrative coherence, the author has altered, combined, or omitted names, identifying details, timelines, locations, and events.

The views, opinions, and interpretations expressed herein are solely those of the author and are not presented as verifiable statements of fact regarding any individual's character, conduct, motives, or behavior. Any resemblance to real persons, living or deceased, is based on the author's subjective experience and is not intended, nor should it be construed, as factual representation or assertion about those individuals.

The author expressly disclaims any intention to defame, harm, disparage, or misrepresent any person, entity, or group. No statements in this work should be interpreted as allegations of wrongdoing or factual claims about any identifiable individual. Additionally, nothing in this memoir is intended to constitute medical, psychological, therapeutic, or professional advice. Any references to health, trauma, treatment, or healing reflect the author's personal experiences and should not be relied upon as guidance or instruction; readers should seek the advice of qualified professionals for any such concerns.

PROLOGUE

"An inflated consciousness is always egocentric and conscious of nothing but its own existence. It is incapable of learning from the past, incapable of understanding contemporary events and incapable of drawing right conclusions about the future. It is hypnotized by itself and therefore cannot be argued with. It inevitably dooms itself to calamities that must strike it dead."

- Carl Jung (1968)

It is a strange thing to realize, after decades of living, that you are only just beginning to truly know yourself. To see that so much of what you believed about your life was shaped by secrecy, false narratives, and the agendas of others. These forces quietly sculpted your sense of self. And yet, with awareness comes freedom: the chance to release yourself from distortions, to step into a life rooted in peace and self-acceptance.

Some forms of harm are easy to spot: a black eye for missing curfew, a child left hungry. These wounds announce themselves. But others remain hidden. They unfold in subtle moments over years, disguised as "normal." The excitement that's met with indifference. The feelings dismissed. The milestones unnoticed by those you love most.

When we voice our needs, we are called "too sensitive." When we set boundaries, we are labeled "the problem." Because these wounds are understated, they often remain unnamed, passed silently from one generation to the next. From the outside, life may look fine. Inside, something vital has been denied.

We know children need food, shelter, clothing. But emotional needs; the need to feel seen, heard, valued, are too often treated as luxuries. The truth is: trauma is not only what happened to us, but also what didn't. Our lives are mosaics, shaped as much by absence as by presence. These hidden traumas matter. They shape who we become, how we move through the world, and how we love.

These writings are for those who have lived under the quiet shadow of emotional neglect, often at the hands of caregivers unable to meet them, sometimes struggling with narcissistic or borderline traits. This is a space to name what was unnamed, and to bring light to what was silenced.

Let this be a cleansing.

Let this be the beginning of a new story: your story.

PART I

THE MEMOIR

CHAPTER 1:
"Don't Deck the Halls"

"Here," he said, shoving a crumpled manila envelope into my hands as he brushed past me. It looked as if it had survived the soak cycle of a washing machine.

Inside: my birth certificate, a few stained scribbles, sun-bleached macaroni art from summer camp twenty years ago.

My father had cleaned out his condo, discarding anything he didn't want, especially anything of mine.

I stared at the envelope, heavy with things he couldn't wait to be rid of, and wondered: Is it normal to feel sad about this? I was never sure. I'd always been told I was too sensitive.

Sentimentality was never his department. That belonged to my mother, who stuffed crayon drawings and old birthday cards into bulging drawers, only to hear him bark from the next room, "Just throw it out!" One was a hoarder. The other, a minimalist. You can probably guess which was which.

In our house, holiday decorations were banned. Anything "excessive" would be mocked until it disappeared. The only décor allowed were artifacts he approved of: Japanese prints of geisha girls fanning themselves,

Egyptian chairs etched with hieroglyphics. Living there felt less like home and more like a museum curated by someone else's taste.

"Your father doesn't let me decorate," my mother would whisper, as if confessing a family secret. Even as a child I wondered: Aren't you an adult? Why do you need permission? What would happen if you just… did it?

I didn't have the language for it then, but I felt it in my body, a stomachache that never went away.

She seemed spellbound by even his most ordinary habits, bending herself into pitiful shapes to please him. Her desperation sometimes flipped into rage, sudden and sharp, sparked by jealousy or something trivial. One moment she was fawning, the next her face darkened, her voice rising into a storm that rattled the walls. My chest would tighten; my fingertips buzzed with anxiety as her anger filled the house.

Possessiveness threaded through their marriage. My mother policed my father's relationships, dismissing friends as "bad influences" or insisting others didn't have his best interests at heart. At one point, she barred him from attending his own brother's wedding, "too far out of the way," she said. Another time she refused to let him pick his brother up from the airport. "He can take a taxi."

These weren't simple logistics. They were quiet acts of control, small severances of family ties. Years later, my uncle told me how much it hurt to look out on his wedding day and see his brother missing. But honesty like that was never possible with my father. He couldn't or wouldn't hear it.

Over time, it wasn't just his brother who disappeared from his life, it was everyone. Anyone who encouraged him to travel, to think for himself, to want more, was gradually cut out. My mother behaved as if her value decreased in direct proportion to the time he spent with others.

Even small things could ignite a fire. Once, my father stepped outside to check the mail without a shirt on. You would have thought someone had been shot from the way my mother screamed. She accused him of trying to get attention from neighborhood women, her outrage spiraling into a full-blown spectacle. He looked bewildered, unsure of what he had done wrong, but after that day he was never shirtless outside again. When you were on the receiving end of one of her overreactions, you learned quickly: it was safer to comply.

It wasn't just strangers she resented. She was jealous of his mother, too. Visiting my grandmother was brutal, not because of who she was, but because of the minefield around it. There were three parts. First, the prelude: my mother throwing tantrums about why we shouldn't visit. Second, the visit itself: her watching every interaction with narrowed eyes, dissecting my grandmother's apartment or her cooking as if it were infested. And finally, the aftermath: a vicious debrief where she accused my father of betrayal for not defending her against imagined slights.

"You just sat there like an idiot," she would persevere. "What kind of man lets his wife be treated like that?"

I watched my father shrink a little smaller after every attack. Sometimes he argued back. Other times he just went silent, retreating to his office to lick invisible wounds.

Phone calls with his mother were no safer. If she mentioned she wasn't feeling well, my father's concern would trigger my mother's rage. "She's faking it. I can't believe you fall for it every time," she'd sneer, before launching into descriptions of her own ailments, louder, more dramatic, demanding his full attention. Visiting, calling, even thinking about his mother became exhausting, guilt-ridden tasks.

Over the years, visits grew fewer and fewer, until my grandmother died and my mother finally sighed with visible relief, as if a competitor had left the field.

As a child, I watched it all. My father was like a tiger pacing behind glass, worn down, panting, resigned. My mother had only two emotional settings: euphoric monologues where the world was glorious, or dark spirals where everyone was out to get her. "People are no good, you can't trust anyone these days." There was no in-between. The weather she created set the forecast for everyone else.

My father was usually painfully passive, saying little until he reached a breaking point. When he finally exploded, it was terrifying. I was four or five, throwing a tantrum, slamming my bedroom door and locking it. He began yelling, "I'm going to break in there and cream you!" His voice reverberated through the door as he pounded and shouted, words blurring together in his rage.

I sat against the wall, too scared to unlock it, praying it was a nightmare I could wake from. Sometimes I waited until his footsteps receded down the hallway. He didn't really want to deal with the door. That would mean dealing with my mother.

The fighting between my parents was constant and trivial, but the consequences were volcanic. I remember thinking they might kill each other over something as small as when to stop for gas.

One minute they were debating, the next they were face-to-face, screaming, threats flying through the air. Even before I knew the word "compatibility," I knew they didn't have it. I often fantasized about them divorcing, just so the house could finally be quiet.

Worse were the times my mother dragged me into their war. She mocked my father's height, called him a pushover, degraded him in front of me. It was confusing and ugly. I didn't want to be her sounding board. I was just a kid.

My father's answer was silence. Withdrawal. Disappearing into himself. Their conflicts ended without resolution, just an uneasy truce until the next eruption.

At home, suspicion hung in the air like smoke. Any time you came back from somewhere, you had to recount every detail: who you spoke to, where you went, what was said. The questions were endless, exhausting. By the end, I often wondered if I had done something wrong, even when I hadn't. Self-doubt became my constant companion. My father mistook my quietness for shyness, never realizing the environment itself was impossible for a child to navigate.

My mother's paranoia stretched beyond our house. On phone calls she would suddenly stop mid-sentence, whispering, "Someone's listening." She invented a code phrase, "Start the tracer!"—then hung up and called back, proud of her ingenuity.

I would just stare at her blankly, wondering: Am I the only one who sees how strange this is? Everywhere we went, danger lurked in her mind, scam artists, thieves, conspiracies. If you questioned her, she'd snap, turning suspicion or anger onto you. It was a losing battle.

This was the soil I grew up in: suspicion, silence, invalidation. Even without the words, I knew, something about this wasn't right.

CHAPTER 2:
"Watch for Geese"

Let me go back in time for a moment to give you a fuller picture of who my parents really were. My mother had been a schoolteacher for a few years and studied library science, but she ended her career as soon as she met my father. I was born shortly after, and she embraced the stay-at-home mom lifestyle at least, in theory.

Ironically, I wish I could tell you something she taught me, but we didn't have those kinds of moments. She seemed like she had once been an enthusiastic teacher, planning creative activities, decorating her classroom. Her face lit up whenever she recalled it. But when it came to me, that spark was gone.

She seemed distant, drained, like life had been flattened out into one long sigh.

At one point, I came across some of her old classroom decorations stuffed into a crate down in our basement, colorful bulletin boards, construction paper art and I would wonder: Who was that woman? I wished I could have seen her in action. Maybe then I would have understood her better.

By the time I came along, her days consisted of occasional laundry folding and calling relatives, with The Young and the Restless constantly humming in the background. She was hooked on the drama. The chaos on the screen or within the family kept her company.

She wasn't the lively, scrapbooking socialite type you sometimes hear about or maybe I just didn't get that version of her. She had me at 39 years old, and as I would later learn, there's a difference between a "young 40" and an "old 40." She was the latter.

I got the sedentary, "leave-me-alone" version. Sometimes I wondered why she even had children at all. It didn't seem like she enjoyed the process or even wanted to be present for it. It felt like she wanted the title "mother" without the responsibilities that came with it: teaching, listening, guiding, connecting.

The truth is, most of what I learned growing up didn't come from my parents.

One source of knowledge came from being babysat by my older brother, whom I'll talk about later. He was one of the few people who invested time in teaching me things, showing me how to count to twenty, explaining who the President was, taking me to places like the Museum of Television and Radio, where you could put on a headset and watch shows from the past eighty years. On another occasion, he introduced me to Indian food, and we made tie-dye shirts in the washing machine with some of his old white tees.

My father, to his credit, taught me how to ride a bike, despite not knowing how himself. He hoisted me onto the seat and gave a giant shove. Off I went. My eyes widened with fear, but it was what I needed to figure it out, feet pedaling furiously. Most of my education about life, however, came from the kids at school.

At school, I watched the other girls closely. Their young moms talked to them about everything from hairstyles to sex, so casually. I envied them. I studied them. I tried to live through them.

But it wasn't the same.

While the others focused on building social and cognitive skills appropriate for their age, I was just trying to make it through the day without drowning in my own mental fog. As I got older, the gap widened. In middle school, when the others were dating, experimenting with makeup, growing into themselves, I still felt lost, like a misplaced, left-behind child.

Part of that feeling came from the fact that my parents were about fifteen years older than most of the other parents. The generational void between us became more visible as the years progressed. Parental age is not always a factor that necessarily makes a difference in a scenario like this, but when paired with minimal relatability, it created a relationship that felt deeply disconnected to me.

When I got my period for the first time, it was uncomfortable and humiliating to ask my mother to take me to the store. She made a passing comment about how "good girls" should only use maxi pads, that tampons were "not for girls like me," whatever that meant. I didn't know what she was talking about. But I got the message loud and clear: Don't ask. Don't talk. Leave it alone.

When my friends would casually talk about their periods with their mothers, I was stunned. How were they able to just bring it up? How was it considered normal?

I was also probably the last girl in my grade to start wearing a bra. During gym class, while the other girls slipped T-shirts over their sports bras, I still had to undress like a little kid, exposed and mortified.

At thirteen, I worked up the nerve to ask my mother if we could buy one. Her response? "What do you need that for?" Annoyed. Dismissive.

Looking back, I wonder what she thought I was asking for. Did she think wanting a bra meant I was trying to be promiscuous? Was she just irritated by my attempt at growing up? Some parents prioritize control over connection, and control often means keeping the child as childlike as possible. Maybe my request for a bra didn't fit the image she wanted to keep of me. Whatever it was, everything between us carried this awkward, tense energy.

I craved simplicity.

UNPARENTED

I craved care.

I wished she would take my hand and lead me in some regard.

After my continued pushing, my mother ended up bringing me to some 80-year-old Jewish woman's shop, lined with the most matronly cream-colored bras. The saleswoman crept around the store, looking as if she were straining her osteoporosis, and held up a few choices with her brown, speckled, wrinkled hands. I picked the first one I saw in hopes of getting out of there as soon as possible. What should have been a small, simple rite of passage felt humiliating. I finally understood that saying about wanting to crawl under a rock and die.

We didn't talk about sex in my family. We didn't talk about the body.

We didn't talk, period.

If a raunchy scene came on TV, my mother would scrunch up her face and squeal, "Ewwww!" like a child. It confused me.

Once, I even asked, "Why 'ew'? They're just kissing." She didn't answer. I think sex made her so uncomfortable she had to regress into childishness just to avoid her own feelings. Maybe she thought it would deter me from the subject, too. If anything, it just made me more puzzled.

She wanted attention from others, but true intimacy seemed to terrify her. When she had it, she didn't seem to know what to do with it.

Growing up, nudity, sexuality even basic bodily autonomy, all felt forbidden. I learned to change my clothes as quickly as possible, to hide under baggy clothing, to feel ashamed of simply existing. I realize now: that shame wasn't mine. It was hers. It leaked onto me. But deep down, I didn't feel the way she did. I didn't want to hide.

Even though we had almost nothing in common, I still wanted to spend time with my mother. But I can barely remember us doing anything together besides grocery shopping at Waldbaum's or an occasional trip to the drugstore for stickers and household items. She seemed afraid to go too far without my father, afraid to venture out into the world alone.

There was one occasion, however, that stood out. She once took me to a park near our house, where a big pond shimmered in the middle, surrounded by white and lavender water lilies. Hundreds of Canadian geese squawked and floated across the water. I, about five or six years old, sank into the moment, watching them flap their wings to shake off the water that streamed down their velvety black feathers. I was entranced.

And then, in an instant, the moment shattered.

I felt a sharp jolt, my mother yanking my arm hard enough to make it red and swollen.

I looked down at my own arm, confused, like it belonged to someone else.

"You stepped right in their poop! What's wrong with you?" she snapped. "Don't you look where you're going?"

She dragged me into a public bathroom and aggressively scrubbed my shoes while muttering insults under her breath. The scolding went on for what felt like an hour.

Why had I done something so stupid? The whole situation made me sad; our rare outing, and I had ruined it somehow.

I dissociated for the first time that afternoon.

I floated out of my body, watching from somewhere far away.

A year later, it happened again.

We were at a restaurant, the kind that brings you endless breadsticks and salad. Excited, I bit into a juicy tomato, and somehow, it splattered across the table onto her new fancy blouse.

The rage that erupted from her was instant and volcanic, berating me in the middle of the restaurant like I had committed some unspeakable crime. I remember how vividly I felt it, even now, thirty years later: the burning shame, the desire to disappear, the way I sank into myself. I couldn't tell her how these situations made me feel, because it would only make it worse.

These moments taught me more than words ever could: that I was an inconvenience. That joy was dangerous, and that it was safer to stay small, silent, and unseen. Most of all, that there were things we didn't talk about things we couldn't talk about.

Not then.

And not for a very long time.

CHAPTER 3:
"You're Getting It"

I turned sixteen before I got my ears pierced for the first time with a friend of my mother's, who couldn't believe I hadn't done it yet. I was the only girl I knew without pierced ears, just one of many things that made me feel different.

I used to admire all the shiny colors of earrings the girls at school wore, how they caught the light, dangling through their hair. Why did it always feel like I was living vicariously through others instead of being the one doing the living?

I had asked countless times to get them pierced, but my mother always said she "didn't believe in it" and that it was "ruining your body." It reminded me of what I call "Catholic School Syndrome," where you're forced to suppress all your carnal urges but instead of turning into a chaste nun like they intended, you just end up with a Britney Spears "Hit Me Baby" vibe.

I ended up with an affinity for tattoos and piercings as an adult, and only God knows if that's a coincidence.

Even the first time I got my nails done was with another family friend; never with my mother. She wasn't one to get her nails done; she said she didn't like other people touching her. It never occurred to her that it might be something I would like to do. Generally, if she wasn't interested in something, we didn't do it at all.

I dreamed of having the kind of mom who I could get my nails done with, take a walk with, and talk about life. Most people have big, exciting fantasies, but that was mine. I wanted those firsts to be with her.

During the day, my mother would often sit in her bedroom and stare off, as if deep in thought, or maybe thinking about nothing at all. Later, I realized this was her version of dissociation: a way to divert attention from being present, from being fully aware of herself and her life. She always seemed internally preoccupied and didn't say much unless we had company over. Then she would talk endlessly about the latest news, animated and lively, as if she had just woken up from a long sleep.

It was like there were two different people living inside her. How could each side be so different from the other? She hid well what I think was actually a very introverted person. Ask most people, and they'd say she was outgoing and talkative — and they wouldn't be wrong. They just wouldn't be right, either.

The dissociations manifested in various ways. One of the ways she detached was by watching the Home Shopping Network or QVC for a good portion of the day. From what I can remember, it was almost always on, flickering in the background as soon as the soap operas grew tiresome.

I'd watch her short, stubby fingers poke through the dial of our old rotary phone whenever something caught her eye: black pants and sweater sets ("They make you look thin," she'd say), whatever tennis bracelet or necklace was featured that day, or some random kitchen gizmo she was convinced she couldn't live without.

Packages arrived every other day, and she'd hide them strategically before my father got home. Of course, since he handled all the finances, he would see the charges at the end of the month, and the fights would start like clockwork.

I'd hear them screaming behind their closed bedroom door. Sometimes the fights ended in returns; sometimes they ended in tears. But it never stopped her from continuing the cycle the following month.

It was like the women on the screen were hypnotists, spinning stories she couldn't resist. Every sales pitch promised a better life, one tiny object at a time. Even a homemade ice cream maker with matching bowls became essential. We had enough clip-on earrings delivered to send one back to every little child in China.

Most of the time, it felt like my mother was living on another planet, if not from dissociation, then from delusion. In response to these distortions, she created this perfectionist image of herself as a mother: generous, doting, indulgent. Over time, she built an entire narrative around it, complete with a catchphrase: "You're getting it," she'd say, envisioning me waltzing through stores getting whatever I wanted.

It was bizarre, because it couldn't have been further from my firsthand experience, often being overlooked so her own needs could take center stage. When I finally told her that wasn't my experience, it spiraled. She snapped, "No matter what you do, it's never enough for her."

If I contradicted her regarding this image she had of me, especially in front of her friends, she became enraged. It felt like I was exposing her, but no one was looking anyway. Afterward, she'd scold me, warning, "Don't contradict!" I didn't even fully understand what that meant at the time, only that I had said something that pissed her off. I was dumbfounded at where these imaginary constructs of herself had even come from. It honestly made me question her sanity.

My mother had other phrases too, repeated like a wind-up doll or one of those toys where you pull the string to hear a moo or oink.

If I declined to do something she asked, it was, "After all I've done for you, that's the thanks I get."

If I didn't shower her with praise, it was, "You're so ungrateful."

If I disagreed, it was, "You're talking nonsense. You don't know what you're talking about."

Most of the time, I did know exactly what I was talking about. But with her, you were either a loyal ally or a traitor, based purely on whether you agreed. It was a treacherous setup. I either had to abandon myself and lie, or endure her disappointment and rage. She made me feel like I owed her eternal gratitude for a debt I could never repay.

When I mustered the courage to tell her how I really felt, it was an exercise in dread and anxiety. Even as a little kid, I wrote her letters, desperate for her to understand how she made me feel. They were disregarded.

I told her more than once that I didn't feel loved; that if I disappeared, her life would go on exactly the same. Her response was always the same: "That's all in your head. You're not seeing it right." She never explored why I felt that way. Never offered warmth or reassurance. I would immediately shut down in the face of her denial. There was no room for nuance with her. I could explain my reasoning carefully, calmly, but it didn't matter. Healthy communication was a foreign concept.

As an adult, phone conversations with my mother became something I dreaded before, during, and well after they ended. She never initiated the call, but every time I reached out, she'd say, "Oh, I was just going to call you, but I didn't want to bother you." Every time. I don't know if that was guilt over how one-sided things were, or if she actually believed it. Maybe it was just another way to maintain control; making it seem like I needed her more than she needed me.

She dominated the calls, turning them into monologues. Toward the end, she'd toss in a question about me, but if I started answering, she quickly turned the spotlight back to herself. I could feel her boredom through the phone line. If it wasn't gossip or somehow about her, it didn't hold her attention.

Much of her conversation centered around trashing other people, which left a sour taste in my mouth. I often wondered how she talked about me to others, but some things are better left unknown.

Despite rarely leaving the house, she always had endless chaotic stories about her daily grievances, delivered with the drama of a radio host narrating the news. Oddly enough, even though I was the one who called, she was always the one to decide when the conversation ended. If I tried to wind down, she steamrolled right over me unless she was the one ready to say goodbye.

My parents both believed the child should cater to the parent, not the other way around. And this was no exception. One day, after years of this dynamic, I finally said, "Mom, you're ignoring that I said I needed to get off the phone." Her enraged reply was unforgettable: "Where do you have to go? You don't have anything else to do."

I nearly dropped the phone. She had no idea what I had planned, but she didn't care. In her mind, she was the most important thing. Time, like everything else, revolved around her needs. That was how her mind worked.

CHAPTER 4:
"Elevator Romance"

My mother was never comfortable saying "I love you." I'd say it to her at the end of a phone call, and she would either just hang up or reply, "Thank you."

"Thank you?" What in the world was that? Maybe you say that to a romantic partner when you're not ready to say it back, but to your daughter? Why were emotions so uncomfortable for her? Every unrequited sentiment stung, even when I wasn't entirely sure I meant it myself. I longed to connect with her. It feels foolish now, trying to create a bond with someone who was never comfortable with herself, let alone anyone else. I can probably count on one hand the number of times she hugged or kissed me as a child.

Instead, my mother seemed to constantly seek love through acts of service. You couldn't walk into a room without being tasked with something.

"Can you just fold that laundry over there? Thanks."

"Could you fix this television? It's not working."

There was always something. You felt trapped, because saying no wasn't just declining a favor—it meant you were the ungrateful child who lived rent-free and didn't help her mother. She did the same thing to my father and brother. No one was immune. You were either "helpful" or "lazy," with no middle ground. She was also a master of dry begging: asking for what she wanted without asking directly.

"Oh, this suitcase is so heavy. I wish I had someone to help…"

"Your makeup is so beautiful. I don't even know where to buy that stuff anymore…"

These were subtle tests. If you didn't immediately offer your help, there would be consequences: sulking, coldness, guilt-tripping. It was manipulative, a way to get what she wanted while preserving the image of being independent and "low-maintenance," even though she was anything but.

Riding in the car with her required mental preparation; deep breathing, and maybe a glass of wine if you had it. It didn't matter who was driving; the experience was always the same. She'd clutch the door handle dramatically and shriek, "Watch the guy on your left!" or she'd grab her hair and scream, "Slow down! You're going to get us all killed!" even if the other car was a hundred yards away.

The agitation she created was so thick you could cut it with a knife, and the rides almost always ended in a screaming match. My father would snap and tell her to be quiet, which would only enrage her more.

Cue the next act: a long, tearful retelling of a car accident she had thirty years ago, which she felt justified her outlandish behavior, as if we were hearing about it for the first time. I could recite the entire story by heart. I used to wonder how someone could experience something so regular as driving in a car and never grow, never heal, never even try. It felt emblematic of the rest of her: wounded, stagnant, stuck.

It's worth noting: if a stranger was driving, especially someone she wanted to impress, she could magically keep quiet the entire ride. Miraculously, she was "healed."

My mother didn't have many long-term friends. She would collect them during her extroverted, smiling bursts and lose them just as easily when her critical eye or insecurities took over. There were a few, a former colleague here, an old school friend there, but eventually, everyone did something she couldn't forgive.

There was always a difference between how she treated women and how she treated men. Around women, she was guarded, competitive, easily offended. Around men, she transformed: flirtatious, giggly, suddenly soft and compassionate. Her voice would change; higher, more helpless. She would smile so much it seemed painful, as if she had read somewhere that this was how to attract a man in the latest Cosmopolitan. I often wondered if other people could see what I was seeing, but no one seemed to.

There was a man in her condo building, we'll call him Jax, known for being friendly with everyone. One day, we were riding the elevator with him.

"Hello today! How are you?" he said cheerfully.

My mother lit up like a Christmas tree, suddenly speaking in this slow, syrupy voice. As soon as he exited, she beamed, "He seems interested in me. Did you see how he looked at me?"

Meanwhile, Jax was married and, from my view, had spoken to her no differently than he spoke to anyone else in the building. But she loved to rewrite interactions to suit whatever story made her feel special. She could idealize or vilify a situation depending on the narrative she needed. I found it strange, even disturbing. Each encounter like this made me feel further away from her, as if there was no shared reality between us. It made her feel unrelatable, untrustworthy.

Men could do no wrong in her eyes. Women were opponents. She told endless stories of women betraying her, a friend dating her ex, another stealing her job interview, another taking "the good room" on a cruise.

Meanwhile, my father and brother? Permanent hall passes. Me? I lived in detention.

I remember a time when a family friend, Carol, finally confronted her about how selfish she could be, how she never asked about Carol's family, how every conversation revolved around herself. I felt relief wash over me. Someone else saw it. Someone else understood what I was seeing.

Carol's son had been sick for months, and after countless conversations, my mother had never once asked how he was doing. When Carol pointed this out, my mother launched into a long, defensive monologue about how "inaccurate" it was to feel that way. There was no apology, no curiosity, no self-reflection.

And just like that, she ex-communicated Carol. Applications for honest feedback were not accepted here.

Every relationship she had seemed unstable, and almost all ended at some point. I realized early that confronting her wasn't an option. It only led to abandonment. So I turned inward.

Barring the occasional chaos, my childhood was mostly quiet and lonely. I spent hours outside, building snowmen in the winter or stuffing dried leaves into jack-o'-lantern trash bags in the fall. I can still smell the rich soil in the spring, and still hear the crunch of ice under my boots. I'd wander down the street to the cul-de-sac, squeeze through a hole in the fence, and swing by myself in the empty playground until the twilight sky turned dark.

Most of my childhood memories were solitary.

I found companionship in David the Gnome on Nickelodeon or in sending my Barbies on elaborate picnics. I dreamed of my mother picking up a doll to play with me, to join me, but that was something she didn't know how to do.

True connection comes through the nonverbals: the attunement, the lingering eye contact, the soothing voice. These silent gestures tell us we are safe, seen, loved. But with my mother, there was none of that.

I disappeared into my imagination instead.

I believe that's where my introversion was born.

CHAPTER 5:
"My Father's Many Daughters"

My father was easily someone I looked up to as a kid, mostly because he was the calmer one out of my two parents, and I paired that calmness with salvation. My mother's emotional oscillations made me cling to him, hoping to dodge whatever the wrath of the day was about.

Occasionally, after dinner, he would sit on the edge of my bed and read me a story. I don't remember the stories themselves, just the lines on his face, the way his eyes moved across the page. I was simply happy he was there with me.

Both of my parents always felt mysterious, like strangers living in the same house. They rarely shared much of themselves. I would gather bits and pieces about them the way a bird might collect scraps to build a nest, overhearing their quiet conversations, connecting the dots alone. That's how I learned that my father had been married several times before he met my mother.

One particular mystery lived on our wall: a framed photo of a baby girl, hanging quietly in the upstairs hallway. I used to stare at it often, wondering who she was. One day, after much persistence, I finally got an answer. Her name was Sarah. My father and his first wife had struggled to conceive, suffering multiple miscarriages before finally having Sarah — only to discover she carried Tay-Sachs, a cruel genetic disorder with no cure. Sarah, unfortunately, passed away shortly after birth.

After that loss, they adopted a daughter.

It's hard for me to imagine my father parenting anyone, ironic as that might sound. I was told that the relationship with his adoptive daughter was tumultuous, full of discord, drug use, and theft as she got older. "She broke into the liquor cabinet!" my mother would say, dramatizing the dysfunction with her usual flair. When his daughter was old enough, she left and rarely spoke to my father again.

I often wondered if she had felt the same things I did: the isolation, the yearning for connection, the unspoken feeling of being unwanted. Maybe her destructive choices were a way of showing her pain. Or maybe she felt nothing like me at all, and it was just my heart grasping for someone else who might understand.

My father's first marriage ended in flames, and true to form, he moved quickly on to the next distraction instead of sitting with the grief. On a flight to Israel, he met his next love. I imagine the conversation: she probably complimented his shirt, he probably beamed at the attention, and soon enough, they "discovered" a connection; the kind you can find with anyone if you're determined enough.

Their relationship progressed quickly, until one day she disclosed that she was dying of cancer. Shattering news to find out as your feelings are developing for someone. They married anyway. I wonder if he ever really sat with that devastation or if he buried it the way he seemed to bury everything else. I wished, in some impossible way, that I could have been there for him then, to show him that feelings aren't fatal. But maybe he wasn't scared of feelings. Maybe he simply didn't have them the way I imagined he should. He was a vault, always.

Of course, in my mother's retelling, the story had a different flavor. She focused on how deceitful it was for this woman to hide her illness, ignoring alternative explanations: that maybe the woman just wanted to live whatever life she had left without pity, or to love genuinely without intrusion. My mother had a way of turning others into villains when they threatened her spotlight. Even the dying weren't exempt.

Loss clung to my father's life the way smoke clings to clothes after a campfire. And maybe that smoke made it easier for my mother to step in, a woman ready to give direction and soak up whatever fractured love he had left. My parents met on a blind date set up by my father's secretary at work. My mother never let me forget that my father had kept her phone number in his wallet for months before calling, even while he was with other women. She elaborated, "That tells you something about him. He always needs a backup plan."

It amazed me, how she could spot the red flags and yet run straight toward them, arms wide open.

Their first date was attending a ballet recital for his adopted daughter. My mother was irritated by it, not just by the awkwardness, but by the fact that any part of his heart might still belong elsewhere. But she was lonely, stating, "After my divorce, I was so desperate, I'd throw a shoe at the wall just to hear a sound." Her tolerance in those early days was a performance, meant to look easygoing, accommodating. She knew how to wait until she had a firmer grip to let the real her surface.

She told me that when they started dating, he still had his deceased wife's robe hanging in the bathroom; still stained with blood. I remember thinking how strange it was that she wasn't more disturbed by it, or at least more alarmed by the way he clung to one life while already building another. But she didn't care enough. Or maybe she cared more about winning.

Over time, the seeds were planted: seeds to distance him from his adoptive daughter, seeds to bury his past. She needed him fully, without distraction. When the relationship between my father and his daughter finally disintegrated, my mother, again, seemed relieved.

What haunted me most wasn't just the silence that followed the endings of these relationships, but the absence of any observed grief. You were erased.

CHAPTER 6:
"The Poison"

We've spent some time unraveling my mother, but the full picture requires stepping into the shadow beside her—my father.

He came to the United States in his thirties and attended CCNY, learning English while working toward a degree. He chose electrical engineering mostly out of practicality: the program was available, less dependent on language skills, and would allow him to graduate quickly so he could start building a life. Before that, he worked odd jobs as a security guard and a chimney sweep, neither of which paid well enough to sustain him. A degree was a necessity, not a dream.

After graduation, he got a job as an electrical engineer in New York City. Eventually, tired of taking orders and clashing with colleagues, he struck out on his own and started his own business. Even though he was passive in many ways, he had strong opinions and found it difficult to maintain long-term, peaceful relationships.

Despite that, he took real pride in his work. Whenever we would drive through the city, he would point out the buildings where he had done the electrical plans, almost like showing off trophies. It made me think that, despite falling into the field by chance, maybe engineering had been a good fit for him. It didn't involve emotions.

Because of his long commutes to various job sites, we rarely saw him before 6:30 or 7 most nights. When he finally walked in the door, my mother would slap some dry meat onto a plate, announcing, "I have to feed your father," as if he were a helpless infant. Then she'd try to drag conversation out of him, performing like a tap dancer hoping to be noticed. Meanwhile, my father sat there detached, barely lifting his eyes from his food.

She would fish for compliments: "I colored my hair today. Do you like it?" And he'd mutter, "It's fine," without even looking up. Other times, he'd comment that it was too short or too dark, with blunt honesty, not realizing that my mother was looking only for positive feedback. I'd watch the pain pool in her eyes and feel her anger and disappointment fill the room.

She often complained that he was "so quiet" and asked, "Why doesn't he talk to me?"

But if she really wanted his attention, she knew how to get it: she'd fake a physical ailment. Suddenly her back would spasm, or her foot would ache, and like clockwork, my father would snap to attention. It was a cheap trick she used often, and he never seemed to realize it wasn't real. Sometimes she wouldn't even bother keeping up the act once he left the room, walking perfectly fine again. She didn't care if I noticed; I was insignificant to her. Not that it mattered—even if I told him, he wouldn't have believed me.

When she ran out of fake illnesses and small talk, she turned her attention to me. Each evening, like clockwork, she would compile a list of my supposed offenses to report to my father—distorted versions of things I said or did. "Wait until your father hears about this," she'd threaten. She'd accuse me of being unhelpful, of talking back, of being disrespectful—all to stoke his anger against me.

Every evening, like a bad ritual, I'd develop a pounding headache, dreading dinner. Most nights ended either with screaming matches between her and me, or I'd sit silently while she unloaded on me until my body felt like it would combust. Other times, I could only cry, the words caught in my throat.

"Ashley left the lights on again. She doesn't even think about how much electricity costs. So inconsiderate." She'd speak as if I wasn't even there, even if I was sitting right across the table. It felt like she purposely chose the things she knew would upset my father the most, like wasting money, just to drive the wedge deeper between us.

There were occasions when I'd leave the table before dinner ended and sit at the top of the staircase adjacent to the kitchen, listening to her whisper lies about me to him. I couldn't stand the injustices and would at times yell, "I can hear you!"

I felt so heavy with the idea that she was poisoning his mind against me, and that no matter what I said or did, I would never be able to undo the damage. I carried the constant feeling of being unwanted.

I can still remember staring down at my plate, wishing my food would swallow *me* whole.

CHAPTER 7:
"Marble Rye"

My mother was born in Philadelphia but raised in New York by an emotionally vacant mother and a father who, in many ways, resembled a Nazi in his personal philosophies. He had strict, unyielding rules about how everything should be done, and he could turn stone cold at the drop of a hat if you disobeyed him. I was told he would be physical with both of his daughters if they ever talked back or forgot that old mantra: children should be seen and not heard.

On the softer side, he would sometimes sit down after dinner and play show tunes on his fancy organ. I would watch his fingers dance across the keys, delicate and fast, like a bird's wings skimming the surface of the ocean. He was talented, charismatic even, at first, but his critical nature poisoned whatever he touched.

I remember him once taking the time to show me how to paint a child, and I appreciated it. It was rare for anyone to slow down for me like that. But with him, everything came with a price: if you didn't do things his way, the relationship would suffer.

He had a way of isolating and exiling you when you disappointed him. His dominance created a ripple effect. Everyone else would pile on, lecturing you to make it right with him. He lived in his own distorted reality, one where everyone existed to cater to him.

I wish I could say something warm about him, especially at the end of his life. You'd hope that staring death in the face might soften a person. But it didn't. In those last weeks, he made it a point to tell us not to help ourselves to anything in his fridge, and declared that he would no longer shake anyone's hand or waste time with pleasantries. Whatever tiny filter of politeness he had for society was gone, and what was left was his raw, unfiltered self.

Even in death, he found a way to manipulate and control. His will and trust were a mess; scratched-up documents, filled with emotional amendments based on isolated slights and perceived betrayals. I was told that before he died, one incident in particular determined whether I would receive anything.

He asked me to pick up a marble rye from his favorite deli. On the surface, it sounded like a simple, reasonable request. But when my grandfather asked for something, what he really meant was: *drop everything and deliver it immediately.* Normally, I would've welcomed the chance to please him. Those moments were rare, and I clung to them, but it was the end of my semester, and I was buried in finals.

I called to explain I could bring it to him in a few days. The silence on the other end was immediate and cold. The line might as well have gone dead.

I hung up the phone with a knot in my stomach, already anticipating the fallout. Guilt crawled over me like a fever. How could I choose myself, even for a moment? But I was exhausted. I was drowning in deadlines, desperate for sleep, for silence, for a breath. And still, I hated disappointing him. I hated how it opened me up to torment from my family.

My reasons for not immediately delivering didn't matter. Silence followed. He stopped answering my calls. And when I finally showed up with the bread, he wouldn't even open the door. I stood there holding the bag like a child with a failed offering. The air felt colder than it should have. My cheeks burned, not from the wind, but from shame. It wasn't just a door shutting. It was love being withheld.

I wasn't mourning the bread. I was mourning the silent message that love was conditional. That being seen, being good, meant erasing myself.

Within hours, the family grapevine was humming with condemnation: I was selfish, disrespectful, ungrateful. All over a loaf of bread. What I didn't realize then was that it wasn't about the bread at all—it was a test. A test of loyalty, of blind devotion. And in his eyes, I had failed.

Because of that one moment, I was cut out of the will. It was like a game: you were constantly being tested to determine whether you'd be in or out. By the end, his decisions changed so often that nobody could even decipher what he really wanted. His daughters lived in constant fear of being cut out too. The sisters clearly despised each other but superficially smiled at one another and insulted each other behind closed doors to avoid a scolding from my grandfather. And that fear outlived him. Even years later, my mother would say things like, "Well, you know, you really should have just brought him that bread." To her, that mindset was normal. One disobedient action, and you were a closed chapter.

My grandmother was a ghost of a woman. There physically but emotionally vacant. There she stood as a shadow for my grandfather. What I remember most vividly are her obsessively white leather house slippers, shuffling around the kitchen as she murmured to herself about old grudges no one else cared to hear: "Karen never paid me back for that rolling pin I got her years ago," she would mutter.

My grandfather was so used to ignoring her that he barely registered when she spoke. She existed to cook, clean, and serve; nothing more. Their romantic relationship had long since ended, eroded by her colon cancer, the challenge of her colostomy bag, and years of emotional neglect. He looked at her with disdain, like she was a burden he was forced to tolerate.

He belittled her constantly. Once, I watched him fling open a kitchen cabinet door so carelessly that it hit her square in the forehead.

As she cried out in pain, he walked away without even a glance. I sat frozen, halfway through my sandwich, not sure if I should say something or pretend it didn't happen. She spent her days scrubbing every inch of the house, obsessively cleaning as a way to dissociate; a pattern I now recognize in my mother.

There were often other women too. My grandfather was a skilled painter, and his art studio in Pacific Beach attracted a rotating cast of young women, some staying longer than just for a portrait. When confronted, he would say nothing, his silence dripping with entitlement, as if to say, "How dare you question me?" My grandmother would find drawings of nude women and say nothing. She lived a life of silent suffering.

Imagining what it must have been like to have him as a father makes me shudder. He was intimidating enough to me as a child, and I was only ever on the edges of his world.

He didn't have an easy childhood himself. His father was a gambler who wasted whatever money the family had. Eventually, his mother, my great-grandmother, had enough. She left with my grandfather, her only child at the time, to build a new life. The separation didn't last, however. His parents reconciled briefly, had a second child: a baby girl, and the old problems resurfaced. When she left again, she could only afford to take one child with her. She chose the baby. My grandfather stayed behind, abandoned by his mother, unwanted by his father, and soon bounced between foster homes.

By the time he was twelve, he met my grandmother in a nearby park. He used to ride his bike to see her, and as teenagers, he began courting her. He would tell me she was "so beautiful, quiet, and mysterious." It's hard to imagine now, seeing how he treated her in the end.

Their romance was interrupted when he was drafted into World War II. He earned many awards, including a Purple Heart, and poured himself into his military career. Maybe the army was the only place he ever felt truly validated. Maybe he thought achievement would finally earn him the love he never got.

After the war, my grandmother and grandfather married in 1945 and soon had my mother and my aunt.

My mother and her sister were at war from the beginning. One of my aunt's earliest memories is my mother telling her she was adopted. She crafted an elaborate story about how no one wanted her, how she had been left on the porch by her real parents. My aunt, devastated, packed her favorite doll and T-shirt and ran away, getting only a few blocks before the neighbor brought her home.

When my grandfather found out, he punished my mother with his belt. And that was just the beginning. Their relationship spiraled into years of screaming matches, backstabbing, and desperate grabs for attention and love.

My grandfather fueled the fire, whispering toxic things to one about the other, manipulating them into rage so he could then step in and punish them. Although my aunt was more rebellious, she was favored; given more money, more forgiveness, more patience. My mother, the more studious one, was expected to be perfect. She was held to a higher standard but received less love. Any achievement from her was expected; from her sister, it was celebrated.

The bitterness took root in my mother early and never left. She grew up feeling like she was never quite enough and that one wrong move could cost her everything.

In a family like that, you either learned to survive through perfection or by disappearing. My mother tried both.

CHAPTER 8:
"The Painted Horses"

My mother's relationship with my grandfather was strained, to say the least. Growing up, she would often say, "You couldn't talk to him." She kept secrets from him for as long as she could remember. Major details: where she went, how much money she spent, what was happening with me or my brother were routinely altered before being shared with him. When I asked her why, she'd simply say, "It's easier this way. He doesn't need to know everything."

Even as an adult, she remained intimidated by him. I remember her once asking what had happened to my grandmother's jewelry after she passed; a simple question that was met with such anger and dismissiveness that she immediately shut down. It was startling to see my mother retreat so completely.

The dynamic between them was transactional, surface-level. They could manage a conversation about food or the weather, but anything deeper tended to end in disaster. He was domineering and critical; she was emotional and quick to react. It was a combustible mix. I still hear him grumble, "Your mother is too excitable about everything," as if emotions themselves were a defect.

Despite everything, my mother still sought his approval, even though she would never get it. One of her most frequently recounted memories was about the painted horses. They had gone shopping together when she was young and came across a pair of beautiful hand-painted horses in a store. She admired them aloud, and to her amazement, he told the clerk to wrap them up. For a brief moment, she believed he had bought them for her, only to watch him take them home for himself. "He was always that way," she'd say. Self-centered, thoughtless, incapable of considering anyone else's joy.

If you had asked my grandfather, he likely would have told you, without a hint of irony, that he was a terrific father. After all, in his mind, providing financially and offering discipline were all that mattered. Attachment was unnecessary. Feelings were a liability.

He devoted most of his energy to his work as an architect, pointing out the temples and schools he helped design like trophies on a shelf. His pride was reserved for projects, not people. Things couldn't betray you or leave you. People could; and in his mind, often did. His emotional detachment was both a shield and a weapon. If you didn't serve a purpose for him, you became invisible.

When my grandmother eventually passed from colon and uterine cancer, he wasted no time revealing what we all quietly knew: he had been romantically involved with her caregiver for years. The same woman who had "helped" the family during that dark time of illness had helped herself to my grandfather's attention, even as my grandmother lay dying just a room away.

Their affair had been an open secret long before my grandmother's death: the suggestive clothing, the lingering looks, the hours spent together. It disgusted everyone, but confronting him would have been useless. In his mind, there was nothing wrong with discarding one object when it was broken and picking up another.

My grandmother's funeral was a grim testament to how little real connection she had nurtured in her lifetime. There were five people in attendance: my aunt; my then-husband and I; the caregiver-turned-lover;

and my grandfather. Bringing his mistress to his wife's funeral was, for him, no different from running an errand.

I'll always remember the incongruity of that day; the crystal blue sky, the sunlight glinting off the water that surrounded the mausoleum, the ducks gliding along as if nothing were amiss. Nature continued, beautiful and unconcerned, even as human failings unfolded under its gaze.

It was almost poetic.

In a world of such callousness and betrayal, the sun still shone.

CHAPTER 9:
"Drugs or Religion"

My father grew up on a kibbutz in Israel; a kind of children's village where every kid had a job to contribute to the whole. Some milked goats; others picked fruit or cooked meals in the kitchen. When my father first told me about it, he described it as "a place where orphans go," kids without anyone to care for them.

Neither of his parents was around. They divorced early in his life—he was about eleven, his brother thirteen—and the boys were left to figure things out for themselves. My father's early life was a blur of movement: born in Egypt, then shipped off to France, and eventually to Israel. His father took a job as a storekeeper on a passenger ship that sailed the Mediterranean, with frequent stops in Marseille. His mother, meanwhile, was more focused on fostering new relationships than on raising her sons. There was no one to play the role of parent.

I have a photo of my father sitting at a long table in the food hall of the kibbutz, surrounded by other boys eating lunch. I like to look at it and imagine he was different then; different from the man I eventually knew. Maybe, in that photo, he was softer. Maybe he still had hope.

It was in that place that my father learned how to work and how to rely on himself. It's striking how similar his story is to my grandfather's: both abandoned in different ways, forced to grow up too fast, learning to bury their feelings of rejection and inadequacy so deep they almost forgot they were there.

I imagine that when you're stripped of your family, you have to turn to something else to survive. Some people turn to drugs; others turn to religion. For my father, I think practicing Judaism became his anchor; something rooted, something reliable. Structure. Rules. Predictability. All the things he craved.

Like my mother, my father seemed to live in a constant tug-of-war between rebellion and a desperate longing for guidance. He stuck close to my mother, even when she bossed him around—and she often did. Despite his resistance, he always circled back, hungry for her direction. It wasn't sweet. It was codependent. Without her, he seemed lost, but not in the tender way that invites sympathy. More in the way that makes you quietly sigh and brace yourself for the fallout.

Still, I was curious about his relationship to religion. I was about ten years old, sitting on our old peach-and-mint-green sofa, tracing the jungle-leaf pattern on the cushions with my fingers. My father sat nearby, reading the newspaper, his tired face mostly hidden behind the pages. My mother was furiously clipping coupons from our local grocery store in the armchair across from me.

I'm not sure what triggered it, but that day my mind started to wander toward the idea of heritage. Every December, I would watch my mother, much to my father's dismay, string Christmas lights onto a fake plant in the corner of our living room, even though I'd been told I was Jewish. It was confusing. Hypocritical, even.

And somewhere in that tangle of contradictions, it hit me: I had no real idea what it meant to be Jewish. As far as I could tell, Judaism was a piece of crispy matzoh eaten once a year. A brittle bread standing in for thousands of years of history I knew nothing about.

If religion mattered to my father, why hadn't he taught me? Why hadn't he passed down even one of the many languages he spoke—Arabic, French, Hebrew?

"I want to go to Hebrew school," I said out loud, half-challenging, half-hoping. Silence followed. Their favorite response. I don't know if they were shocked, pleased, or annoyed. They never said. I sat there wondering what they were thinking, but I already knew better than to ask. If I was going to buy into anything, I needed to learn about it myself.

And so, I enrolled. I wandered the long, cold hallways that smelled of stale coffee, clutching my notebook, eager to ask questions. There were two back-to-back classes: the first focused on Jewish history, the second on learning Hebrew. I found myself disengaged and feeling different again but in a new setting. I felt the same there as I did at home: disconnected. Isolated.

The other kids seemed to recognize something in each other; a shared thread I couldn't find in myself. I was the observer again, not a participant. Always at the edge of things, never woven into the fabric.

I stayed just long enough to "graduate" but didn't stick around. If anything, I felt even more confused than when I started. Years later, that early search for meaning evolved into a larger question I carried with me into my doctoral research: Why hadn't I found connection there? Why didn't it click, even though all the makings for community were technically there?

If bagels and lox can't bring you together, I thought, what can?

The answer was both comforting and lonely: some of us are just built to keep searching.

CHAPTER 10:
"The Motherland"

As the years went on, I decided to travel to Israel, now as an adult, wide-eyed and still hopeful about igniting my connection to the ethnicity. I wanted to absorb the culture, to understand my roots more deeply. Maybe, I thought, I would finally feel tied to those who had suffered before me so that I could have a future.

A big part of me wanted to see the kibbutz where my father grew up. It felt like a missing piece of the puzzle—a tangible link to him, and maybe to Judaism as a whole. But if I had to sum up the trip in one word, it would be this: uncomfortable.

To be fair, the trip had been my father's idea first. He was already planning to go when I asked to join, thinking maybe we'd both see it as an opportunity to bond. He seemed enthusiastic when I asked, and before I knew it, I was boarding a plane at JFK.

After fifteen and a half hours from California to Israel, I was beyond relieved to hear the flight attendant announce our landing. My legs ached, but the excitement for what lay ahead pushed me forward. I was eager to reunite with my father upon landing, and images of us laughing together and eating fresh local cuisine made me buzz.

We had made a plan: meet by the large water fountain at the center of the arrivals terminal, a landmark he assured me was unmistakable. He said he would track my flight and be there waiting.

But when I arrived at the fountain, I didn't see him.

"Maybe he's grabbing food," I thought. "Or in the restroom."

I wandered the terminal, checking the bookstore and the watch shop, scanning the faces rushing by, but there was no sign of him.

It quickly became clear that English wasn't as widely spoken as I had hoped. I tried asking airport staff for help but was met with blank stares. I felt my skin flush hot and my eyes blur with disorientation.

Finally, a man at a SIM card booth took pity on me. Maybe I looked as lost as I felt. I bought an Israeli SIM card, found a fat armchair to sink into, and dialed my father's number.

Ring. Ring. Ring.

An hour passed. Then two.

Here I was, in a country I'd never been to, unable to find my father.

Historically, my mother had been the more reliable one of the two. If she said she would be somewhere, she would be there. However, I didn't think my father would ever put me in a situation like this, especially in a foreign country. I started to wonder if something had happened to him, and guilt crept in for feeling so frustrated.

After hours of waiting, calling, and searching, I decided I would buy a return ticket home.

The thought of another fifteen-hour flight was nauseating, but the idea of staying felt even worse. The idea of a trip built around connection followed by the core feeling of being alone was crushing.

And then, as I approached the ticket counter, I saw him.

My father.

Sitting in an armchair.

Laughing, drinking coffee with a friend.

He hadn't called. He hadn't looked for me. He hadn't even tried.

I stood there, stunned, watching him casually sip his coffee like nothing had happened. When I approached and explained how long I'd been searching and calling, he barely looked up.

"Well, I'm here. What's the big deal?" he said flatly.

For a moment, I wanted to unleash all the anger and hurt that were bubbling inside me.

But I didn't. His nonchalant perception of my last harrowing few hours felt painfully familiar—disappointing, yet unsurprising. The images of him and me bonding immediately exited stage left, but I told myself not to ruin the trip. Against my better judgment, I stayed and kept my mouth shut.

"It'll be okay," I whispered to myself, even though everything inside me screamed otherwise.

Tel Aviv was beautiful, but different from what I expected. Teenagers boarded public buses with massive semi-automatic weapons slung over their shoulders, pushing and shoving to squeeze into narrow trains. The energy felt tense, urgent, like everyone was fighting for the last gallon of milk on a shelf.

I still didn't feel like I was coming home. I felt even more misplaced and wondered if my strained relationship with my parents had anything to do with why Judaism, and now Israel, felt so foreign to me. Maybe if Jewish practices had been part of my life from an earlier age, I would feel differently.

From the start, the experience with my father was cold and detached, centered around his friends and interests. They were people I had never heard of—friends who had never visited the States, who now seemed to light him up in ways I had never seen, complimenting him and wanting to know every detail of what he was doing. They exclaimed emphatically at each statement he made. My father looked unrecognizably happy in their presence.

At dinners with them, the conversations stayed in Hebrew. No one bothered to translate. I sat silently, feeling invisible. We hadn't had one meal that involved just the two of us. During one of the ongoing group dinners—overwhelmed and miserable from the repetition night after night—I asked if we could leave.

"You can walk back on your own if you want," my father said coldly. "I'm not leaving."

I didn't know where I was. I didn't even know how to get back to the flat we were staying in. I just knew I had to get out of there. The layers of rejection I felt from him were overwhelming. I got up from the table, exasperated. A friend of his followed me out—not my father, but someone who had only just met me and cared enough to check if I was okay—while he sat chewing away on his Chilean sea bass.

That night, I cried into my pillow, wishing the days would pass faster until it was time to return home. My father's emotional vacancy was louder than any argument could have been. He seemed oblivious to my sadness, or maybe he just didn't care. The immersion of time with him, without any actual engagement, was suffocatingly difficult.

One of the days toward the end of the trip, desperate for a sliver of comfort, I asked if we could pick up a fresh-baked challah from a street vendor. Food had always been one of the few ways I felt tied to Judaism, and I thought, when in Israel.

"We don't have time," he said without hesitation and without eye contact. The silence that followed felt deafening.

It wasn't about the bread. It was about being seen. And once again, I wasn't.

Sitting there, feeling small and foolish, I realized how much I had been chasing him; just like my mother had chased him. I hated seeing myself in that role.

When we finally returned to the States, I tried to talk to him about how the trip had made me feel. I thought maybe, just maybe, we could reach some kind of understanding.

But a few words in, he shut down.

"You invited yourself, so what do you expect?" he said sharply. "I never get to see my friends."

There it was.

For me, the trip had been about building a father-daughter connection. For him, it had been about seeing old friends and basking in their adoration.

I felt a cold wave settle into my stomach. Maybe it was my fault for assuming we wanted the same thing. For projecting meaning onto an experience that, for him, meant something completely different. Seeing these complete strangers appear to be closer to my father than I ever was surreal to observe. It was clear, however, that they were attracted to the surface version of him. They didn't really *know* him. I had to remind myself of that so that I didn't melt into a complete puddle of self-pity.

Needless to say, that was the first and last time we ever traveled together.

CHAPTER 11:
"Red like a lobster"

The feeling of neglect and emotional abandonment from my parents had begun years before all that, though.

Let's rewind to 1991. Can you picture it? Poofy dresses with shoulder pads, big hair, and patent leather shoes were a prerequisite.

I was around five years old when I was asked to be a flower girl at a wedding for a family friend. It was expected that everyone participating would have their hair done a certain way—curls and all.

It was my first time in a hair salon. Dina, wearing sequined pants and chewing gum loudly, approached to comb through my tangled bee's nest of hair.

Phil Collins crooned through the speakers: You could practically feel it coming in the air tonight.

A few minutes in, Dina whispered something to another stylist. Before I could process what was happening, four women surrounded my chair, each armed with a bigger comb and a pair of scissors.

I didn't realize yet that this wasn't normal.

My hair was so heavily matted and neglected that it was stuck to my scalp, impossible to brush through. I sat on the booster seat, feet dangling, while the first stylist tried to work through the mess with her comb, sighing and shaking her head. I could feel her tugging for what felt like hours, then giving up. She turned to my mother and said gently, "Most of this will have to be cut off."

My mother's reaction was quiet and dissociative, finding some way to pin it on how I was "too difficult" to comb properly. I hadn't had my hair brushed in months. I glanced down at my arms, dirt encrusted into my skin, camouflaging my freckles. The women looked over at my mother with disgust.

I sat still, silent, as giant clumps of my dark hair fell to the floor. It wasn't a haircut; it was damage control. When it was over, I was left with a ragged little bob that barely grazed my chin. I had started out with hair down to my waist.

I didn't feel cute or clean or cared for. I felt a sudden, deep shame, even though I couldn't yet intellectually explain why. It was like my body understood something my mind couldn't piece together.

I felt like there had been proof of something wrong with me, and now everyone could see it.

It carried an unspoken truth: that no one had been paying attention. That I had been left, on my own, to manage things a child shouldn't have to. And that the people who were supposed to protect and care for me had failed.

To this day, my mother has never addressed it; never responded to the women's glances, never acknowledged what had really been exposed: a visible aspect of the neglect.

Did they not notice? Or did they just not care?

My parents seemed completely indifferent to the basic activities of daily living when it came to me. My father deferred everything to my mother, believing it was the mother's role to tend to personal matters, especially since she wasn't working outside the home. He expected this, just as he expected dinner on the table every night at six o'clock without question, without thanks.

When I eventually asked my mother about the hair incident, she simply shrugged and said, "Well, you didn't like it brushed, so I stopped."

And there you have it. The beginning and end of the conversation. No further questions.

Somehow, it was always my fault. So simple. So complicated.

Her conflict avoidance, dissociative passivity, and complete lack of parenting skills all sat together at the corner diner, ordering pancakes and pretending nothing was wrong. It wasn't just my hair.

The neglect ran deeper. It threaded through every aspect of my care, or lack thereof. My teeth were of a similar nature. When I was four and five years old, I had major root canals multiple times a year. I would wake up screaming in pain and be rushed to the dentist over and over. I didn't realize at the time that most kids brushed their teeth daily, or that someone, anyone, was supposed to show them how. That kind of basic nurturing was absent in my world.

The experiences felt similar to those of a child whose parents were either dead or chronically ill. But mine were very much alive. I craved some kind of guidance, some kind of presence. Instead, I stood at the top of an empty well, calling out and hearing only echoes.

One of the stories my mother loves to tell about my childhood, told with a laugh, as if it's endearing, is about my very first car ride home from the hospital after I was born. Sounds sweet at first, right? Except the story goes that I spent the entire forty-five-minute drive baking in the sun, strapped into the back seat, turning "red as a lobster" by the time they pulled into the driveway.

Severely sunburned on the very first day I was breathing oxygen outside the womb. My mother found the whole thing funny. It didn't occur to her that maybe this wasn't a charming anecdote. That maybe a mother who had just carried a baby for nine months should be slightly more concerned. But she wasn't. She never was, not if it meant she could be at fault for something.

And that absence of responsibility followed me through childhood like a shadow.

I had walked over to the neighbor's house one afternoon to play. The family had housekeepers who had just mopped the marble basement floor. At some point, I slipped and hit my head so hard I lost consciousness. When I woke up, one of the housekeepers, who spoke little English, was leading me back to my house. She pointed to my head, indicating something was wrong.

I don't remember the fall itself; just the blinding, throbbing pain. I felt like an object being returned to the lost and found—an object nobody had even bothered to look for because they had already moved on.

When my mother opened the door, she barely reacted. No hug. No panic. No concern.

I had hoped she would scoop me up, inspect my head, rush me to the doctor. But there was nothing. No hospital visit. No questions.

We just moved on with the day, as if it hadn't happened.

It was like living with two robots: cold, mechanical, sterile; concern only flickering to life if it somehow inconvenienced them. I wasn't expecting grand displays of love, but even a simple acknowledgment would have meant the world.

When no one validates your existence, you start to wonder if you were ever really there at all.

Another young memory of this nature surfaced at Jones Beach—a typical summer outing for a New York family: cars packed with chairs, umbrellas, salami sandwiches, icy coolers full of cans of Coke, and endless "just in case" supplies. It always felt exhausting getting there, even before the day began.

One day, my dad said, "We're going into the water." Panic flickered inside me, but he placed his hand warmly on my back.

"It'll be okay. I'm going in with you."

We entered the bluish-green water, cold against our skin, raising little goosebumps. He kept moving farther in. I called out for him to wait, but he didn't turn around. My feet struggled to touch the ground. The shore slipped farther away. I didn't know how to swim but tried to mimic what I had seen others do. I wasn't proving very graceful, and the realization that I was in too deep sent fear coursing through me.

When I tried to turn back, a huge wave slammed me sideways.

I was pushed underwater, disoriented, unsure which way was up. Rocks and shells scraped against my legs. My lungs screamed. I flailed, weakening with each movement. Water flooded my mouth. My survival instinct kicked in—and then quickly gave way to the terror of giving up.

Then…a hand. Someone pushed me up from beneath. A stranger's face blurred by my disorientation. He laid me on the sand. I coughed up seawater and stared at my own blood dotting the beach.

Minutes later, my dad strolled out of the water. "Oh hey, kiddo," he said casually.

He had missed the entire thing. He asked why I was bleeding, as if he couldn't possibly connect the dots. He joked about it.

You were supposed to make sure I was safe, I thought.

He had seemed so sincere about wanting a shared experience, but in the end, he couldn't even see that I needed him. He was oblivious to my fear. I felt like I could have disappeared completely that day, and no one would have blinked an eye.

And yet, each time and in each memory, I blamed myself for expecting something different. Over the years, I created a phrase to describe the feeling: I was the last kid waiting at the bus stop—filled with hope that someone would come pick me up, only to be left standing there.

I realized this wasn't occasional. This was the norm.

I was minimized and forgotten.

CHAPTER 12:
"I don't know what to tell you"

Sometimes when you're young, you trust without question, and I paid the consequences for it later.

I was working at a psychiatric hospital at the time, a local acute setting where clients demonstrated mental health symptoms ranging from command auditory hallucinations (voices telling them to do things) to forensic patients awaiting trial. I had just finished a particularly taxing therapy session and plopped down on one of the hard wooden chairs lining the office, relieved to have a few minutes to collect my thoughts.

As soon as I exhaled, someone from Payroll marched up to my desk.

"Looks like you have some sort of issue with the IRS?" she said, with a questioning, almost disparaging look.

"You'll want to look into this," she added, handing me a notice. My wages were being garnished to repay some kind of debt: a word that felt foreign to me. I was obsessively diligent with my bookkeeping, driven by anxiety to stay ahead of anything that could go wrong.

A wave of panic washed over me: hot and cold at the same time, instantly nauseous. I'm a Type A, everything must get done a week in advance kind of person. So, what was happening? I reasoned it must be a mistake. Surely the IRS would dismiss it when I provided evidence of payments.

After hours on hold, I was told there were significant back taxes due from ten years ago, when I was still a minor and my father's accountant had handled everything. Confused but hopeful, I called my father, thinking he could quickly clear this up.

When I told him what had happened, I was met with a tone of irritability and resentment, as if I were bothering him. I explained the amount owed, an impossible sum for someone scraping by on minimum wage, still unlicensed and waiting for a career to begin. He simply replied, coldly, "Well, I don't know what to tell you. You'll need to figure it out."

A deep and again familiar loneliness filled my stomach, like the sound reverberating through the skin of a tight drum. It felt clear that, in his mind, I should just be grateful his accountant even did my childhood taxes; never mind the life-altering mistake that followed. What other choice does a child have?

I stared at the phone, stunned. My body felt suspended in that charged silence; cold anxiety curling deep in my gut, slowly rising and igniting into a simmering anger. I wanted to scream, to demand answers, to plead for accountability. But instead, I said nothing. I stayed quiet, not because I didn't have words, but because I knew they wouldn't land. He was a brick wall, immovable in his stubbornness, incapable or unwilling to examine what was unfolding. There would be no reckoning, no shared responsibility. Just silence on his end, and survival on mine.

As I hung up, the reality of the situation flooded in all at once. If I couldn't resolve this quickly, I wouldn't have enough to pay rent. I wouldn't be able to buy food. I wouldn't be able to care for my dog, which relied on me completely. The weight of it was suffocating, and all of it could have been avoided.

Thankfully, a good friend stepped in and helped me navigate the chaos. I was able to pull myself out, piece things together, go on a payment plan, and keep going. But the memory of it lingers. I will never forget the way my father left me to clean up the mess alone, as if my well-being, my security, my life, were nothing more than collateral damage.

That incident reminded me of a time back in New York during my college years, which I'll expand on later. My father and I were driving home from the bus station that took me from Boston to Manhattan on a cold winter day, snow blanketing the roads. He was nice enough to offer to pick me up on this particular day, so I took him up on it. I noticed, however, that my father wasn't wearing his glasses. He was blind as a bat without them, and before I could even process it, he sideswiped the car next to us.

In shock, we pulled over. I braced myself, knowing he didn't handle accountability well. Sure enough, he stormed out of the car and immediately started yelling at the other driver, blaming him. The driver looked at him, dumbfounded by the sheer distortion of reality unfolding before him.

It was obvious. We had veered into their lane. It wasn't even a question. Later, when the insurance company ruled him at fault, he still maintained how "ridiculous" it all was.

Moments like these revealed who he was: someone utterly incapable of taking responsibility. Rules never applied to him. If a sign said "Do Not Enter," he'd boldly stride through anyway. "Just act like you own the place," he'd say. "No one will question you."

He saw most people as lesser; not just in passing moments, but as a guiding principle. There was a casual condescension in the way he spoke about others, a constant undertone suggesting he believed himself smarter, more capable, more deserving. Waiters, store clerks, employees, even friends and family, were often dismissed as incompetent or naïve. It wasn't always overt cruelty, but rather a chronic belief that rules and expectations simply didn't apply to him.

That mindset seeped into every area of his life. Over the years, he faced multiple lawsuits tied to his business dealings: clients who accused him of wrongdoing or negligence, partners who claimed he broke contracts. Even in his personal life, there were similar patterns. He'd hire contractors for major construction projects and then refuse to pay them in full, always convinced that their work didn't merit the cost, or that he could find some excuse to withhold what was owed. Accountability was something he dodged with skillful deflection.

At one point, he owed the IRS a significant sum; a debt he minimized or joked about, as though it were someone else's mistake or an inconvenience he could charm his way out of. But underneath the bravado was a man operating under the belief that consequences were negotiable, or meant for other people.

But it was always someone else's fault. Now I know: he was the common denominator.

He also struggled, profoundly, with empathy. It wasn't just that he failed to comfort or nurture; it was that he seemed incapable of even recognizing when those things were needed. In the moments I needed him most, he wasn't just absent; he was indifferent.

When his mother, my grandmother, passed away, I was still a kid. I remember us cleaning out her condo, the air thick with dust, grief, and a strange sense of urgency as he rummaged through her belongings, laser-focused on sorting and salvaging.

In the chaos, I accidentally slammed my hand in her heavy metal door. The pain was instant and searing, followed by the hot gush of blood spilling onto the black-and-white checkered floor.

I couldn't move my hand without seeing stars. I stood motionless and shocked, overcome with nausea. I vividly remember shaking, and because I couldn't get words out, waiting for someone to notice.

He barely looked up. My mother asked if they should take me to the hospital, and without pausing, he muttered, "She's fine." That was it; his medical assessment, his emotional response, his paternal instinct all wrapped into two dismissive words.

No one checked with me. No one looked closely. No one asked if I was okay. I wrapped my hand in my shirt, watching as the fabric turned dark with blood. Eventually, he tossed me an old scarf from one of my grandmother's drawers, not out of concern, but as a practical solution to keep the mess from spreading. The symbolism of that action was not lost on me. Taking me for medical care would have disrupted their mission. His priority was efficiency, not tenderness.

Thankfully, I didn't need stitches, and the bruising healed over time. But what stayed with me wasn't just the physical pain, or even the lack of treatment, it was the apathy. The fact that I could be hurt, bleeding, scared, and still somehow be irrelevant. That moment branded something into me: the understanding that my needs, my pain, my voice would always come second to his agenda.

That kind of disregard showed up again and again, in big moments and small ones, quietly teaching me how little space I was allowed to take up.

CHAPTER 13:
"The Green"

Money was always a strange and constant subject in my family. It was the biggest focal point, yet rarely spoken of directly. Growing up, I never knew our financial standing. I assumed we were a family of modest income. I wore shoes from Payless Shoe Source and ate at McDonald's weekly. In areas my parents valued, however, like travel or fine dining, there seemed to be no limits. My father would buy sapphire, emerald, and ruby necklaces for my mother, as jewelry was her favorite indulgence.

This was how they showed "love" to each other, not through affection, understanding, or real connection, but through objects that, from the outside, suggested they cared. It always felt more about appearances than anything real.

As a child, the way money was used made me feel like a second-class citizen. When I asked for something, as children naturally do, I was quickly dismissed: "Just appreciate what you have" or "Stop being so selfish." These responses were so constant that I believed I was ungrateful before I even fully understood the word.

It wasn't until much later in my life that the truth began to surface; not through anything they told me, but through the things they let slip, the inconsistencies I pieced together. My parents had far more than they ever let on. Only as I got older did I begin to notice the quiet clues: the luxury purchases, the investments, the multiple properties. They had more than enough, and yet somehow, I had grown up believing we were always on the edge.

They simply reserved their generosity for the things they valued; their own interests, while others', including mine, barely registered. Even in small decisions, it showed. If I liked the green dress but they preferred the blue, we bought the blue. If I shared my feelings about that, I would be shamed for not being grateful to have a dress at all. I didn't understand why I was treated differently, but I learned early that in my family, money wasn't currency; it was control.

By the time I was a teenager, this control felt unbearable. I vented one afternoon to a friend, a senior I knew from my art class, where we spent hours building giant papier-mâché cows in the name of "creativity." Over grilled cheese sandwiches, she asked, "Why don't you come work with me at the bakery?"

In New York, you technically couldn't work officially until sixteen, but I was desperate. To me, a job meant freedom, choice, and eventually, escape. Staying in my childhood home felt like being trapped in golden handcuffs: looking polished from the outside but tightening every day. I learned what emancipation was and often fantasized about it, especially on the tougher days. I immediately said yes.

My friend spoke to the bakery owner for me, and a few days later, she high-fived me after school. "All right, you start Friday. Don't be late."

Excitement flared in me, quickly followed by anxiety. There was no hiding it from my parents. I knew the conversation would be a battle. My mother's reaction was exactly what I expected: "What do you mean you got a job? We give you everything. You're not doing that."

She seemed less concerned about me working and more about how it would look, how it would reflect on her. In her mind, a working teenager suggested financial hardship and, by extension, bad parenting or low income. "We'll talk to your father about this," she said, her usual tactic when she wanted to shut something down.

To her dismay, my father didn't oppose it. He had started working young himself and, for once, saw my point of view. Hard work mattered to him, and for a brief, rare moment, I felt aligned with him. It was a tiny, almost imperceptible victory; a moment of connection that I carried with me.

Despite my mother's continued opposition, she stayed quiet after his decision, unable to come up with a convincing argument against it. Part of me wondered if her resistance was tied more to her own insecurities, a reminder that she wasn't contributing financially either. And just like that, it was settled.

Before I knew it, I was standing behind rows of chocolate éclairs and cinnamon babkas. The scent permeated all the way down the street. The bakery's owner, an older woman with silver hair, looked down at me through thick glasses, scanning me like a shopkeeper examining merchandise. She mumbled instructions as she showed me the back kitchen, a world of giant mixers, hanging metal tools, and surfaces dusted in flour like fresh snow.

The cash register was a relic, its keys wiped blank by decades of use. I had to memorize what each button once said. On my first day, I was also thrown onto the bread slicer; a terrifying machine that demanded respect if I wanted to keep all my fingers.

Customers trickled in; mostly elderly women, pointing their bony fingers at pastries and barking demands.

"Not that one, I want the cookie all the way in the back!"

Even though the job had its moments, I would have plunged toilets if it meant a paycheck. By the end of that first shift, I was exhausted but buzzing. I had begun carving a path toward independence.

I stayed at the bakery for the rest of high school and picked up work as a camp counselor during the summers; anything to stay away from home. That early exposure to hard work would shape my adulthood, fueling my drive to build my own business and fiercely protect my financial independence.

It's not that my parents were incapable of generosity. They were often giving in their own ways, but it always came with strings attached. Accepting their gifts meant inviting guilt and resentment into my life. Even thanking them was a trial. I had to thank them each separately: "thank you, Mom," "thank you, Dad" or my mother would erupt, "It's my money too!"

Very few things they provided could ever just be appreciated; everything was a transaction, a future debt.

Their relationship with money extended into death and inheritance. When relatives passed away, my parents seemed more focused on what they stood to gain than on mourning the loss. I rarely saw grief, only a rush to claim furniture, jewelry, and possessions, as if life itself were a scavenger hunt.

Funerals became performances only when there was something tangible to collect. When my maternal grandmother died, there was no monetary inheritance, since my grandfather was still living at the time. With nothing to gain, my mother simply didn't show up. There wasn't a single tear, nor a flicker of grief. Her absence spoke volumes, but her indifference said even more.

When my grandfather later passed, the frenzy began again. My mother and aunt devolved into bitter arguments, not over memories or grief, but over *things*. It wasn't mourning; it was looting in slow motion, dressed up as grief.

Watching them pick over the remnants of lives they barely seemed to care about was one of the most eye opening experiences of my life. Each argument over a decorative Buddha or a dusty telescope only underscored the hollowness of their connection to the people who had passed. It was as if the value of a life could be measured in furniture, as if claiming an object could somehow compensate for decades of emotional absence.

By contrast, I began to understand something they never seemed to grasp: that meaning isn't found in what's left behind, but in how we show up for each other while we're still here. The quality of our relationships; the presence, the compassion, the love we offer, is what gives life weight and memory its power. No inherited item could ever replace what was never nurtured. Watching them, I didn't just witness dysfunction. I learned what I didn't want to become.

The more they battled over the scraps, the more I vowed to build a different kind of life.

CHAPTER 14:
"Butter"

It became clear early on that my parents and I had different philosophies on life in general. There was one compassionate girl in one of my high school classes that year who took a liking to me. We seemed to have a lot in common. I even invited her over to my house to watch a movie; a rare occasion for me, since I generally tried to keep my friends and parents separate.

After she left, my mother came into my room, sat on the edge of my bed, and said, "You know, people will judge you based on who you're friends with." She didn't have to explain. It was clear in her tone and gestures: my friend, who was a different ethnicity and heavier set, didn't fit the image my mother expected for me. She feared how others would judge her based on my associations.

My mother had old-school ideas about who I should befriend: girls who were clean-cut, straight-edged, and white, often the exact opposite of who I felt drawn to. Her expectations created constant contradictions in my life: she would either exert extreme control or disappear into neglect. I only seemed to get their attention when they were overprotective or judgmental. It felt as if any time I was my authentic self, I was punished for it. I had to remain formal and polished at all times, rehearsing every move, crossing every *t*, and dotting every *i.* It was subtle but understood. Realizing I could never naturally meet their expectations created deep internal anxiety. I started to believe something was wrong with me. Over time, I hid more and more of myself until there was almost nothing left.

Eventually, the friendship faded, worn down by my parents' pressure and subtle disapproval.

The irony wasn't lost on me: my mother, who had long struggled with her own weight, had been harshly judged by her father. He regularly insulted her, calling her "obese" and "unhealthy," reminding her how unlovable someone like her was. I would hear her crying after these verbal assaults. Yet somehow, she passed those same judgments on to me and my friendships, as if handing off a baton in a race.

Food was a frequent crutch for her; a language she had spoken since childhood. She once told me that if she didn't drink her milk as a child, her father would pour it over her head. In her family, food wasn't just nourishment; it was discipline, guilt, survival. It's no surprise that, for my mother, food became intertwined with emotion. She ate to celebrate, to mourn, to cope with anxiety. She rarely talked about her feelings; instead, she literally stuffed them down with food.

Her relationship with food was impulsive and indulgent, as if Julia Child were her spirit guide. She often launched into crash diets: Weight Watchers, Jenny Craig, only to lose a few pounds and abandon the effort. Health wasn't the goal. Attention was. Thinness equaled attractiveness, and attractiveness equaled worth. True self-care, of either mind or body, didn't seem to enter the picture.

Her self-loathing often came wrapped in humor. She'd joke, "I was born a size 13," or "I have shoulders like a football player." I internalized those comments, eventually seeing myself through the same critical lens. I tried to blend into the background, afraid to take up too much space.

As a child, I was often called an "old soul," which I now understand can be a euphemism for "someone who's experienced trauma too early." I became an observer, not a participant. In gym class, I was the one no one wanted to partner with. I froze in terror at the idea of moving my body in front of others. When someone threw a ball at me, I stood motionless, arms glued to my sides.

I remember being around nine when our class made a gymnastics video for our parents, set to "Eye of the Tiger." Watching myself stumble awkwardly while my classmates nailed their routines was gut-wrenching. A class bully laughed loudly at my clumsy attempt, nudging others to join in. Even now, hearing that song can make my palms sweat.

The idea of being seen made me feel like I would die. My mother reinforced the idea that "our family isn't athletic" and "we don't do sports." I believed her, as kids do. It was like being told you're sick, so you never even try to leave the house, only to realize much later that you were fine all along.

I spent much of gym class hiding in the bathroom, hoping the teacher wouldn't notice I was missing. My mother's approach to feeding me didn't help either. Since my father got home late, dinner was often an afterthought. Meals that were easy were usually chosen, those with heavy sauces or fried. Nutrition wasn't a topic anyone discussed. Everything on the plate had to be eaten or comments were made. "She's wasting her food," my mother would tell my father as we all sat around the table. Food was both guilt-ridden and comforting; a complicated relationship that began early.

Looking back, I realize her insistence that I overeat was less about nurturing and more about seeking company in her own coping mechanisms. "Finish it," she would say, almost pleading. I once heard her admit that eating was the only reason she lived, a brutally honest confession.

I read once that when food becomes our primary source of comfort, it's often because it was the only reliable form of nurturing we had as children. Emotional needs went unmet, but food was always there; predictable, soothing. I can see now how that cycle became ingrained, how food became not just sustenance but survival.

The unhealthy habits I had around eating started shockingly young. My parents loved to recount the story of taking two-year-old me to an Italian restaurant, laughing as they described how I devoured squares of butter straight from the breadbasket, resulting in an emergency bathroom trip. They told this story with glee, oblivious to the glaring negligence it revealed. That would have been an appropriate time to stop your baby from doing something harmful or self-destructive; to teach them right from wrong.

From early on, it was clear that my parents and I didn't think the same way. They seemed unaware of how their actions shaped me. For much of my young life, I was furious without knowing exactly why. Only later did I understand: I was angry because my basic emotional needs had gone unmet.

At just seven or eight years old, I weighed 132 pounds. I rotated between a few shirts that barely fit, often crying in front of the mirror before school. I felt disgusting but didn't know how to fix it.

After two years of feeling trapped in my body, something shifted. At ten years old, armed with AOL dial-up internet and a fierce determination, I typed "how to lose weight" into the search bar. I learned what a carbohydrate was. I pestered my gym teacher for healthy eating tips. By cutting out soda and fried foods, the weight began melting off. I lost twenty-five pounds and felt lighter, physically and emotionally.

My passion for healthy living grew so strong that I wrote a book about it, with help from my brother. It was my safe outlet, my way of offering hope to others like me. But after putting my heart into it, I rescinded it, too ashamed and vulnerable to share my story with the world. I already felt like a target. I couldn't bear to make myself even more visible.

Looking back, I realize how unusual it was for a nine-year-old to show such fierce self-motivation. That book wasn't just a project; it was my first attempt at reparenting myself. I became the advocate I needed but never had.

Feeding a child the way I was fed should be considered a form of abuse. While I'm grateful I had food at all, the poor choices made by my parents, despite having the resources to do better, made my life exponentially harder. The frequent trips to fast food chains and frozen meals made it easy to put on unnecessary weight, and as a young child, I really didn't know any better.

Children who experience neglect or abuse often develop a strange duality: the desperate need to be seen and the overwhelming fear of it. I learned to make myself physically smaller; always clutching something in my lap, always slumping my shoulders, trying to disappear. What I truly craved was attunement, attention, a parent who noticed and cared.

Being unseen offers protection, but it also brings profound loneliness.

Cognitively, school became a battlefield. In fifth grade, we were assigned to read *The Lion, the Witch and the Wardrobe*: a book full of fantasy and intricate details. If you didn't absorb every word, you were lost. Our teacher, who looked perpetually sour, would cold-call on students daily to summarize random passages.

When she called on me to discuss the concept of a centaur, something I'd, of course, need for my future, my mind would flood with panic, and go blank. Even as it was, I couldn't focus and dissociated for a large portion of the day, only tuning back in when hearing my name or the word, "test." I begged my parents for help, telling them how mortifying it was. Their response: "Just pay attention." As if attention was a simple switch I could flip.

It never got better. I scraped by academically, but the damage was done. My self-concept was in shambles and I was still left unable to concentrate on anything for much time at all.

Even now, the memory of that teacher's withering gaze makes me cringe. I internalized the belief that I was stupid, not because I truly was, but because no one encouraged me to believe any different.

CHAPTER 15:
"A Special Kind of Freedom"

As I moved through my teen years, I kept struggling in some areas at school, especially with math. It was like my brain would just shut off at the sight of numbers and cue up the theme song to *Growing Pains*. I'd cry at the first sign of difficulty, overwhelmed, feeling defective and worthless. My emotions came in tidal waves: short-lived but strong enough to knock me off my feet.

My dad would sit down with me at the kitchen table and try to help me work through the word problems my teacher had assigned. I'd barely get halfway through a sentence before I had no idea what the question was even asking. I still wonder how many apples Joey had left after starting with forty-two, sharing some with his dog, losing six when they fell off the cart, and spiraling into an existential crisis. Word problems were like a foreign language I just couldn't decode.

I had mixed feelings about those kitchen-table math sessions. I hated them—they spotlighted my struggles, and my father and I would argue back and forth—but part of me also craved that time with him. Still, it felt like he wasn't really talking with me, just at me. His mind was analytical; mine was emotional and creative. We spoke different languages, and neither of us could translate. After years of this, I can honestly say I know no more math now than I did when we started. It was discouraging, and eventually I internalized the belief: *I'm just not good at math.*

In early high school, I discovered singing. I was pretty withdrawn by then, but one of my closest friends, more like a sister, made me feel safe enough to share my voice. We harmonized in a way that felt magical, carrying a tape recorder everywhere, covering songs by BBMak, Mariah Carey, Boyz II Men, the Dixie Chicks, and Amy Grant. We'd listen to our recordings on repeat, trying to get better each time. Weekends were spent finding new bands and songs to replicate.

When I sang, I felt something new; a special kind of freedom. I felt heard. It was terrifying and exhilarating all at once.

By my junior and senior years of high school, I decided to perform for NYSSMA, the New York State School Music Association. You'd pick a song of varying complexity and perform it for judges who scored you on technical accuracy and stage presence. I practiced for months. I asked my parents if I could show them what I was working on, hoping maybe they'd be proud. They were often too preoccupied to attend to me. After a while, I stopped asking. It felt like sitting across from someone on a date who couldn't wait to leave.

On the day of the performance, I walked in with sweaty palms and a racing heart. But I sang. I sang with everything I had. Somehow, I was able to belt it out for people I didn't know and would never see again. It felt beautifully anonymous. When I finished the last note, a surprising calm washed over me. Maybe, just maybe, it had gone well.

The judges asked me to step outside while they deliberated. When one of them handed me an envelope, his serious face broke into a smile. "Well done," he said.

Inside was a blue ribbon.

I sat in the hallway for a few minutes, overwhelmed by emotion. "I did it," I whispered to myself.

The ribbon shimmered like a star in my hands; a tangible piece of proof that I had done something that mattered. I wished I could have shared it with my parents. But even if I couldn't, I appreciated the moment.

When I turned eighteen, I decided to celebrate with my first tattoo. A good friend designed it, and another came along for moral support. It felt like marking the start of a new chapter; a small, personal denotation of adulthood.

It was all fun and games until I had to put on a swimsuit. Early-2000s tankinis didn't do much to cover it. As I leaned over to put on sunscreen, my mom's eagle eyes zeroed in.

Immediately, the rapid-fire interrogation began. I lied to her at first and said it was a wash-off, but her suspicious look told me she wasn't buying it. I eventually admitted the truth, knowing there wasn't much she could do at that point. I apologized for lying; however, I maintained that I had no regrets.

But she didn't let it go.

Years later, decades later, she would still bring it up at holidays, in front of others, turning it into a story of betrayal. Over time, she even rewrote the facts, claiming I'd been underage and had done it "illegally," a pattern I recognized well. When control slipped from her fingers, she'd rewrite history to seize it back.

My mother could never seem to let things go. She'd perseverate on mistakes, rehashing them until any guilt I might have felt hardened into resentment. Naming my "deceptions" gave her the upper hand, even if it meant twisting the truth.

But it was never really about the ink; it was about the power. It was the fact that I had made a decision about my own body without asking for permission. That I had claimed even a small sliver of autonomy.

The ink was permanent, yes, but more than that, it was symbolic. It represented a break from their control, a declaration that I belonged to myself. That I could make choices; bold, visible, unapologetic ones without needing their approval. And that terrified them. For them, love was often tangled with obedience, and identity with conformity.

Getting that tattoo wasn't just rebellion. It was reclamation.

Even birthdays felt controlled and performative. My parents would ask where I wanted to eat, only to reject my choices every time. Eventually, I learned to skip the song and dance and just say, "Wherever you want." Being asked was a formality; a box checked so they could believe they were generous, when really, it was always about them.

I was asked to make the dinner reservation for my own birthday at the restaurant they wanted. It felt more like a chore than a celebration. I was a background player, an employee carrying out assignments under the illusion of inclusion.

Year after year, excitement turned to disappointment, and disappointment turned to resignation. If I wasn't thrilled about making my own birthday plans or going to a place they personally liked, I was "ungrateful." There was no warmth. No recognition. Only expectations. I didn't feel celebrated; I felt managed.

Looking back, I wasn't a daughter to them. I was a symbol of commonality between them—a symbol of my mother's accomplishment where her career hadn't developed or materialized. I was there to hold things together, to fill spaces, to distract from what they didn't want to face in their relationship with each other or in their lives in general.

No wonder I always rooted for the underdog in movies. I was rooting for myself without realizing it. I wasn't the star of the show. I wasn't even in the credits.

My math struggles came back around when it was time to talk about college. My dad thought I should study finance or business and go to school in New York.

It was almost laughable; as if he had completely forgotten the years of kitchen-table meltdowns over basic word problems. He didn't see me; he saw an idea of who he wanted me to be. He saw himself.

Meanwhile, I was spending late nights online, searching for universities that actually sparked something inside me. One day, I remembered a story my sister-in-law had told me about her time at

Boston University. Something about it stuck. I scheduled a tour, and when I stepped onto the campus, I knew.

Snow-dusted sidewalks, cozy cafés, students hunched over battered paperbacks; it felt like a place where I could finally exist outside the narrow blueprint I had grown up under. It felt like possibility.

I decided to apply, even though I knew my parents would disapprove due to the school was out of state and not the cheapest option. At that point, hope was a risky thing for me, so when the acceptance letter came, it didn't feel real at first. I read the words "Congratulations on your acceptance to Boston University" over and over until the letters blurred.

For the first time in a long time, I saw a version of my future that actually belonged to me.

I approached my parents, trying to present it logically, calmly, a kid giving a PowerPoint presentation to an audience that had already decided the answer was no. My mom stayed silent, visibly annoyed. My dad's first reaction was to call it a "waste of money" and remind me that if they helped pay for college, there'd be no financial help for a future wedding; a transaction, not a milestone. This was a trade, not a celebration; a transaction, not a turning point.

My excitement quickly fragmented into dread at the possibility of missing this opportunity. I wished, just once, that they could see the whole picture; the actual person standing in front of them, not just the price tag, the distance, or their own desires. I was so excited to get accepted to the school and wanted, more than anything, for my parents to share that with me.

They couldn't.

But I knew the dance: stay calm, don't push too hard, because any sign of defiance would only make them push back harder.

After a lot of pleading and problem-solving, and sacrificing a few dreams along the way, they agreed. It felt less like support and more like winning a negotiation you weren't supposed to win.

But still; it was happening.

The kid who never expected much of herself was about to step into a life of her own making; not because anyone held the door open, but because she found a way to pick the lock.

CHAPTER 16:
"Witch Trials and Chowder"

College was a place of enormous growth for me. Coming from a home where I wasn't even allowed to go to the mall unsupervised, I suddenly found myself sailing in the Mediterranean with people I had just met and living the full red–solo–cup experience at every house party on the block. Boston—with its dense cluster of universities and young transplants from every corner of the world—felt like an explosion of everything I had been denied.

Sweet, stunning freedom.

My parents had bounced between overbearing control and total absence, and now there was no one watching. No one policing who I spoke to or what I wore or how I spent my days. It was terrifying, and it was exhilarating.

It felt strange going from the cookie-cutter, preapproved friends they wanted me to have to meeting people from all walks of life; different cultures, religions, sexual orientations. My mind stretched wider than I knew it could.

I found myself falling in love over and over with new experiences: basking in Harvard Square beneath towering oaks and maples that looked as though they were born out of a storybook; visiting the North

End with its intoxicating Italian dishes; tracing the edges of Paul Revere's statue with my eyes. I signed up for every ghost and witch tour in Salem, tasted enough clam chowder to write reviews, and practiced my Boston accent. I allowed myself to get completely lost in the quiet breath of my favorite part: the libraries. Sitting between stacks of hundred-year-old books made my world feel infinite.

I remember thinking: *This is what being alive feels like, and how tragic it would have been to miss it. I knew then there was no going back to New York.* The thought of it felt like returning to a locked room full of ghosts. I was becoming someone new, someone with boundaries, curiosity, and, finally, the beginnings of self-respect. I'd still visit for holidays, but after a day or two I was itching to leave; back to the bus station, back to Boston.

My mother made sure I felt the guilt of it.

She accused me of abandoning her by going away, though she barely acknowledged me when I was home. It felt like something she said more to hold me in a guilt-ridden state than because she actually meant it. At times, it felt as though she was fishing for things to be upset about. It was as if the idea of me leaving threatened some fragile part of her identity, not because she truly missed my presence, but because she missed the distraction I provided. I also think she viewed my decision to leave as a direct rejection of her.

Some of the few times she would come out of the woodwork when I was home visiting were to listen to my personal phone calls. She'd stand outside the door of the bedroom I was staying in.

"Who ya talkin' to?" she'd inquire. As if it were any of her business.

Her questions always came fast and sharp, a tactical game meant to trap me in some kind of lie or to find out personal information that could be used later for her own gain. She believed everyone was trying to deceive her, so she operated like a detective rather than a parent.

When I once brought up the idea of boundaries, she looked confused. After I explained, she said, "You're my daughter. What do you mean? We should tell each other everything." What she meant was that I should tell her everything. The exchange was never mutual.

She read my diary more than once. I'd know because she'd accidentally reference things

I had never told her. For her, privacy was disrespectful. Asking for space made me the villain. Going "home" didn't feel like returning; it felt like stepping into someone else's script again and I didn't want the part.

Connecting with my father wasn't any easier. Once, I sent him chocolates and nuts for the holidays since I was away at school. He called to say the chocolate had melted, the nuts were stale, and to "stop wasting money with things like that." Another time, I told him I planned to buy us tickets to a stand-up comedy show, hoping we could share a laugh together. He shut it down before I could finish the sentence. "I never heard of him. Probably no good. Skip it."

He didn't value the time together, only the utility of an experience he already approved of. It was never about connection. It was hard to stay motivated to reach out when I knew it would only leave me feeling foolish.

There was one exception. One small moment that stood out as uncharacteristically kind.

During my second year at BU, I lived in a single room in Myles Standish Hall; more broom closet than bedroom, but I loved the privacy. One week, I came down with a brutal virus. I could barely stand. A friend down the hall helped me get to the campus infirmary, and the staff called my parents.

To my surprise, they drove from New York to check on me. They brought cold medicine.

They bought Kraft mac and cheese. Then they went home.

It was the most care they'd ever shown me, and I still wonder what it was about that moment that cracked something open for them.

Why then?

Why only then?

I've come to believe that unless I was physically sick to the point where it was visible, there was no urgency. It was the only language they seemed to understand: visible, measurable suffering. And even then, only if the stars aligned could they attune to the situation.

And it made sense, in a way. My mother had always spoken in the dialect of ailments. Every need was translated through illness.

And I had no idea just how much her health would come to take center stage in our lives.

CHAPTER 17:
"A Different Kind of Sickness"

During my junior year of college, I came home for one of the holiday breaks and found myself in the kitchen making a batch of cinnamon French toast. My mother shuffled in, her slippers whispering across the wooden floorboards the way her mother's once had.

As I let my mind drift, my eyes scanned her absentmindedly—and then caught on something.

"Let me see that," I said, gesturing toward the back of her leg.

"What? Ugh, I have all these growths. Don't get old," she muttered, brushing me off.

But this wasn't just a random bump. It shimmered slightly, grayish-green under the kitchen light. An odd shape. It stood out from the map of freckles, scars, and age spots I'd grown used to seeing on her skin.

"I think you should get that checked out," I told her.

She actually took it seriously. She scheduled a doctor's appointment soon after—her annual visit was coming up anyway. A few days passed, and life went back to its rhythm: my father experimenting in the kitchen, my mother watching her "stories." None of us gave it a second thought.

Then I went back to school.

A week or two later, I got a call.

Her voice had that anxious tone I knew too well, but this time it wasn't just nerves. "They told me I'm already stage IV. Skin cancer. It's metastasized melanoma."

The words landed but didn't sink in. They floated there, unprocessed, as my brain went blank. I said all the right things, expressed sadness, support, asked questions about treatment, but I was running on autopilot.

My mother, as always, filled the air with chatter. She was never comfortable sitting in silence, especially not the kind that begged to be felt.

In a blur, she was connected with doctors at NYU Medical and began radiation and experimental trials. Traditional chemotherapy wouldn't do much at that stage, they said.

My dad wheeled her down crowded city blocks to appointments. She'd yell that he was pushing her too fast or too carelessly. Nothing was ever quite right.

I remember feeling sorry for them both, but for entirely different reasons.

The doctors encouraged her to join a cancer support group. A space to speak freely, to share the unshareable. She declined without hesitation.

"I'd rather just not think about it."

That one sentence told me everything. Even with her life on the line, she remained tightly sealed, emotionally padlocked. I wanted to beg her, just once, be unfiltered. To let herself fall apart.

But that wasn't who she was. She was the woman who wore makeup to bed. The woman who followed you around the kitchen to make sure you didn't get fingerprints on her cabinets. She could undergo radiation but not reflection. She could take poison into her bloodstream but not let a feeling touch her heart.

As treatments progressed, there were moments of hope. Her doctors spaced out appointments to give her a better quality of life. We began to breathe again.

But then her scans changed. The cancer was growing back aggressively. She needed lymph node removal, which led to lymphedema. Her legs swelled painfully, and with her preexisting obesity, mobility became almost impossible. The surgery crushed what little morale she had left.

My mother always had a glass-half-empty outlook. Now she had gallons to draw from.

She called everyone she knew to detail every symptom, every medical injustice. There was something unnerving in how animated she became while describing her suffering, how her voice perked up as she recited her ailments. I believe her pain was real, but it often came with a strange theatrical edge. She seemed to glow under the light of concern. It became a soap opera she made sure everyone watched.

One day she was dying; the next, she was "miraculously better." The inconsistency made it hard to trust what was real. And if I'm honest, it made compassion difficult. I never told her that; it would have crushed her, and we were already barely holding on.

But emotionally, I felt like I was being whiplashed. I wanted to get off the ride, but the child locks were on. Time passed strangely; slow and fast all at once. Years went by.

Eventually, her doctors declared she was in remission. The experimental treatments had worked. "You'll just need to come back for annual checks," one of them said, words we'd clung to for so long.

She was cleared to travel. Her color returned. Her energy climbed back.

But something I hadn't expected happened: she acted as though none of it had ever occurred. There was still no gratitude for life, no softened edges, no change in how she treated me.

I'd held on to the hope that this brush with death would shift something in her—that maybe she'd see me differently, or more clearly. But the roles snapped back into place like a rubber band. I watched her resume her life: shopping and dining out with my father. And even though I was still carrying the weight of our complicated relationship, part of me was glad she was okay.

Then came my graduation from BU.

The snow had melted, and bright yellow daffodils bloomed across campus.

Despite her improved health, my mother told me she wouldn't attend the ceremony. She said she was "still too sick."

I was confused. She'd been out and about, living normally. I asked why she couldn't make it, gently pressing.

She grew agitated. It was clear: don't ask again.

On the day of my graduation, I walked across that stage, shook my professor's hand, and felt a hollow space in my chest. If my child were graduating, I remember thinking, I'd die trying to get there.

A few weeks later, she and my father went to Vegas.

Apparently, she had a miraculous recovery; the kind only slot machines and buffets can inspire. It would've been laughable if it hadn't hurt so much.

CHAPTER 18:
"Hawaii is Where Honeymooners Go"

Timing is everything.

Had I not stepped into a particular elevator that first year of college, I would've never met my first husband. First husband. Even saying it tastes bitter. It sounds like failure; but that's not the story I want to tell, not here.

What I want to remember, or rather, what I can't seem to forget, is the engagement. Not just for what it meant to me at the time, but for how quickly it was minimized.

We had been together for six years. My ex-husband had been sweating bullets trying to plan the proposal. He chose a quiet horse trail we used to walk often. He got down on one knee, nervous and sincere, and when I said yes, we sat together on a picnic bench for a while, soaking it in.

I did what most daughters might do at that point: I called my parents. My hands were shaking. My face hurt from smiling. I was glowing in that wide-eyed, twenty-something way when the world still feels elastic and full of possibility. I wanted to share the news, to pull them into the joy with me. I wanted them to say they were happy for me, that I deserved love and stability and a future that looked nothing like the one they had created for themselves.

But what happened next, their reaction, taught me more about our dynamic than perhaps anything else up to that point.

"Well, did he get you a ring?" That was the first thing out of my mother's mouth.

The air went out of me. I felt like I was floating outside my body, staring down at this strange, disjointed moment where joy met judgment head-on.

There was a long pause. Then came a "Congratulations," forced and hollow, like a placeholder in a greeting card.

I had imagined that moment a thousand times, picturing joy and connection, but when it finally came, all I wanted was for it to be over.

There was no rejoicing afterward. No mother-daughter bridal shower. No shopping for wedding dresses, cascading down the aisles and bonding over lace, ribbons, and bows. I think I watched too many episodes of *Gilmore Girls*, and even though I knew most people didn't have that kind of relationship, my heart still ached with the lack of even an inkling of it.

My mother had survived cancer, made it through something life-altering and yet she still couldn't show up for me in these simple, symbolic ways.

Thankfully, others stepped in.

One of my closest friends from graduate school offered to throw a bridal shower. She went all out: finger sandwiches with curry chicken salad, cucumber tea rolls topped with tiny edible flowers, hand-crafted invitations, and a Zoom call set up with two of my best friends across the country. Her home was filled with laughter, love, and people who showed up for me. I felt so special for the first time.

I was overwhelmed, in the best way, by the care she poured into it.

Six months passed between the engagement and that shower. Six months when my mother could have offered something, anything.

Instead, she waited until she found out my friend had planned the event. Then she swooped in with an offer:

"I can throw a shower here in New York!"

New York, where I no longer had a network of friends. Where I no longer lived. New York, where the guest list would be her friends, not mine.

It wasn't about me. It was about her. Her guilt, her image, her need to perform motherly duties on her terms.

"No, thanks," I said. And meant it.

But the disappointments didn't stop there.

On the wedding day itself, she couldn't even give me that.

We had created a slideshow—cheesy music, baby pictures, milestones. The kind of thing people do at weddings to make you laugh and cry and remember. As it played, my mother stood up, back to the screen, and started chatting loudly at her dinner table about something completely irrelevant, as if nothing meaningful was happening. Guests had to lean around her teased hair just to see the screen. She didn't notice. Or maybe she didn't care.

How do you miss the signal that it's not your moment? How do you talk through your own child's wedding tribute?

Because in her world, nothing mattered more than her.

Later, my then-husband and I told my parents that we weren't taking a honeymoon just yet. We wanted to save some money. I was still in school, and my ex was just starting out, but we had a dream. It was our own.

"Iceland," we told them, smiling. "To see the Northern Lights, soak in hot springs, pet some reindeer."

My father wrinkled his nose. "It's cold and dark. Why would you want to go there?"

My mother chimed in, "That's no place for a honeymoon."

I felt foolish for sharing something that was meaningful to me—a feeling that was familiar. Like I was a child again, constantly being told my instincts were wrong, my dreams misguided.

Then came a phone call. My mother's voice was practically giddy. "I have a surprise! We decided, you're going to Hawaii! Just like your father and I on our honeymoon! Isn't that great?!"

There had been no conversation. No asking what we wanted. Just a declaration, as if our preferences were irrelevant.

It was packaged as a gift, but it wasn't for *us*. It was about *them*; their memories, their image, their idea of how the story should go. Our quiet little wish was replaced by something bigger, louder, shinier but emptier.

I paused.

Because it was generous. It was thoughtful on the surface. Many families don't do this for their children, and I appreciated that. But it was controlling again. I was voiceless. Erased. She hadn't even paused to wonder whether this trip reflected our wishes.

"Hawaii is where honeymooners go," she kept repeating.

When I didn't react with immediate gratitude, her tone snapped. I was "ungrateful." I was "impossible to please."

I hadn't even had time to process it.

Once again, it became a choice: go along with her plan and keep the peace, or say no and rupture the already fragile relationship.

We went to Hawaii.

And somewhere in the background of every sun-drenched photo, the Northern Lights flickered quietly, waiting for us.

But we never got to Iceland. They gave us paradise, but not permission. And so we wandered, smiling, through someone else's dream.

CHAPTER 19:
"A Female Role Model"

I never did move back to New York after that. Instead, I stayed in Boston to earn my master's in counseling psychology. I'd drive along snow-laced roads into Cambridge, headed to Lesley University; a cozy, artsy-fartsy program where people took off their shoes in class and believed in the healing power of finger painting.

It was even more of an adventure than undergrad: quirky professors, warm classrooms, the smell of chai tea wafting from someone's thermos. I learned quickly that "therapist attire" meant chunky sweaters and loafers. There was one professor who'd sit on the edge of his desk, stroke his beard with exaggerated thoughtfulness, and talk about Freud like he was the Messiah. Half the class rolled their eyes; the other half scribbled notes furiously. I floated somewhere in between, absorbing everything.

Part of the program included a clinical internship, and mine was at an outpatient day program in Beverly, Massachusetts. Beverly had a quiet, faded charm slightly run-down, but with a personality all its own. Well-worn laundromats and empty storefronts, once home to shining businesses, lined most of the streets.

I was thrilled. This was the real thing, no longer role-playing in classrooms or writing hypothetical treatment plans. I was working with actual people. Real stories. Real struggle.

And their charts God, those charts. They were thick, the kind you could barely close, and filled with brutal truths: stories of cult abuse, of people hung from ceilings and made to drink bleach; histories of chronic sexual trauma. Others had long battles with schizophrenia, major depressive disorder, bipolar disorder, diagnoses that lived not only in their charts but in their bodies, their language, their eyes.

It was terrifying and sacred. This was where I truly learned what psychosis looked like.

What deep, untethered depression felt like.

To my pleasant surprise, the staff welcomed me with open arms. They encouraged me, coached me, and gave me the freedom to lead groups, test out therapeutic tools, and stumble with dignity. They believed in me, maybe even more than I did. And that belief . . . it moved something in me.

For the first time, I felt nurtured not by family, but by mentors, colleagues, people who took the time to care about my growth. My self-worth started to bud, not because someone told me I was valuable, but because I was becoming someone I respected.

The work itself was grueling and beautiful. I learned that sitting with people who've been shattered by life is one of the greatest honors you can have. They trusted me to hold a piece of their pain. And even though I was still learning, I held it carefully.

That place will always be important to me.

When I close my eyes, I can still see the faded yellow wallpaper in the group room, smell the lingering coffee and burnt toast from the kitchen, someone was always burning toast and feel the worn mahogany desk under my palms as I reviewed worksheets and planned sessions.

Sometimes I miss it. It felt like home somehow.

At lunchtime, I would walk across the street to the café with my coworker Susan to grab a chicken cutlet sandwich. We'd debrief about clients, ethics, theory, and what it meant to help. It was cozy in there. The time we chatted elapsed quickly, and we'd need to scurry back to our desks after a short while to lead one more group for the day, either on healthy coping skills or maybe leading a drum circle.

Being around like-minded people in the field made me feel warm, seen. It was like wrapping myself in a knit blanket. I felt like I belonged.

When it came time for graduation, however, I didn't go.

I skipped it altogether. The idea of scanning another crowd and not seeing my family there, not feeling their pride. I didn't want to put myself through that.

You can't be disappointed if you don't show up, I thought.

But the truth is, something else was happening too: I was beginning to appreciate my own accomplishments without needing their applause. That felt like growth.

After graduation, I decided to keep going with my education—this time, across the country. San Diego.

It was a big move, but I had a good reason. A mentor of mine, Dr. J, had given me some advice I couldn't forget. She was seventy-seven years old, silver-haired, electric-spirited, and in the process of earning her JD—after already having a PhD. People would ask why she wasn't retired, why she wasn't playing golf or gardening or doing something more "age-appropriate."

She'd shrug and say, "I'm not dead yet."

Dr. J was the first strong female role model I'd ever had. She was fiercely independent, relentlessly curious, and had a presence that was both warm and steady. She was the one who urged me to pursue higher education. She said, "As much as you may love a man or feel you can depend on someone else, get your doctorate. That way, no matter what, you can take care of yourself."

Those words hit deep.

Then and now.

I imagined what life would've been like if she were my mother. How differently I might have seen myself. How differently I might have grown up; less eager to please, surer of my worth. Because if Dr. J was my model of motherhood, then my actual mother was her foil.

Where Dr. J said, "Learn, grow, be independent," I could almost hear my mother in the background, like a scratched record looping: "Find a rich Jewish man to take care of you and stop working as soon as you can." The difference between the two was seismic—one urging me to step into my own power, the other nudging me to shrink into someone else's shadow.

I remember sitting in Dr. J's office one afternoon, staring at the colorful stained glass adorning her windows. Sunlight filtered through in soft blues and deep ambers, casting a kaleidoscope across the floor. I was anxious after a difficult exam, spiraling in self-doubt, wondering if I was cut out for any of it. She looked up from my paper, then directly at me, and said gently but firmly, "You have a voice. Use it. The world doesn't need more women who disappear; it needs women who dare to take up space."

That sentence cracked something open in me. For the first time, someone wasn't just telling me I was smart, they were telling me it mattered.

Though she was always professional, she made the space feel safe; like you were being held without ever needing to be touched. Just being in her presence made me feel seen, but never exposed. Guided, but never controlled. She had a way of making you believe you could do hard things because she already saw you as someone who could.

Dr. J saw something in me: intellect, potential, grit, and treated those qualities not just as valid, but as sacred. She spoke to me as if I were capable of building something with my mind, not just my appearance.

Her belief in education wasn't transactional; it was transformational. She didn't just teach content, she modeled a life of agency.

It was different strokes for different folks, sure. But for the first time, I saw clearly that I didn't have to follow the script my mother had handed me. I could write my own. And I would, word by word, choice by choice, degree by degree. Dr. J gave me permission to want more, and the audacity to go after it.

CHAPTER 20:
"Don't Call Me Doctor"

San Diego felt safe from the start, like a place where I could finally exhale. I began building the foundation of my career, and for the first time in a long time, I felt at home. I decided to hold on to those rare pieces of life that felt that way, the few shards of my mosaic that actually brought comfort.

Determined to be independent, I tore through a five-year doctoral program in just three years, putting my neuroticism to good use. I buried myself so deeply in school and work that when I finally emerged, it felt as though I was a bear crawling out of her cave after a long, punishing winter.

I had loved what I was studying, and I was good at it, but somewhere in the process, I had lost parts of myself. Elements of softness, spontaneity, even joy had quietly slipped away while I was sprinting toward survival and success.

Still, I had done it. I had achieved something few people do. My doctoral graduation wasn't just a ceremony. It was supposed to be momentous, a symbol of everything I had endured, everything I had fought to overcome. It was the physical manifestation of my worth: hard-earned and undeniable. I imagined the applause, the regalia, the acknowledgment—and perhaps, the redemption. This was supposed to be the moment when the people who had overlooked me, forgotten me, hurt me, especially my mother and father, would finally see me.

But there was no sign of my mother. Again.

Deep down, I hadn't expected her to come, but that didn't spare me the sting of disappointment. It's a strange thing; to brace for absence and still feel gutted when it arrives. I guess some part of me still held on to hope, that small, stubborn ember of a child's wish: that if I accomplished something big enough, my family would finally show up, or finally value me.

Her absence was more than just an empty seat at a milestone. It was the silence after years of effort. The echo of all the times I had wanted her to be proud and had gotten indifference instead. I had climbed the mountain, but when I reached the top, I found I was still alone.

Her absence echoed long after the ceremony ended. I had crossed the finish line, but instead of feeling triumphant, I felt hollow. The degree was real, the achievement immense, but without the recognition I'd always longed for, it felt oddly untethered. I had spent so many years chasing this moment, imagining how it might stitch something back together in me. But the applause couldn't drown out the silence that mattered most. It was a sobering reminder: healing doesn't always come in the form of milestones. Sometimes, it's what happens after.

After graduation, I began working at a local psychiatric facility. My colleagues started calling me "doctor," and something strange happened; I cringed. The title felt foreign on my skin, like a costume I hadn't earned. I felt undeserving, even ashamed. I kept insisting people use my first name instead, but that only seemed to confuse them more.

Over time, though, something began to shift. As I kept hearing the word doctor spoken with respect, not sarcasm or skepticism, I slowly began to internalize it. And with that came a deeper realization: my self-esteem had been running on fumes for years. I hadn't even noticed how thoroughly I had come to doubt my own worth. The problem hadn't been the title. It was me, and the parts of me still waiting for someone else to give me permission to believe I was enough.

The more I confronted my inner world, the more I let the title settle, let my voice emerge, and allowed myself to feel pride, the more other truths began to surface too. With clarity comes consequence. I could no longer numb myself with productivity or hide behind the next goal. My body was tired, my mind frayed. I was burnt out, exhausted, and only then did I begin to notice cracks in my marriage that I'd been too preoccupied, or perhaps too afraid, to see before.

As my sense of self began to change, so did my perception of the relationship. What I started to see more clearly was this: I had married someone who, in many ways, mirrored my parents. Emotionally distant, avoidant, absent.

If I wanted to talk about something meaningful, I had to ask him to sit down with me. He'd look away, shut down, or sometimes cry; tears that pulled me back into the caretaker role again. I always ended up soothing him. That dynamic, that constant emotional labor, left me depleted. I didn't want to be the emotional shepherd in my marriage, too.

To be fair, he wasn't cruel. He was kind, and different from my parents in many ways. But I felt ornamental, like a fixture in the background of his life. As he trained to become a pilot, our conversations dwindled to air traffic and flight patterns. He rarely asked about me beyond a generic "How are you?" and spent more time away than at home. If someone had asked him my favorite hobby or who my closest friend was, I'm not sure he could have answered.

After more than a decade together, it hit me: he didn't really know me. Not in any meaningful way.

Our social circles had started to reflect the divide. His friends were technical, reserved, straight-edged. Mine were tattooed, artistic, emotionally open. The gulf widened.

And underneath it all was a core absence, a dull ache that whispered: This isn't enough. It looked fine on paper, but I felt like I was floating in space. We hadn't been emotionally connected in years. I think he loved me the most he knew how, but he didn't have the capacity to see me.

After eleven years together; years marked by quiet loyalty, suppressed needs, and as the emotional distance between us grew, the latter part of our marriage was consumed by agonizing self-inquiry. I had begun peeling back layers of myself, confronting childhood wounds and naming long-ignored truths. And in doing so, I reached a painful realization: I was wearing my invisibility cloak again. The same one I had worn growing up, the one that taught me love was something to be earned through silence, service, and staying small. I couldn't do that anymore. Not after how far I'd come.

We tried couples therapy with a specialist. I went in hopeful, maybe even desperate. For months, we showed up, sat on the couch, and took turns speaking. Or so I thought. But every time the therapist gently challenged his perspective on our lack of intimacy, on the emotional deadness that lingered between us, my husband grew defensive. He said the therapist was biased, that he was being ganged up on. The walls only grew thicker. The air between us more strained.

I remember one session in particular when the therapist asked him how he thought I might be feeling. He shrugged and said, "She's probably fine. She always is." It was a sentence that gutted me, not just because it was wrong, but because it reminded me so viscerally of my childhood. It took me back to being overlooked, to screaming inwardly just to feel seen.

The sessions went nowhere. We weren't partners trying to find our way back to each other; we were strangers sitting in the same room, holding different maps, pretending we were headed in the same direction. That's when I realized I had been in a marriage that echoed the very dynamics I had spent years trying to escape—emotionally unavailable, conflict-avoidant, and unwilling to do the hard work of truly seeing me.

It wasn't anger I felt in the end. It was grief.

Grief for the woman I had been, for the love I had poured in, for the hope that something might shift. But even grief, I learned, can be a form of clarity. And clarity became the compass I could no longer ignore.

I knew then: it was over.

Ending the marriage was the hardest decision I have ever made. Because I wasn't just losing a partner; I was losing my closest friend, my main support for so many years. Guilt washed over me. I couldn't shake the feeling of being responsible for other people's emotions, even those of grown adults.

When I told my parents I was considering separation, they brushed it off as if I'd mentioned switching laundry detergents. My mother said, "Yeah, well, sometimes it doesn't work out."

Sometimes it doesn't work out?

Eleven years of my life, wrapped around this person, through career changes, moves, grief, and growth, and that was all she had to say? No questions. No empathy. No curiosity about how I was feeling.

It hurt more than I expected. Not just because they didn't care about my marriage, but because it confirmed what I already knew: they didn't really care about me either. Not in the way a parent should.

There was no guidance, no warmth. Even though both of them had gone through divorces themselves, they offered nothing; no wisdom, no reassurance. Instead, the conversation pivoted back to them, as it always did.

My mother would do this thing: nodding incessantly with vacant eyes, a look that never quite met mine. She'd respond with some generic platitude that made it obvious she hadn't heard a word I said.

I remember recounting this to my individual therapist, Tony. I needed a reality check.

Was I overreacting? Being self-centered?

Tony didn't hesitate.

"Can't they just let you have something for a minute? Even a divorce? Jesus."

He got it.

Week after week, I'd bring stories about my parents into session to try to make sense of it, and Tony would repeat his best advice like a mantra: "Don't take the bait."

He meant that not every comment they threw my way deserved a response. Not every wound needed to be reopened. Other people's ignorance didn't have to poison our peace.

His advice became my grounding force.

It taught me how to detach from the chaos, how to recognize when someone else's storm didn't need to become my own. Their moods, their projections, their limitations could all live outside of me.

And in that detachment, I found a small but steady kind of freedom.

Tony was monumental in my healing. He helped me rewrite the narrative not to erase the pain, but to understand it, and to know that I didn't have to keep carrying it forward.

CHAPTER 21:
"The Facebook Reunion"

After more than over three decades of marriage, my mother began started to gain traction in her suspicions. She often felt uneasy about my father, who would claim he was going out to a museum and then disappear for the rest of the day. He began taking phone calls outside and guarded his phone like a bank vault. He grew distant, more critical, and I watched her internalize it all, ingesting it like black licorice, bitter and unwelcome.

Details of what was happening at this time between my parents at that time remained elusive, as they were notoriously secretive about their transgressions. To this day, I've never seen them kiss or embrace. You didn't show affection in public. You didn't talk about private matters. There was a sterility to their behavior that touched every part of our family.

One day, with little more than my father's vague disappearances as evidence, my mother announced that he was leaving her for an old girlfriend from his teenage years. They had reconnected via Facebook, that online graveyard of rekindled golden years. Her words hit me like a hammer. His recent evasiveness suddenly snapped into focus.

My father had always been quiet, but for a long time, I mistook that quiet for stability. He was the kind of man who rarely raised his voice, who prided himself on logic and routine, and who seemed most comfortable when discussing data or the inner workings of a machine. As a child, I interpreted his distance as calm competence. He wasn't warm, but he was there.

I came to equate his presence with safety, even when it was silent and detached. There was a steadiness in how he methodically chopped up carrots and onions of equal size to make a big pot of soup, or how he read *The New York Times* cover to cover every Sunday without fail. But now, looking back, I wonder if that quiet was just emotional vacancy in disguise; if I had learned to cling to the illusion of consistency because it was all he ever offered. When his attention shifted away from us, I felt it instantly, even if no one said anything. His silences grew heavier, more calculated, and somewhere in that space, the man I thought I knew simply evaporated.

While I stood in shock, my mother stood with fury, boiling over with disbelief. The infidelity had come to light through a glance at some strange texts on my father's phone. The messages, labeled as being from a male colleague, were clearly not. A technique my father likely thought was clever. My mother, always one step ahead, wasn't fooled. My father underestimated her determination; maybe he wanted to be found out, or maybe he was just that careless.

When she confronted him, he denied everything. But eventually, under pressure and constant badgering from my mother, he admitted the truth. From that point on, things only got worse. My mother's emotional volatility increased; my father grew more detached. And I became the unwilling emotional sponge for both of them. Their feelings didn't just exist in the space; I absorbed them.

It was as if my body became the battleground for emotions they refused to process themselves. I carried the anxiety my mother projected when she felt ignored, and the cold silence my father wrapped himself in like armor. I learned to read every shift in tone, every subtle cue, like a weather forecaster trying to predict the next storm. If I could anticipate their moods, maybe I could keep things from erupting. Maybe I could make things okay. We either sat in thick, suffocating silence or witnessed their hostility spill into screaming matches. Their arguments were cruel, often laced with sarcasm and disgust, each seeming to loathe the other but unable to let go. It was as if they used each other as mirrors for their worst selves, and I was caught in the crossfire, trying not to shatter.

Being the emotional sponge meant no one checked in on how I was doing because I was too busy managing how they were doing. I became hyper-attuned, over-functioning, and emotionally exhausted. Their volatility didn't just shape the environment; it shaped me. I didn't have all the language for it at the time, but I was parentified, absorbing emotional labor that no child, adult child or not, should have to carry. And though I appeared "fine" on the outside; helpful, and composed, I was silently crumbling under the weight of emotions that were never mine to begin with.

In the quiet between their battles, I tried to build some kind of structure for myself; anything to keep from unraveling the way my mother was. I buried myself in my work, often staying hours past when I needed to, volunteering for projects that didn't require me but gave me a sense of purpose. Anything to create some reprieve from my divorce or their chaos. I liked the predictability of client appointments, the calm rhythm of clinical notes, the sterile comfort of diagnostic criteria. It was the only space where I felt like I wasn't failing or falling apart.

Sometimes I would take long walks after sessions, just to hear something other than the static of my own looping thoughts. On particularly hard days, I'd open my laptop and type out pages of stream-of-consciousness thoughts with no punctuation, no structure, just raw, feverish attempts to make sense of things. I never reread those entries. They weren't meant to be anything but a release. I was slowly replacing my family with routine, trading connection for control. It was a quiet coping.

"You know he abandoned you too, right?" my mother would say, hoping to pull me into her grief, oblivious to how such a statement could fracture a person. I was no longer her daughter; I was her therapist, her echo chamber, her required ally. Her need to be comforted eclipsed her role as my mother.

Completely overwhelmed by both of my parents' emotions and behaviors, I turned to my older brother for support. Twelve years my senior, with a different father and his own family across the country, he had always felt a bit like a third parent to me growing up. I looked up to him. When we were younger, we used to sing Disney songs in goofy voices and eat late-night Cheerios while whispering secrets in the dark. He was smart, steady, funny, someone I had always believed would tell me the truth when I needed to hear it, but gently. I thought that maybe, if I could explain what was happening, he could offer me some kind of grounding. A voice of reason. Some validation that I wasn't crazy or too sensitive. I wasn't expecting him to fix anything; I just wanted to be heard.

I called him and launched into a breathless account of what I'd been managing: Mom's emotional spirals, Dad's increasing detachment, the screaming matches, the unbearable tension. I barely got two minutes in when he cut me off, sharp and abrupt:

"I don't have time for this. You're too much." Then click; he hung up.

I stared at the phone, stunned. The silence on the other end was somehow louder than the chaos I had just described. It took a few moments for the words to sink in. *You're too much.* It echoed in my head like a sentence I hadn't realized I'd feared hearing all my life.

I had expected compassion, or at the very least, curiosity. Maybe a simple, "That sounds awful. Are you okay?" But instead, I was met with complete dismissal. It surprised me, not because he had ever been particularly nurturing, but because I had clung to the idea that he could be. That buried beneath the distance, the years, and the different lives we now led, there was still some remnant of the brother I once knew. The one who looked out for me. The one who knew the version of our mother I was describing, because he had lived it too.

I had said something like, "I just need someone to talk to. I don't know what to do anymore." But what I didn't say was, I need you. I need to not feel so alone in this. I need to know that someone else in this family sees what I see.

Instead, I was left holding that need by myself. And in that moment, I didn't just feel dismissed. I felt abandoned.

In hindsight, the signs were there. His life was already full: triplet daughters, years of IVF, a draining career. I had hoped that, just once, we could reconnect like we used to. But that moment made it clear: whatever bond we once had was gone.

There had been breadcrumbs of our relationship disintegrating over time. Years earlier, I'd called him after being invited to do a radio interview about anxiety disorders. It was a big moment for me. I was excited, nervous. But his response? "Anyone can get on the radio. It's not really a big deal." His words deflated me. I was his little sister, craving pride and support. That should have been the first red flag of our changing relationship.

Meanwhile, the chaos at home escalated. My parents battled endlessly—over belongings, properties, who would live where. It was eventually proposed that my father would go back to New York to stay at their condo, while my mother would remain in San Diego. My mother felt she deserved everything because she was the wronged party. My father, meanwhile, disappeared into his new relationship, claiming his girlfriend didn't want him speaking to my mother.

"Oh, she doesn't like it?" my mom would yell. "How about the fact that your wife doesn't like it?"

They spent over a year in court, burning through thousands of dollars. Meanwhile, my mother spiraled. She constantly pressured me to "talk to him," as if I could somehow talk him out of his new relationship.

"Ask him why he would do this to his family after I did everything for him."

She sent unrelenting emails and messages to my father, refusing to take no for an answer. Other times, she'd concoct stories about dates she'd supposedly been on to make him jealous. She obsessed over his new girlfriend's appearance.

"What does she have that I don't?" she'd ask. "I looked at her pictures, she's so ugly, with a horse face."

She lied to my brother and me about how often she tried to contact him. She pretended she was moving on. There was shame in her attempts to win him back, but it was fleeting, quickly transmuting into overt desperation. I'd see the messages on her phone or email during the times she asked me to fix something on her old, clunky laptop. They were impossible to miss. It was pathetic and painful to see them all, a list of dozens. He was the only person she had tried to reach.

Then it got worse. My mother began researching the woman my father was seeing in more detail this time. She tracked down phone numbers and addresses, even messaging the woman's daughter and ex-husband. She told the daughter that her mother was a homewrecker. I still cringe when I think about the boundaries that were crossed. My mother couldn't just fall apart on her own, she needed to drag others into the wreckage.

After these anger-inducing conversations, she would repeat parts of the dialogue out loud to herself and pace around the house, as if trying to find answers among the empty rooms.

There was even an awkward phone call between my mother and my father's girlfriend at one point. Insults and hostility were slung back and forth. I remember his girlfriend saying, "Karma will get someone like you," as her parting words. The irony of that statement was almost comical, coming from the woman who had chosen to be with someone who was married, but really, the whole scene was enough to make onions cry.

You'd think my father would have drawn the line at that cringeworthy exchange. But he said nothing. As my mother and his girlfriend screamed at each other, he stayed silent, as if the whole thing had nothing to do with him.

"She won. I give up. She won," my mother eventually said. It wasn't about love. It was about ego.

At first, I couldn't quite name what I was feeling. It was like standing in the middle of a house that had been slowly burning for years, only now realizing the walls were ash. I walked around stunned, trying to be the calm one, the helpful one, the one who kept the pieces from flying off the table. My father had always been cold, yes, but I'd still held onto this quiet, unspoken hope that he would someday show up for me in a way that felt real. His detachment from the chaos he created, his willingness to let me clean up the mess while he played house with someone new—it pierced me in a way I wasn't ready for.

After the betrayal, the grief took its place. Not just for the marriage that ended, but for the family I realized had never really existed the way I thought it did. I grieved my brother too—the version of him who used to sing with me at 2 a.m. and ask about my dreams. That grief settled in slowly, like dense fog.

But eventually, something else began to form; something quieter, but sturdier. I started to pull back. I stopped answering my mother's baiting questions. I let the silence between my brother and me stretch longer without rushing to fix it. I realized that not every sinking ship is mine to save.

And with that came space. Not peace, not yet, but space.

Everything around me was crumbling. I was surrounded by people who never spoke the truth, who buried their feelings until they boiled over in cruelty or manipulation. I was treated as the problem for making waves, for acknowledging reality. I felt completely alone. And maybe, for the first time, I was.

But I also began to see things clearly. My mother had, perhaps unconsciously, chosen a man cut from the same unforgiving cloth as her father; men ruled by ego and ambition, unmoved by emotion, disloyal in both word and deed. Each had served in the military, each had made a living parsing data and systems with clinical precision, and each wore his coldness like armor, mistaking detachment for authority.

My father had no boundaries. My brother had checked out. And I? I was the only one still trying to make sense of it all, still trying to stay grounded in a family that had long since stopped caring about the truth.

This was the beginning of understanding what it means to survive not just abandonment, but emotional exile.

And still, I endured.

CHAPTER 22:
"The Transformation"

After decades of emotional distance, my father began doing something unexpected: he started looking in the mirror. Not the kind of glance a man gives to adjust a tie or smooth back a rogue hair. No, he became consumed. He worked out furiously in the gym tucked inside his New York condo, flexing muscles that had long since gone dormant. He bought sleek, European-cut clothing that looked better suited for a man half his age. And best of all, he decided to surgically remove the bags under his eyes.

My mother got wind of this transformation and called him in disbelief. "You're having a senior life crisis," she spat into the phone, her voice thick with derision.

He denied the surgery was cosmetic. "It's for my eyesight," he said.

How exactly did removing eye bags improve vision? I had to laugh. The absurdity was textbook Dad; he didn't care if his lies were obvious; he just needed a line to offer.

Then came the inevitable. He wanted me to meet the woman. A therapist, of all things.

Suddenly, he was fascinated by psychology, insisting we had so much in common. He even suggested I consider working with the military, something I was already doing, not that he knew. He never asked about my career. His awe for this woman made me queasy.

I put off the meeting as long as I could. Meanwhile, my mother applied pressure from the other side. "You won't sit and eat dinner with her, will you? That would be a betrayal of me," she'd say.

Her voice was sharp with abandonment and fear, cloaking her pain in ultimatums. No matter what I chose, someone would feel betrayed.

One afternoon, she looked me in the eye and asked, "What do you have to be so upset about with the divorce? This only affects me. He was my husband."

Her words stung more than I expected. Her blank stare told me she meant it. As if being an adult child of divorce rendered me immune to grief.

Her questions grew more invasive. "Do you think they slept together in my old bed?" I told her not to talk to me like that. She exploded.

"You're my daughter! Who else am I supposed to talk to?"

When I set boundaries, she accused me of taking his side. In her world, neutrality was treachery. Everything was binary.

It was dizzying; one parent emotionally volatile, the other vacant. Trying to stabilize them both was like standing upright in a canoe.

After much of my father's prodding, I eventually caved and agreed to dinner. Just one.

His girlfriend brought a book on psychology, clearly trying to bond with me. My father made cauliflower soup and brisket; the condo was warm with the smells of effort. He smiled more than I'd ever seen, giddy in her presence. She was dressed elegantly and radiated calm. When he put his arm around her, she stiffened, eyes flicking to mine. She wanted me to like her. I wasn't used to someone paying me that kind of attention.

I stayed surface-level. I already had one mother flooding me with inappropriate emotional content; I didn't need a second. Still, I made polite conversation because it mattered to him. She asked about my practice, my hobbies. I asked a few things in return. Her answers felt rehearsed.

When dinner ended, I escaped to my old room, the one I stayed in when home from college, shoulders unclenching like I'd just finished a debate speech. I sat on the bed, tracing the green and burgundy circles on the carpet with my eyes. Outside, thirty-five stories down, dots moved along Manhattan's avenues. I imagined being one of them, unmoored, disconnected.

Over time, my father traveled to her hometown, but his updates grew strange. He stayed in hotels. He hadn't met her friends. Even a year in, she wouldn't introduce him to her adult children. It was as if she was hiding him. The irony wasn't lost on me.

Still, he was smitten. He bought her blue lapis jewelry, her favorite. He stared at his phone like a lovesick teenager. But slowly, she pulled away emotionally, answering his calls less and less. She spent more time out with friends and family, and less with him. He filled the silence by calling my mother, getting her hopes up before ghosting her again. It was a carousel of manipulation.

Eventually, he stopped mentioning the woman. When I asked, he blamed my mother. "She was scared off by her behavior," he said.

But I didn't buy it. She wasn't afraid of my mother. She just didn't want my father. The man she'd imagined from decades ago no longer existed; the army hero with thick, lustrous hair. Their worlds no longer aligned in politics, spending, or family. The past wasn't enough to sustain them. My father couldn't see it. He clung to a fantasy version of them that wasn't real.

After it ended, he sat alone in that cold condo for another year, unwilling to date or join anything that might offer community. He was unraveling. Our weekly calls were mostly silence. He told me he walked for miles across New York City each day to stay busy.

"Please don't walk alone at night," I told him. He ignored me.

Then one evening, he said he'd fallen and had to have a stranger help him up off the concrete. He'd tripped over some sidewalk debris, cutting his knee and his face. I felt chilled, worried for his wellbeing, but even after the incident, he continued the same routines. It reminded me of how he handled most everything else: unwilling to learn from his mistakes.

I visited a few times. The condo was barren. No more of my mother's knickknacks, no warmth in any corner. Just a man in his sparse museum.

He told me he'd gone to therapy. I nearly choked; that was never something he would have done when he was married to my mother. His girlfriend had encouraged it when they were together, and I wondered if attending was his way of reconnecting with her in his mind.

"What was that like?" I asked, trying not to pry too deeply.

He shifted in his seat. "The therapist said I might have narcissistic traits." Then he changed the subject abruptly. Soon after, he stopped going altogether. It felt as if he immediately regretted cracking open the lid, like he'd stirred something too messy, too real, and now all he wanted was to shove it back in and pretend it had never been there.

Something shifted inside me that evening. I stopped trying to fix him. I still called, still checked in, but I let go of the hope that he would become someone different.

He looked in the mirror, but he still couldn't see.

CHAPTER 23:
"Not Even The Ocean"

It became impossible to see my mother without her obsessing over my father. I remember one Mother's Day when I planned a special outing for the two of us, a lunch at a beautiful ocean-view restaurant. The balcony was framed with pink and yellow hibiscus, their fragrance drifting through the dining room. The waves lapped against the sand below, creating a sleepy rhythm in the background. I had hoped the outing would be a chance to connect, to mend our strained relationship. Instead, it was hijacked by her relentless questions about my father.

Since I was the only one still in contact with him at the time, I became her personal information pipeline, an emotional treasure trove she couldn't stop digging through.

"Where was he? What did he say? Did he ask about me?" Her focus remained solely on him, leaving no room for us. Each question stoked my anger and resentment, pushing me back into the role of messenger. I felt like a stagehand at a concert, there to facilitate the main event but never to be seen under the spotlight. Even the ocean couldn't compete with her obsession.

My mother had become terrified of being alone. "What if they rob me or rape me?" she would murmur whenever I suggested she try dating someone else. I helped her create online dating profiles, though it quickly became clear this wasn't about finding a partner—it was about provoking my father. She would send him ridiculous, fake messages: "Can't wait to see you tonight!" followed by, "Oops, that was for someone else."

Despite the absurdity of these attempts, he bit. His jealousy fed into her game, and soon she was back in the cycle of desperate manipulation. It baffled me that he didn't see through it. She played the part of the vulnerable woman while he fed her delusions, and she relished the power it gave her.

I tried to detach from their drama, but it was impossible. Her tactics were transparent, yet effective, and I was left watching, helpless.

My mother's obsession with my father never truly ebbed. It wasn't just about missing him—it was a compulsive need to keep him in her orbit. And when he pulled away, she would spiral, endlessly rehashing every slight, every betrayal.

Her thoughts circled him like a predator stalking its next meal. She created stories to justify her behavior, convincing both herself and me that she was the victim. And as always, when she needed to vent, I became her sounding board.

It wasn't long before she began sharing things about him I knew she never would have told me if they were still married. She would spill secrets, only to later retract them with a simple, "I never said that." It was a twisted version of reality one where facts and feelings were interchangeable.

After a period of painful separation, my father reappeared in San Diego just as my mother had inherited money from my grandfather. And, just as predictably, he reentered her life, not because he wanted to reconcile, but because he wanted to take something.

While she was in the kitchen preparing lunch, he rifled through her belongings and helped himself to several valuable netsuke—small, intricately carved Japanese sculptures. When she returned, she noticed they were missing. He admitted to taking them, but only after she pressed him. It was a childlike confession, and the power imbalance was staggering.

She begged me not to tell him I knew. The fear in her eyes was palpable. If we rocked the boat, he might leave again. She couldn't bear that. So, of course, she forgave him without much questioning. This was their cycle: manipulation, forgiveness, and moving forward as though nothing had ever happened.

A simple gesture from him was amplified and endlessly celebrated whenever they were getting along. My father was taking piano lessons during this time, and even though he used one finger at a time to strike the keys, my mother would exclaim, "He's amazing, Ashley. You have to hear him! He's a regular Beethoven."

She would beam from ear to ear at how incredible she thought he was, making the whole thing feel performative—superficial, detached from reality. The dynamic was bizarre to me. I often questioned whether I was seeing the same thing she was.

The extent to which she infantilized my father went beyond exaggerated admiration. She spoke about him like a doting mother heaping undue praise on a spoiled child. She would monitor his eating habits, often inserting into conversation that she needed to "feed him soon," as if referring to a toddler whose appetite had to be managed and maintained.

As usual, I was the only one to recognize how strange it all was. Her reactions were never proportional to what was in front of her. The narrative swung wildly from my father being a disgusting, horrible person to a perfect angel. Complete whiplash. Black and white. I was expected to flex with the tides, moment to moment. It's no wonder I was often left disoriented just being around them.

My parents would go from this stage of idealization straight into their reemerging issues; namely, my father keeping black-and-white photographs of women he had dated thirty years earlier, women in bikinis or smiling up at him adoringly. It sent my mother into a fit whenever she caught him looking at them.

He had a short fuse around this matter and made it clear she would have to learn to live with it. His most recent response to her was to tell her to "go to hell" if she expected him to let go of those photographs. Very romantic.

One night, everything came to a head. I received a call from my mother at 10 p.m. Her name appeared on my phone, not as "Mom," but with her full name. The title didn't feel fitting anymore.

"Uhh, Ashley," my dad's voice boomed through the line. "We need you to come here right now. Mom's on the floor, and I can't get her up."

In the background, I could hear her crying.

"He pushed me onto the floor. I could have hit my head."

It was one thing to manage their volatile emotions, but now they were putting hands on each other. It felt surreal.

His calm response: "Yeah, I didn't push her. Can you just come right now?" was infuriating. He showed no concern for her injury, no empathy for the situation. I wanted to scream, to tell him to fix his own mess. But I didn't.

I told them we'd be right there. Moments later, they called back. They didn't need me after all. They'd called the doorman instead. I was left with a gnawing sense of confusion and dread about what had just happened. And as always, I was expected to move on as though nothing had occurred; just another unresolved trauma swept under the rug.

A few months later, my mother visited my father in New York. She promised to be on her best behavior. But within a day, she was demanding details about his affair with the other woman. When my father refused to answer, she threw a glass of water in his face. He retaliated with his own. And then, in an instant, he told her to "get out."

My seventy-five-year-old mother trudged into the snowy streets of Manhattan with her suitcase, and my brother reluctantly took her in. Even he, who had always stayed distant from their chaos—was stunned by my father's coldness. They didn't speak for almost a year. And yet, like clockwork, their cycle resumed.

CHAPTER 24:
"Holiday Tension"

Throughout the course of time, my parents forgave each other once again, minimizing the impact of their past conflicts. They began chatting more often but continued to live separately. It was the longest they'd gone without conflict; six months, with no major incidents reported. I thought things might finally be settling.

Both of my parents expressed interest in spending Thanksgiving together at my house. I hoped for a peaceful gathering and assumed as much, especially since eight of our friends were also attending the holiday. I wanted to believe that, this time, things would be different.

The dinner table was beautiful, adorned with a burgundy tablecloth woven with silver threading. Chocolate turkeys sat on every plate. Despite my efforts at creating a calm atmosphere, it didn't take long for things to unravel.

One of our friends began asking everyone at the table how each couple met and invited them to share "their story." One friend recounted how they had met on a double date and ended up liking each other's partners better, switching mid-way through the evening. Another couple shared that they had met while traveling abroad.

Stories flowed, and laughter rang through the dining room as we all shared memories. We skipped over my parents, as everyone knew they were no longer together. However, my mother is not one to pass up an opportunity to talk about herself.

Unable to hold her tongue, she began recounting the story of how my father had abandoned her for another woman. She burst into tears, making the entire table uncomfortable. My father, mortified, sat in silence.

I broke the tension with a joke about who wanted a cocktail, but the damage had already been done. Her emotions spilled over in front of an audience this time. For a moment, I felt less alone in witnessing this chaos, but it didn't make me feel any better.

Neither of my parents ever spoke of the incident again. They pretended everything was fine, their specialty. Yet I could tell my mother was still struggling with the uncertainty of their relationship. She wanted them to be married again, to put it all behind them, to live the life she had imagined in her mind.

Her difficulty coping with their separation only amplified her distorted thoughts. She would claim that my father had bought her a gorgeous perfume as a sign of his affection. Later, I learned she had asked him to buy it—and never paid him back. To her, though, it was a symbol of his love, an illusion she clung to.

Even simple acts held the potential to trigger something volatile. We never knew where the landmines were buried. After a lunch I had with the two of them, we decided to take a walk along the San Diego Bay, which bordered the restaurant. Rather than joining us, my mother chose to wait on a bench until my father and I returned. When we did, she erupted in fury, accusing us of abandoning her. It wasn't the first time, and it wouldn't be the last. Navigating her emotions was like steering a paper boat through a hurricane. She couldn't tolerate the uncertainty of their future. Between her constant neediness and her obsession with my father, there was no room left for me.

In the end, I realized their relationship functioned through a kind of shared, willed ignorance. They couldn't be emotionally present and survive together. There was no room for reality, only cycles of manipulation, forgiveness, and deceit. The irony? My mother maintained a close friendship with her ex-husband, my brother's father. Despite their messy divorce, she kept that relationship on her terms. Had my father ever done the same, she would have gone ballistic. But he never questioned it. That was the secret to their survival: denial. Without it, their relationship would have crumbled long ago.

It's a lot of work, protecting a house of cards.

CHAPTER 25:
"The Rebuilding"

As I was rebuilding my life after my divorce, neither of my parents checked in on me—not once. It was clear they could barely manage their own chaos, let alone be there for me. But isn't that what parents are supposed to do? See if you need anything, ask how you're holding up, make sure you're still breathing? Instead, the dynamic was often reversed. The expectation was that I would always be there for them.

Meanwhile, I spent countless nights alone, trying to figure out my next steps in a life that felt disorienting. I'd sit cross-legged on the floor of my half-furnished apartment, sifting through bills and scribbling half-finished to-do lists in the margins of old notebooks. Some nights I paced the kitchen until sunrise, chewing the inside of my cheek, wondering how to stretch my budget to afford groceries and rent.

I was running on a mix of adrenaline and dread, trying to chart a path forward while still carrying the emotional rubble of the life I had just left behind. My phone barely buzzed; not from the people who should have known to ask. I wasn't just rebuilding logistics; I was trying to reassemble my sense of safety, my identity, my hope.

I had always wondered what it might feel like to have a parent I could truly turn to for guidance; someone steady and present, who could help me navigate life's harder moments with care and wisdom. That longing never really left me, even as an adult. During one stretch, I asked my father for advice. I was trying to restructure my business to reclaim some balance, to make it more sustainable after too many long hours.

He had run his own company for years, and I thought maybe he'd have something meaningful to offer. This business wasn't just my livelihood; it was my lifeline, the thing I had poured my heart into when everything else felt unstable. It was something that was truly mine.

He barely looked up from his phone. "Just shut it down," he said flatly. "Work for someone else. It's easier."

I stared at him, stunned; not just by the dismissal, but by how effortlessly he discarded something that meant everything to me. In that moment, the silence between us grew cavernous. I hadn't necessarily come to him for a business plan; I just wanted to know he had some semblance of faith in me. But he couldn't give me that.

That was it. No curiosity, no questions, no encouragement. He didn't ask what I was building, who my clients were, or what my goals might be. It wasn't just discouraging, it was dismissive. It made me feel foolish for even trying, as if I were asking for something frivolous. His words felt undermining, as though my aspirations were burdensome fantasies rather than something real.

That exchange left a mark; a quiet confirmation of what I had long suspected but tried not to believe: that I couldn't count on him, not even for the smallest gesture of support. Still, some part of me kept hoping things might be different the next time. That maybe, in a more pressing situation, he would show up.

When I found a house I loved, a place that felt like the fresh start I desperately needed, I reached out again. This time, I asked him for a small, short-term loan to help with the down payment. I had the means to repay him within a few months; I just needed a bridge.

His response? "No, I'll be selling my condo and buying a new one soon, so I need the money." The speed of the dismissal stung more than the refusal itself. This was a man in his late seventies, a multi-millionaire, who couldn't even feign deliberation or offer a basic kindness. He never did sell his place.

I wasn't looking for a handout. I was looking for empathy, for even a moment of recognition that times are different now, that buying a home today isn't the same as it was when he was starting out. I explained the shifts in the housing market, the rising cost of living, the reality of stagnant wages, massive student loans, and soaring property taxes, especially in California. But he refused to acknowledge any of it.

"Homes cost more, but you get paid more, so it's all relative. This generation has nothing to complain about." It was a complete oversimplification, a wall I couldn't break through, no matter how much reason or evidence I laid before him.

Did he really think young people just didn't want homes? That no one worked hard anymore? The people I knew were burning out just trying to get by, delaying children, relocating to more affordable states, working multiple jobs. To me, the shift was obvious, or at least worth discussing. But with him, there was never a real conversation, only dismissal. Talking to him always left me feeling more alone.

Maybe acknowledging this reality would have forced him to confront his own privilege or guilt—maybe even a sense of responsibility to help. Or maybe he just didn't want to. Above all, it seemed he was simply incapable of empathy.

The house I'd been so hopeful for sold. When I eventually bought another place on my own a few months later, aspects of it turned out to be a disaster. The foundation had problems that hadn't been identified in the inspection. One New Year's Eve, after a heavy rainstorm, the house flooded like a river.

It started with a small pool forming, and within a few hours, six inches of water cascaded from the front yard into the living room, seeping up through cracks in the foundation. Much of that night was spent fruitlessly scooping water into buckets and pouring it down the sink. Every towel and mop in the house was exhausted. The water kept flowing for hours, and I was too afraid to sleep terrified of what I might wake up to.

My savings were wiped out fixing it. We had to tear the place down to the studs, rip out baseboards and the new flooring we had just installed, build drainage systems, and pay for mold remediation. And, of course, neither of my parents offered to help financially or emotionally. Not a call. Not a kind word. Nothing.

As I was trying to hold myself together emotionally, financially, spiritually, my father decided to inform me that I wasn't an equal in my mother's will. My brother had been named the sole executor. It wasn't about money. It was about what the role symbolized: trust, respect, belonging. Another slight.

Being treated as an equal would have meant I was trusted, that I mattered, that I was seen as capable and important within the family structure. Instead, I felt like a footnote. I wasn't just overlooked; I was deliberately excluded. My father's casual announcement that my brother would handle everything wasn't just news, it was a wound. It screamed, *You're not the one we believe in.* And what hurt most was that they never seemed to think I might notice, or care. As if I wouldn't register being cast out of the inner circle. As if I hadn't spent most of my life trying to earn my place in it.

The challenge was getting my parents to see this for what it was: a matter of acknowledgment, not assets. But I also knew how they viewed things. For them, the role of executor was about favoritism, about who had earned the honor. It was a symbolic crown reserved for the "worthy." I wasn't even in the running.

If my parents were still together, I doubt my father would've told me at all. It felt like a petty move, a jab at my mother during one of their on-again, off-again fallouts. Most of the time, the only way I learned anything about their relationship was when they tried to weaponize information against each other, using me as the unwilling messenger. I tried to act unaffected, but I wasn't. All the old wounds reopened: not being good enough, not being seen, not being chosen. I was never an equal.

I carry pain physically when I keep my feelings inside, so I knew I had to say something to my mother. Not because I expected her to fix it, but because the silence was choking me. I couldn't keep making small talk about the weather or some movie she'd seen on Netflix, pretending everything was fine. It wasn't.

When I brought it up, her reaction was predictably evasive. My mother was more concerned with how I'd found out angrier that someone had revealed her secret than that her daughter had been hurt. She seemed surprised I knew, and immediately redirected her frustration toward my father. Then came the classic freeze-out: the blank stare, her face slack and still, like the lights were on but no one was home. She had a way of going completely vacant whenever she didn't want to deal with something. It was as if she left her body behind in the chair while her mind drifted off to some parallel universe.

What hurt most was knowing I was the only child living in San Diego, where she now resided. If something happened to her, shouldn't I be the one prepared to handle things? But she didn't trust me, and that's what stung. Not just the silence, but what it implied.

I would've preferred a blunt rejection. Something definitive: I don't trust you because of X. At least then I'd know where I stood. But this silence, this vague erasure, left me to fill in the blanks with my own worst thoughts. That I was unworthy. That I was a mistake. That I'd been born not out of love but convenience—another tool to tether my father to her, or to avoid facing the world on her own.

In my family, conflict was a balloon you simply let float away. If something became too uncomfortable, you popped the conversation before it could fully form. Change the subject. Pretend it didn't happen. Blow another bubble and watch it disappear into the summer sky.

CHAPTER 26:
"What House?"

It was June 2022, time for my brother to host a birthday celebration for his three daughters. My boyfriend and I flew with my mother from San Diego to New York to attend their Bat Mitzvah, held on a rented boat. Flying with my mother is no easy task. She requested a wheelchair to get through the airport, even though she was perfectly capable of walking. She complained constantly; about everything from the café staff touching her straw to the length of the security line. Her suitcase was enormous, packed with nearly every outfit she'd worn over the past five years.

My father would have typically accompanied her and managed these behaviors, but they were separated at the time. Still, their emotional entanglement lingered, an unresolved, ever-present undercurrent.

A Bat Mitzvah, if you're unfamiliar, is a significant milestone in Jewish culture, marking a child's transition into adulthood. Given my father's role in raising my brother, he had been invited to attend and participate in an important tradition: cutting the challah bread and offering a blessing. It was a gracious gesture, especially considering the fractured family dynamic.

My father, avoidant as ever, refused to go. Worse, he didn't have the decency to inform my brother that he wouldn't be attending or to formally decline the honor. I encouraged him to make the call, to at least acknowledge the invitation, but he wouldn't budge. To this day, I don't know whether his absence was driven by guilt or shame over what he had done to my mother, or whether he simply didn't care anymore. Most likely, it was a blend of both.

His silence created a ripple effect that defined the tone of the entire event. Instead of finding joy in having her children gathered to celebrate such a meaningful occasion with her grandchildren, my mother cried over my father's absence. His void eclipsed everything else for her. She clung to hope, even in the days leading up to the event, that he might change his mind and show up. He didn't.

My brother made it clear that he no longer wanted my father to attend. Still, my mother ignored his wishes to preserve her own fantasies, endlessly trying to convince him to come. The hypocrisy stung. Had it been me who refused to attend, my mother would've berated me endlessly for being unsupportive. But my father? He could do no wrong. His absence was always somehow forgivable sometimes even excusable.

After the party, we returned to my brother's home for some additional gathering while family was in town together. There, I was greeted by my sister-in-law's aunt, a lively former photographer with an air of practiced charm. As she floated through the kitchen assembling a snack tray, she beamed, "So, don't you just love your brother's new house on the water?"

Amazing, right?"

"I'm not sure what you mean," I said.

"What do you mean?" she replied, taken aback. "Don't you talk to your brother?"

I was stunned. *What house? What was she talking about?*

Later, I asked my mother, assuming she'd be able to clear things up. Instead, her silence filled the room like the scent of an old woman's perfume: thick, invasive, and impossible to ignore. A familiar vacant stare came over her, her expression reminding me of an animal playing dead, hoping its predator would keep moving. In my family, silence was always an alarm bell. It signaled secrets, lies, or an attempt to dodge the truth.

I didn't let it go. I pressed.

Reluctantly, she admitted, "Your brother bought another house. He told us not to tell you. I told him it was wrong and that you'd find out eventually, but he didn't want you to know."

She was quick to throw him under the bus with barely a nudge. There was no cohesive explanation, no logic to her story; just deflection. The only conclusion I could draw was that my brother thought I'd be jealous. But even that didn't make sense. His possessions didn't impact my life or diminish my own accomplishments. We lived in completely different worlds, more than a decade apart.

What hurt more than the lie was what it revealed: the same pattern of secrecy that had threaded through generations of our family. My brother, in keeping this hidden, showed just how much he'd become like our mother, habitual in deception, self-righteous in the aftermath.

When I confronted him, he immediately denied doing anything wrong. It was almost impressive how effortlessly he sidestepped the issue, minimizing and rationalizing his behavior. It was as if he'd rehearsed this dance many times before. There was no acknowledgment of my feelings, no apology, not for hurting me, nor for the deception itself. His tone was casual, as though he were commenting on the weather. "I wasn't hiding it," he said. "Just didn't think it was such a big deal."

My mother, of course, refused to take any responsibility. I told her that enabling one child to withhold information from the other made her complicit. I was tired of being on the outside, tired of being the last to know, but my words seemed to drift past her. It felt like a betrayal, and it hurt.

At times, my mother looked almost pleased with herself, as though she relished sowing tension between her children. She had a habit of telling each of us different stories, fueling suspicion and resentment, as if doing so maintained her place as the emotional center of our fractured family. If we never got too close, she remained essential. I wondered if this was one of those scenarios she thought wouldn't be traced back to her; a moment when she could plant seeds of doubt in the family garden.

That night, after the party and after learning about the house, I lay awake in bed, staring at the ceiling, feeling a familiar ache crawl up my spine, the ache of being outside something I once believed I belonged to. I wasn't jealous of the house. I was angry about the lie. Angry at how easily I'd been excluded, how effortlessly my family could make decisions that treated me like an afterthought.

This wasn't the first time something significant had been kept from me, and I knew it wouldn't be the last. Moments like this reminded me that, in my family, closeness was conditional. If you didn't follow certain unspoken rules; rules no one ever explained; you were gradually, quietly moved to the margins.

I felt myself tighten inside: my jaw, my stomach, my chest. There was no room for my pain in this family unless it could be repackaged into something useful for someone else's narrative. If I expressed hurt, it was dismissed or minimized. If I asked for honesty, I was accused of stirring up drama.

What hurt most was the repetition of it all; the predictability. This was how my family operated. My father disappeared, and everyone adjusted their expectations downward. My brother absorbed our mother's habits and then denied he'd done anything wrong. My mother floated in the middle, somehow always the victim, even when she was the architect.

And me? I was always the one pointing out the smoke while everyone else insisted there was no fire.

I was exhausted; drained by the constant effort it took to get the people closest to me to be honest, to stop hiding behind deflection or denial, to treat me as a real member of the family instead of just a variable in their emotional equations. I couldn't stop thinking about how the cycle kept repeating itself, how secrecy seemed to pass down through generations like a prized heirloom. My mother had never felt the need to be truthful with her children or even with herself and now my brother was following the same path. Both of them used omission as a form of control, a way to preserve power.

Meanwhile, I had grown up needing the truth like oxygen, but I was constantly expected to breathe through a straw.

That trip cemented something for me; a slow, painful realization I had tried to avoid for years: I wasn't part of their inner circle. I was adjacent to it, orbiting it, welcomed in when convenient, excluded when uncomfortable. And the worst part? I kept showing up, wishing it might be different this time.

But it never was.

CHAPTER 27:
"Being the Parent"

As time went on, I watched many of my close friends become mothers. Some enjoyed it more than others, but most ultimately embraced that path for themselves. Baby showers, stroller photos, holiday cards with matching pajamas, they all began to blur together like a slideshow of a life I never quite felt called to. Motherhood never felt congruent with who I was. I had a deeply nurturing side, yes, but at the same time, I felt estranged from love itself. It was foreign to me, like a language I had never learned to speak.

I didn't know what it was like to receive love consistently and without conditions, so the idea of giving it in its purest form, especially to a child, felt strange, even frightening. I wondered why I didn't have that same internal instinct that seemed to strike most women like clockwork.

And of course, the pressure came right on schedule, that familiar parental refrain:

"Why don't you have a kid? We'll watch it!"

It.

They always said it like they were offering some grand solution to a problem I didn't have. As the words left their mouths, I wondered if they truly believed what they were saying or if they were aware of the complete bullshit of it all. I couldn't even get them to help watch my dogs on the rare occasions I'd asked.

"Can't make it. Sorry," my dad texted from his condo, retired and alone, with nothing else on his calendar. He was so bored he'd started looking into volunteer opportunities just to fill his days, yet still couldn't be bothered to help me. Nothing stings quite like rejection from someone with every opportunity to show up and still choosing not to.

I knew exactly how it would play out if I had a child. In the beginning, my parents would visit for an hour or two, just long enough to snap a photo and post it online, their proof of being a loving, involved family. Maybe I'd see them again on a random holiday, long enough for them to have something to brag about to a neighbor in their building, short enough to slip away before any real needs arose.

When they weren't there for me, how could I trust they'd suddenly be there for someone even more vulnerable?

The thought of having a child without any reliable support system felt like trying to swim with weights tied to my ankles. I felt suffocated just thinking about it. It would only create more opportunities for disappointment and I was already drowning in the ones I had.

More than anything, I feared what it would feel like to watch my own child experience the same kind of pain I had. I worried they would grow up feeling invisible, as I once did. I wasn't interested in handing that legacy to another unsuspecting soul. We don't need more children who feel unloved and unseen. Sometimes we convince ourselves our upbringing wasn't that bad until we imagine whether we would want another child to live it. Then we get our answer.

I had spent so much of my childhood being parentified; emotionally responsible for my mother, constantly walking the tightrope of her moods, offering advice no child should have to give. I was the emotional warden, the mediator, the keeper of her stability. I never truly got to be a child myself, and the idea of giving up my freedom now, as an adult, to care for someone else felt like surrendering the small slice of autonomy I had finally earned.

When we are denied a balanced, healthy childhood, it leaves us starving for one later in life. Either that, or we resign ourselves to living a muted version of who we might have been, forever unfinished. Even though I considered myself mature in most ways, I was surprisingly childlike when it came to the thought of becoming a parent myself.

My parents could never fathom that one of the main reasons I chose not to have children was because of how alone I felt during my own childhood. If it had been full of warmth and laughter, holiday traditions without conflict, family dinners that felt welcoming instead of tense, I think I might have been open to the idea.

I've always loved the image of a full house: people coming and going, barefoot kids running through the living room, someone always grabbing an apple from the fruit bowl like in a sitcom. That kind of life seemed so simple, so whole.

From where I stood, that kind of warmth existed only on television. In our house, the fruit bowl was mostly ornamental; polished but untouched, more for show than for substance. I used to mourn what was missing. It felt like living inside a sketch, waiting for someone to color it in. But no one ever did. So I learned to draw my own lines, with bolder strokes, in spaces where love might finally have room to grow.

CHAPTER 28:
"Congratulations"

It was a Saturday morning, with banana nut pancakes flipping and jazz music playing. I was enjoying the slow pace of summer, feeling content that it was the weekend...until I got a call from my parents. A strange feeling hit me immediately, the same unease I'd felt before during that phone call when they'd gotten physical with each other. My stomach dropped in anticipation. Was this going to be another situation like that? Maybe answering the phone just isn't for me.

For context, this was shortly after the awkward netsuke-stealing brunch charade. As if my thoughts were floating in a speech bubble, my dad's words suddenly pierced through them: "We wanted you to know that we decided to get remarried!"

Was I hearing this correctly? Was I the only one seeing the insanity in their choices?

Silence fell over me; a mix of both shock and no surprise at all. It was a feeling I had experienced many times with them. I noticed my mother wasn't saying anything, and after what felt like an eternity, I quietly muttered, "Congratulations." The word hurt as it left my throat. I don't know if it was the inauthenticity of the gesture or the quiet acknowledgment of this never-ending dysfunctional cycle between them, but I ached. I can still hear the pompous tone in his voice, as if he had never left and the townspeople should build a monument in his honor.

Sensing my lack of enthusiasm, they quickly changed the subject to their plans for later that day. I often have trouble shifting from one emotion to another, and this time was no different. My mind was still racing, and all I could think about was how to end the call as quickly as possible.

In prior conversations with my mother about their relationship, she'd had the audacity to tell me they "never had any real problems" and that I should "just be happy for her" now that they were back together. She'd crafted a fantasy in which, if not for the "debaucherous woman" who ruined everything, they'd still be living in paradise, singing *kumbaya*. The delusion was so thick it was impenetrable.

In the pit of my stomach, I felt as though everything I'd done to take care of my mother through this entire ordeal had been erased along with their history. All the effort, all the emotional labor, gone.

I've always thought of myself as intuitive, and everything inside me said this reunion was wrong. But it was also none of my business, something my father wasted no time reminding me. My parents had only just begun speaking civilly again, and a remarriage felt abrupt, reckless even. These people felt like strangers anyway. Why did I still expect them to tell me beforehand, or at least show some hint of change some sign that this time would be different?

They were the same people, repeating the same patterns, having learned nothing. After such a messy, destructive, and expensive divorce, they had changed nothing at all.

As a psychologist, the logical part of me couldn't ignore the research I'd read about how rarely remarriages to the same person actually last; especially when no effort has been made to rebuild trust or form a new bond. I wanted them to be happy. I wanted my father to look at my mother the way she'd always wanted to be looked at, not because he was approaching eighty and had no other prospects, but because he genuinely missed her.

I worried about my mother's fragile, labile emotional state. After spending the last five years crying and obsessing over his return, he was suddenly back in everyone's life. It reminded me of people who win the lottery and lose their minds because the shift is too rapid for their brains to process. This was like that, just not as cool.

The next day, I was surprised when my mother called me. She whispered into the receiver, "I'm scared, Ashley. I don't know if I can trust him."

I think that was the first time she had ever expressed a genuine emotion to me. It wasn't for attention or manipulation, it was real. I could hear the fear in her voice. I tried to stay neutral. The last thing I wanted was to feel responsible for her decision, knowing they would never let me forget it if I said the wrong thing.

Two days later, they made it official. There was no invitation to the ceremony. It took place twenty minutes from my home, and, like so many other things, I had to pretend it didn't bother me. It was one of those situations where you don't want to go—but still want to be invited. It's what people do. Parents invite their children to their wedding. But these were not typical parents.

Maybe I wasn't invited because I didn't belong in the fantasy they were trying to recreate and maybe that's okay. What I carry forward isn't their story; it's mine.

I felt a door close inside me, one that held both positive and negative feelings. I no longer had to take care of my mother. My boyfriend and I had spent years chauffeuring her to doctor's appointments, helping her buy new cell phones, taking her to lunch, and filing her taxes. Now my dad was back to do all those things. With that relief came a wave of rejection. It was clear I no longer had a role in her life. I didn't want to believe I had only ever served a specific purpose, but I knew in my heart that was the case.

The holidays she had only recently begged to spend with me, so she wouldn't be alone, were now centered around catering to him again and his visiting Israeli friends. She still hated when his attention was pulled away, but she did everything she could to keep him from leaving again. She put on her fake smile, her bright red lipstick, and off she went. It was like being trapped in a time capsule, back to before my father left.

I was no longer the host of Thanksgiving, after years of doing it. I was no longer needed. Even when she visited my home, she would groan and limp around, claiming her mobility was limited and that she could only stay for a couple of hours. Yet during that same period, she managed to take a trip to Israel with my father. She said her legs were stiff from lymphedema following cancer treatments, but somehow she was fine sitting on a fifteen-hour flight and touring another country.

When she wanted to do something, she did it. She feared him traveling alone and meeting someone else again. She had lost him once and was determined not to lose him again.

I wished I had held that kind of significance in her life the kind that made her fight to maintain connection with me. As I've mentioned before, my mother never took much time to teach me things or offer guidance, but one thing she used to say stuck with me: something about *fair-weather friends.*

"It's when someone leaves you for someone or something better," she once told me.

As a little girl, I didn't think much of it. But as an adult, I began to understand why that phrase mattered to her. It was both what she feared most and who she became. She was the perfect embodiment of it. I was only relevant when I was useful. She showed me the true meaning of it through her actions.

It's a strange feeling to grieve someone you never really had. But I suspect that's something we both now understand.

CHAPTER 29:
"The Dress"

Several years after my divorce, my boyfriend became my fiancé, and we decided to get married. I was excited and hopeful in a way I hadn't allowed myself to feel in a long time. That week, I met my parents for lunch to share the news. I expected, or at least hoped for, a moment of happiness or support.

Instead, my father looked at me across the table and said flatly, "Relationships are only good in the beginning." It felt like he had flicked a switch, turning off any light in the room. It was a strange sentiment for a father to offer his daughter on the cusp of a new chapter, but not an unfamiliar one. My parents had spent years in a dysfunctional, on-again-off-again relationship marked by volatility and resentment. Even after their separation, their dynamic never truly ended; it simply mutated into quieter forms of toxicity. My father had grown cynical, emotionally walled-off, and deeply distrustful of intimacy. He hadn't healed—and he certainly hadn't reflected.

When I shared my engagement, it wasn't just my news he was responding to. It was his own unresolved grief. His bitterness over how his marriage to my mother had unraveled, his regret over lost time and missed chances, and a life that hadn't turned out the way he imagined. My joy was a mirror, and he didn't like what it reflected back. He couldn't step outside his own pain long enough to see me; his daughter, trying again, trying to love again. He couldn't offer joy, only projection.

Despite his comment, and despite everything I already knew about their limitations, I still found myself wanting to include them. Maybe it was habit, or some leftover strand of hope I hadn't yet cut. Maybe it was the part of me that still believed that if I kept showing up, they might eventually meet me halfway.

Even though they hadn't shown up for my first dress fitting years earlier, I asked them to come with me this time. It wasn't because I believed they'd changed or would suddenly show genuine interest. It was because I was tired—tired of being the only one who cared, the only one carrying the weight of disappointment. I just wanted them there, if only to witness a moment that mattered to me, even if I knew they wouldn't feel the same.

Looking back, I'm not entirely sure what I was hoping to gain by continuing to be vulnerable with them. Maybe recognition. Maybe connection. Maybe just one fleeting moment where I didn't feel like a stranger to the very people who raised me.

On the day of the wedding dress fitting, I stepped out in my ensemble, puffed up with excitement, only to find my dad glued to his phone, texting his Israeli friends. He didn't even glance up, completely oblivious to the moment unfolding in front of him, as if the billion blazing sequins I was wrapped in were imperceptible. It was almost impressive how unaware he was.

For once, my mother noticed the joy drain from my face. She looked over at my dad and asked, "Do you need to do that now?" He ignored her, eyes still locked on his Facebook messages. When she felt safe to do so, she rolled her eyes at me behind his back. I felt tears welling up but forced them down. I didn't want to ruin the day, even though it already felt ruined. I wanted so badly to be acknowledged, but I knew I wouldn't be. He never noticed my tears and strangely, I was okay with it. I just wanted to get it over with. The purpose of having them there had vanished.

Even when paying me a compliment at the fitting, my mother found a way to make it about herself.

"You're so beautiful, we must make an excellent pair," she said, meaning her and my father. She stared at him after saying it, waiting for agreement, hoping for confirmation that she was his perfect match. He, of course, ignored her and nodded vacantly.

The irony of her comment wasn't lost on me. I had altered many physical aspects of myself over the years in a thrilling swirl of self-loathing—working out obsessively, controlling my diet, wearing colored contact lenses, getting cosmetic dental work, permanent makeup, acrylic nails, hair coloring, and dozens of tattoos. Natural wasn't the word I'd use to describe myself.

A few months later, after the ceremony, I invited them to join us for dinner. They came, although they looked anything but thrilled to be there.

"Are you sure you want us to come?" my mother asked repeatedly.

I still have no idea why she asked that so insistently, or what kind of answer she hoped for.

There was no warmth that evening. I had imagined us sitting around the table like a Hallmark movie, sharing stories, laughing, toasting to love. I only had myself to blame for that idealization. Instead, it felt transactional again, as though they believed I'd invited them out of obligation, or worse, to foot the bill.

Maybe they felt guilty for not including me in their own wedding, but I doubt it. That kind of reflective thinking wasn't in their wheelhouse. They couldn't genuinely enjoy being there because the spotlight wasn't on them.

I had to remind myself again: It's not you. I realized that love, presence, and emotional safety can't be orchestrated, even under perfect circumstances. It's not about lowering your expectations; it's about knowing who you're dealing with and choosing to release the fantasy. Because even in a room full of sequins and second chances, you can't make people see you if they've already decided not to look.

CHAPTER 30:
"Just Take a Nap"

Over the next few months, I began experiencing a series of concerning medical symptoms. I struggled with uncontrollable fatigue; overpowering that I would fall asleep during the day without warning, sometimes mid-sentence while speaking to a client. I'd jolt forward in my chair, catching myself just before hitting the desk. As a therapist, it was not only alarming but humiliating. I felt as though I were losing control of my own body.

There were other strange symptoms, too: I was constantly cold, my sleep disrupted, my thinking cloudy, and my mood unstable. At times, I felt as if I were slipping in and out of consciousness, just trying to get through the day; going through the motions, fighting to function while figuring out what was happening to me. It was exhausting.

During the height of these symptoms, I had a phone call with my parents. They casually asked what I was up to, and I mentioned that I was on my way to get blood work done. I briefly explained what had been going on, expecting at least a flicker of concern or curiosity. Instead, my father immediately cut in with theatrical certainty: "You need to just take a nap. There's nothing wrong with you."

His tone was so flippant, so arrogantly dismissive, that my heart began to race. Even though it was exactly the kind of response I'd come to expect from him, it still stung.

Later that week, when my labs came back showing signs of nervous system dysfunction, elevated inflammation, hormonal deficiencies, and restrictive GI patterns; likely indicative of an autoimmune condition, I didn't even consider sharing the results with them. They never asked.

I couldn't help but laugh when my doctor asked, gently but directly, "Have you experienced long-term trauma or stress?"

I wanted to scream, *Yes. Meet my parents and you'll understand.*

As far as my parents were concerned, nothing I went through could ever measure up to what they had endured. My mother always managed to position herself as just a little more of a victim than whoever she was speaking to, and my father prided himself on being the ultimate authority on everything. No matter the topic: restaurants, relationships, illness, he knew more, knew better, and made sure you knew it too. My feelings, my experience, my health all landed in the same category: irrelevant.

The silence surrounding my symptoms began to mirror something deeper, a familiar void where acknowledgment should have been. As my body kept faltering, so did my sense of self. I had always prided myself on being sharp, high-functioning, dependable, someone who could hold space for others, carry emotional weight, and show up no matter what. But some days, even getting through a single session with a client felt like scaling a mountain with no summit in sight.

The brain fog terrified me the most. Words would drift out of reach mid-sentence, or I'd forget what I was saying entirely. Sometimes I'd pause, silently pleading for my mind to catch up. It's a disorienting thing to watch your inner world go dim while the outer world keeps demanding clarity.

And then there was the guilt.

Guilt that I wasn't performing at the level I expected of myself.

Guilt for canceling plans, for needing a break, for letting emails go unanswered.

I had internalized a belief somewhere along the line that being exhausted, unwell, or emotionally depleted wasn't a valid reason to stop. That belief had roots, and those roots pointed straight back to my family.

I realized how deeply I had been conditioned to override myself; to push through, to minimize, to repeat the same hollow reassurance: *You're* fine. My father's voice had become a ghost in my ear, whispering on loop every time I tried to rest or advocate for myself.

And yet, beneath the guilt and fear, a quieter awareness began to form. I had spent most of my life as a caretaker, managing other people's emotions, tending to their chaos, being useful. But now that I was the one struggling, they weren't there for me in the same ways. No one was asking the questions I had always asked: *How are you, really? What do you need? How can I support you?*

I realized then that I had never been granted the luxury of fragility.

These symptoms didn't just strip me of energy; they forced a reckoning. They held up a mirror and asked: Who are you when you can't perform? When you're not useful? When you need help instead of offering it?

It was a question I wasn't prepared for. Somewhere along the line, I had learned that being needed was the same as being loved.

It's strange how the body starts screaming when the soul has been whispering for too long. Mine had been whispering for years. The symptoms, in some twisted way, became the most honest reflection of my emotional landscape: confused, depleted, unattended.

And just like in my childhood, I was left to figure it out on my own.

CHAPTER 31:
"The Birthday"

I decided to call my mother for her birthday and plan a celebratory dinner. She usually had a list of ideas ready for what gift she wanted, so I thought I'd get a head start.

"When's good to celebrate? Why don't we do the eighteenth on the actual day?" I asked.

My mother and father, who were on speakerphone together, suddenly went quiet. I could hear whispering in the background.

"Can we do the week before?" she finally replied.

Normally, this would have been a simple question. But this time, it carried more weight. After some hesitation, and what sounded like an attempt to concoct a reasonable excuse, they revealed they were going on a family trip to Vegas with my brother, his wife, and their kids.

It was clear: I wasn't invited to celebrate her birthday.

It felt like the popular kids were planning a holiday party, and when the outcasts found out, they had to come up with a lesser event just to appease them. In that moment, the familiar feeling of being an outsider in my own family resurfaced. It was like the last tether of connection had snapped.

I let a few days pass before responding, giving myself time to think clearly.

When I finally reached out, I told my parents how much it hurt to feel left out. I asked why we couldn't all go together to celebrate.

My father's response came quickly and sharply: You could have arranged your own trip for your mother's birthday, but you didn't. You need to just be happy with what you have."

I was confused by his comment. Somehow, I was being cast as selfish again. Did he really think I just wanted a free trip? His response left me with a deep, unsettling sense that he couldn't, or wouldn't, understand the real issue. I didn't want a vacation. I wanted to be part of my family.

I felt myself regressing into an old, childlike mindset, trying to explain that I just wanted to belong in meaningful ways, but all I met was defensiveness. The more I tried to express myself, the more it felt like talking to a wall.

But it wasn't just my father's cold dismissal that hurt; it was my mother's silence. She said nothing. Not a word. I didn't even matter enough to be acknowledged.

I couldn't keep doing this. I couldn't keep begging for acknowledgment, investing in a relationship that felt more draining than nurturing. The realization settled in slowly but firmly: I was never going to get anything different from them. No matter how many times I tried to explain myself, they were incapable of understanding.

The toll it was taking on me mentally, emotionally, physically was too much.

My body couldn't handle the stress anymore.

Before I could fully process it, my emotions spilled out, an unrestrained torrent of everything I had been holding in for years. I sent texts to both of them, unloading my anger, my hurt, my grief. It wasn't planned. It felt like I blacked out and just... vented. Normally, I would have wanted to discuss something this serious face-to-face, but I knew, deep down, it wouldn't matter anyway. I had tried every possible approach before: letters, phone calls, in-person talks, and nothing ever changed. The exhaustion had finally caught up with me.

My father's response? "Well, your brother had no complaints about his childhood, and you were given the same treatment. We did our best."

I couldn't understand what my brother had to do with any of this. Why did his experience invalidate mine? Why was I always compared to him? And what did *doing your best* even mean? To me, it was just an excuse. I wasn't asking for perfection. I was asking to be seen, to be considered. But apparently, even that was too much.

What my father failed to understand, or chose not to, was that my brother and I had vastly different childhoods, shaped not only by time but by temperament and role. We are more than a decade apart. He was a latchkey kid, left to his own devices, and he quickly learned that showing emotion got him nowhere. Instead of questioning the dysfunction, he avoided it. Instead of feeling safe enough to express pain or confusion, he minimized it all, telling himself it wasn't that bad, because acknowledging otherwise might have been unbearable.

He survived by suppressing his feelings, by becoming emotionally detached. He avoided confrontation, which likely earned him less scrutiny and more approval. That coping style eventually created a wedge between us: while I tried to process pain by naming it, he avoided it entirely. His silence and dismissal often left me feeling erased, and his alignment with the family narrative reinforced my role as the problem. We grew up in the same house, but lived in emotionally different worlds.

In many ways, he aligned himself with our mother, perhaps because it made things easier, more stable. He saw a different version of her, one shaped by his silence and compliance. But silence doesn't mean peace; it often means fear or resignation. Just because he never complained doesn't mean he wasn't hurt. It just means he chose a different way to survive.

I didn't.

I couldn't.

My father seemed more interested in defending himself than in listening to what I was actually saying. My emotions didn't matter unless they matched someone else's.

What is "doing your best" if it's not enough to keep your child from feeling unloved, unseen, or emotionally neglected? How can you claim to have done your best when you won't even consider your child's perspective?

As I continued to process, I realized something fundamental: in a family, love isn't measured by what you give like birthday gifts, a house, material stability. Those things matter, but emotional caregiving, understanding, and empathy are essential. When they couldn't understand that, I knew I couldn't keep pretending everything was okay.

I was done with the secret-keeping, the exclusions, the constant self-doubt, the begging for recognition. I was done pretending that our relationship was anything other than toxic. Every interaction left me feeling like a shell of the person I once was. I realized I had been giving them more leeway than I would give anyone else in my life, simply because they were family.

Dr. Sherrie Campbell, in her book *But It's Your Family...*, writes that toxic family dynamics are like incurable, progressive personality disorders—patterns that prevent families from ever treating their members with the love and respect they deserve. The idea that some people are incapable of change resonated deeply with me. I had presented my pain to them time and time again, and it was always met with defensiveness, denial, and dismissal.

They would tell me to "let it go," or warn that I'd regret not talking to them when they were old or sick. But you can't just *let go* of something that's unresolved. You can't heal if you're not heard. And with them, I had no hope of ever being heard.

I was sick of the same refrain: "Just forgive them—they're your mom and dad." That wasn't enough anymore. The emotional damage they had caused was too deep, too relentless.

I was done with the invalidation. Done with being ignored. Done with hating myself for wanting their love and approval. I was no longer willing to accept being ostracized, judged, or invisible.

This wasn't just about the past either. It was about the way they still triggered me in the present. Leaving this relationship wasn't merely a choice; it was a survival mechanism. It wasn't about memories anymore, but about how those memories shaped my reality today.

One of the hardest truths to face was that neither of my parents were all good or all bad. They were a mosaic of gray complicated, human, and deeply flawed. Ending the relationship felt like throwing out the baby with the bathwater, but that was the price of breaking a long-overdue cycle of dysfunction.

In those final texts, I told them that as long as they continued to deny and invalidate my feelings, we couldn't have a relationship. The irony was how much I still loved them—despite everything. I didn't want to end things. I wanted to laugh with them, hug them, tell them my fears. But those things were illusions. The heartache and rejection sat heavy on my chest. It was a painful paradox. They were gone, but they had never really been there in the first place.

I couldn't find the right word for that feeling, but it was agonizing.

That was the last conversation I ever had with my parents.

CHAPTER 32:
"The Confirmation"

Even though my father lied to my mother, cheated on her, stole from her, and told her never to speak to him again, she still pursued him relentlessly. She contacted him through every possible method, unable to let go. In contrast, I wasn't worth a text or a phone call after expressing my hurt feelings and needs. I wasn't even worth the effort.

It confirmed everything I had felt in my gut about our relationship: I didn't matter to her, or to them.

My mother had everything she needed now: her new-old husband to drive her around, her son who catered to her every whim. As for me, I had no purpose left.

I had been writing to her since I was a child, long before I had the language for disappointment.

Speaking had often proven useless, so I learned to pour myself into letters, pleas, really, that were never once acknowledged. Each silence accumulated like stones in my chest. But the last silence, the one that followed my confession that I felt unloved, still haunts me.

How does a mother remain quiet in the face of her child's pain? How does she continue to live alongside that silence? Isn't there supposed to be an instinct stronger than pride, some ancient pull to protect? A mother bear in the wild defends her cub with her life. Where was my mother when I needed mine?

Instead, she chose to focus on the man who had discarded her when she was no longer convenient and on the son who perfected the art of deception, the one who smirked behind her back with his wife while eating at her table.

If there is a God, I imagine that in the aftermath of life, he might take her hand and show her the truth: that the loyal one, the loving one, was overlooked, dismissed, and denied. I want her to see that her silence preserved only her ego, while it erased me.

It is the hopeful, however fantastical image of that moment that has, at times, kept me sane. In a healthy relationship, when people don't see eye to eye, there's an exchange of ideas, feelings, and information. There's room for disagreement without it turning chaotic or combative. But for us, bringing up conflict was always an ordeal; intense, dramatic, exhausting. And in this case, there was the opposite of that: no effort, no communication, no willingness to solve anything. Instead, I was left overwhelmed with anxiety and sadness, wondering why they didn't even try.

When someone is upset, the goal should be to avoid upsetting them again, not to debate whether they have the right to feel that way. My mother used to say she'd "do anything for me"… anything except apologize or acknowledge my feelings.

I thought about all the times I was left to handle my emotions alone whether as a child, a teenager, or an adult. I thought about how I had been robbed of my own presence, always needing to "just get things over with" to ease the anxiety that came from being around them. I thought about how they never invested in knowing me outside of the disobedient, entitled child they believed me to be.

Eventually, my brother continued his quiet tradition of blind loyalty to our mother without ever hearing my side of things. He told me I'd left him with a "huge burden" by no longer communicating with our parents. Never mind the years I had cared for our mother during the divorce; those didn't seem to count. He hadn't been concerned about the caretaking then, but now, suddenly, it mattered.

What hurt most was that I had to ask him why he was being so distant. I kept reaching out, trying to stay connected, checking in even as his replies dwindled to silence. There was no conversation, no curiosity, no effort to understand. Just a blunt verdict: I was "full of negativity," and he wanted nothing more to do with me. When I asked if we could talk it through, he declined.

His words didn't just sting, they scorched. They burned through any illusion I had left about who we were to each other.

And then it hit me: my semblance of a family was gone.

CHAPTER 33:
"The Reflection"

In the months that followed, I found myself experiencing a strange mix of sadness, relief, and disorientation. The silence was deafening at first; like stepping out of a loud, chaotic room where your ears are left ringing, and suddenly you're alone with your own breath. I missed my parents, though not in the ways I expected. I didn't miss the tension, the eggshells, or the unpredictability of who I'd be speaking to on the other end of the line. What I missed was the idea of them, the simple notion of having parents at all. It was difficult to let go of the fantasy I had carried for so long, the imagined version of who I had hoped they could become.

There were moments when I still reached for the phone out of habit, forgetting that the number I once dialed with muscle memory now led to a dead end. Grief didn't come in clean waves. It arrived in small, unexpected moments: hearing a joke I knew my dad would've laughed at, or a Rod Stewart song that made me think of my mom singing along—half right, half wrong, always offbeat. I had flashbacks to the three of us sitting around the kitchen table playing gin rummy, my dad pretending to win, everyone throwing down their cards before he'd grin and say, "Just kidding." These are the ghosts that linger. I still feel the space they once occupied.

And yet, alongside the ache, I felt something I hadn't expected: peace. A quietness that had never existed in their presence. Without the constant emotional chaos, I began to hear my own voice more clearly. I no longer had to brace for the next passive-aggressive comment or decode someone's silence. I wasn't defending myself against projections or walking backward through old landmines. The calm was unfamiliar but I was learning to trust it.

There was guilt, too. Guilt for feeling better without them. Guilt for choosing myself. But every time that guilt rose up, I reminded myself of what it had cost me to stay: my sense of self, my emotional safety, my sanity.

Cutting off contact wasn't a clean break. It was a series of emotional reckonings. I had to face the parts of myself that still longed for a parent's love, even if it had never been offered unconditionally. I had to sit with the realization that some wounds don't close just because we finally walk away. Some remain open, aching not from fresh injury but from long-term neglect.

And in that ache, I began to meet myself and to create understanding.

I often heard friends and clients talk about distancing themselves from their families, followed by how, after creating space, they were bombarded with calls and messages begging them to return. Most people resented that constant contact. I was left with the opposite problem: no one reached out to me. The emptiness of that still haunts me. I was unwanted.

Each person in our life perceives a different version of us. Some see us as beautiful and capable with little effort, while others view us through a distorted lens—angry, selfish, or inconsiderate shaped by their own histories and pain. I often wondered how my parents saw me, and why their perception of me had been so warped, so unfair. Worse still was how their perceptions bled onto others, like my brother, coloring their view of me black.

There's a saying that people can only love to the extent that they love themselves, and in a strange way, I found comfort in that thought.

Perhaps the way they treated me was a reflection of how they felt about themselves.

As Charles Blow of *The New York Times* wrote, "One doesn't have to operate with great malice to do great harm. The absence of empathy and understanding are sufficient" (Blow, 2012). My parents weren't bad people. But cruelty isn't always the problem. Sometimes, it's the absence of empathy that is most destructive. You don't have to be overtly cruel to be toxic. Toxicity often hides in inconsistency; the emotional highs and lows, the erratic behavior, the love tangled with neglect.

I once came across a metaphor about fruit that cannot ripen in poisoned soil. Even with a healthy core, it won't reach maturity if the environment is inhospitable. People are no different. In toxic conditions, we don't evolve; we adapt for survival, often at the expense of our own growth.

CHAPTER 34:
"It All Started to Make Sense"

Becoming a clinical psychologist wasn't a conscious decision, but more of a natural gravitation. I never asked myself what I wanted to do; I just started doing it. I began collecting books on psychodynamic theory, attachment, and abnormal psychology, treating them as prized possessions. I was hungry to understand what makes relationships work, or fall apart. What creates resilience? What is trauma, really? How can someone thrive without ever feeling loved? Or is that impossible?

My parents felt so foreign to me that I thought if I could objectively study family dynamics, I might find meaning, some explanation for why things were the way they were.

It's often said that children whose emotional needs go unmet grow up to become adults who compulsively take care of others. We are the ones who tend to everyone else's emotions. We become the entertainers, the hard workers, the fixers. We give financially, overextend ourselves, and blur boundaries in the hope that someone, anyone, will reciprocate and take care of us in return.

Most of these drives operate beneath awareness, born from a quiet desperation to be seen and valued. But the more we give, the less others tend to meet our needs, and the more they come to rely on us to keep giving.

I realized I had been searching for a home in everyone I met and everywhere I went. I carried keys to locks that didn't exist. At the same time, I learned to hide myself because when you feel like a burden, you make yourself small. You become who others want you to be, hoping to earn love and acceptance. I was a stranger to myself, and I couldn't help but feel regret for all the time I'd given to people who didn't deserve it.

I had spent years trying to explain myself to people who were committed to misunderstanding me. Studying psychology didn't just give me answers—it gave me back my voice. It gave shape to what I had lived through and offered language for what had always been wordless. It allowed me to grieve the parents I never truly had and to begin becoming the person I needed.

It was as though someone had turned the lights on in a room I had been stumbling through in the dark my entire life. The chaos finally had a name. I wasn't broken. I wasn't dramatic. I was reacting—appropriately—to something deeply unhealthy. Through my work, I came to the chilling realization that my mother and father exhibited symptoms of borderline personality disorder and narcissistic personality disorder, respectively.

And suddenly, it all made sense.

PART II

CONCEPTS AND RESEARCH

This section seeks to contextualize personal experiences within established psychological theories and empirical research, offering clarity, insight, and validation to readers whose stories may resonate with the one shared here.

In understanding this narrative, it is crucial to recognize the character structures and diagnoses that influence the family dynamics, along with their impact. Even when destructive behaviors are directed at one individual, each family member responds and internalizes these moments differently. What follows is a combination of objective research findings and personal reflections based on my own familial experiences.

Understanding Narcissism

Let's first align on what we mean by narcissism. Narcissistic Personality Disorder (NPD) is a term we hear frequently, but what does it truly entail? To understand its depth, it's helpful to begin with a psychoanalytic perspective—particularly Freud's.

Freud proposed that our relationships with others evolve from birth onward. If we are raised in an environment that is cold, invalidating, or rejecting, we may develop insecurities about ourselves, others, and the world. These insecurities give rise to defense mechanisms designed to protect us from emotional vulnerability. In narcissism, these defenses often take the form of projection assigning fault to others rather than acknowledging it within ourselves.

At the core of narcissism lies a profound sense of insecurity. This insecurity drives individuals to avoid anything that might expose their perceived weakness. As a result, their need for distance in relationships often manifests as anxiety and emotional detachment, since closeness is seen as a threat. Narcissistic individuals may also fear rejection so deeply that they preemptively reject others first.

Although these tendencies exist to some degree in everyone, those with a clinical diagnosis of NPD experience significant distress and dysfunction as a result of them—particularly in their personal and professional relationships.

Common narcissistic traits include an inflated sense of self-importance, a constant craving for admiration, limited empathy, and rapid emotional fluctuations ranging from rage to depression, sometimes within minutes. Other hallmarks include hypersensitivity to criticism, fear of failure, and chronic shame.

These traits inevitably lead to interpersonal difficulties. For example, consider a workplace review: if a person responds to constructive feedback with anger or blame, they may jeopardize their job.

Similarly, if a friend shares their struggles and the narcissistic individual fails to acknowledge or validate those feelings, the relationship will likely suffer.

People with NPD often minimize the experiences of others, distorting reality to preserve their own narrative. They might say things like, "You're remembering it wrong," or "You're overreacting." When others attract attention or admiration, a narcissist may attempt to undermine them through gossip or slander, seeking to reassert control and reduce their own anxiety.

Initially, narcissists can appear charismatic and engaging, often using this charm to build trust that can later be exploited. The term "flying monkeys," inspired by *The Wizard of Oz*, refers to those who unquestioningly support the narcissist's agenda helping them manipulate or control others. These enablers rarely recognize the manipulation at play and often comply in exchange for approval, belonging, or perceived benefit.

This dynamic is common in stories and real life alike. In many Disney films, for instance, the villain is surrounded by loyal subordinates who reinforce their authority—like Jafar and Iago in *Aladdin* or Ursula and her eels in *The Little Mermaid*. These "flying monkeys" bolster the narcissist's power. And when they finally begin to question the behavior, they are either discarded or become the next target.

Narcissists thrive on external validation, often behaving altruistically only when it serves to enhance their image. Their self-concept is fragile, and even mild criticism can trigger obsessive thoughts or emotional outbursts as they work to redirect attention away from their perceived flaws.

Long-term relationships are particularly challenging for individuals with NPD. Their inability to accept critique or engage in healthy conflict resolution often leads to ruptured connections. They tend to view others as competition, distrusting motives and intentions, which further isolates them. Despite their ambition and drive, these interpersonal difficulties can significantly hinder their personal and professional growth.

People with NPD are primarily motivated by achievement, control, status, and admiration; things not easily obtained. This drives them to associate with individuals who enhance their sense of self-worth. They need to remain the focal point in any setting, and when attention shifts elsewhere, they become visibly uncomfortable. Envy often plays a central role, as they long for what others possess particularly if it reinforces their own sense of superiority.

A sense of entitlement frequently accompanies this envy. Narcissists believe they inherently deserve what others have and will construct elaborate rationalizations to justify that belief. Any evidence contradicting their worldview is dismissed to avoid feelings of inadequacy or shame. Their pursuit of material wealth or power is often rooted not in greed but in a distorted quest for security: to them, ownership equates to protection.

This entitlement is closely tied to exploitative behavior. One of my patients with narcissistic traits once said, "If my friend was dumb enough to lend me that much money, he was asking to lose it." On another occasion, he remarked, "I slept with someone else, but if she wasn't smart enough to realize I needed more physical contact, that's her fault." In both cases, the narcissist framed others' trust as weakness—something to be manipulated for personal gain.

Arrogance is another defining hallmark of narcissism. Individuals with NPD often see themselves as superior to others and therefore entitled to act without regard for consequences. Those around them are viewed less as equals and more as obstacles or stepping stones. Interestingly, their charisma and confidence can propel them into leadership roles. Their commanding presence and persuasive abilities often attract admiration, even when their ideas lack true depth or substance.

Subtypes of Narcissistic Personality Disorder

Narcissistic personality disorder (NPD) is not a one-size-fits-all condition. Although all individuals with narcissism share core traits such as a lack of empathy and an intense need for validation, the disorder manifests differently from person to person. Understanding these distinctions can help clarify how narcissism appears in real life, particularly within families.

Research by Russ, Bradley, and Westen (2008) identifies three distinct subtypes of NPD: grandiose (or overt), vulnerable (or covert), and high-functioning (or exhibitionistic).

Each type has unique characteristics:

Grandiose/Overt Narcissists

These are the classic narcissists we tend to picture first bold, entitled, and often reckless. They display overt arrogance and a sense of superiority, believing themselves to be above the rules that govern others. Some may have legal troubles or a history of aggressive behavior. Unlike other subtypes, they rarely struggle with self-doubt or insecurity. They believe they are special and expect the world to treat them accordingly.

This subtype often overlaps with traits associated with antisocial personality disorder, including manipulative behavior, a disregard for consequences, and an inflated sense of superiority. They can be the most dangerous and destructive form of narcissism, particularly when occupying positions of power or influence.

Vulnerable/Covert Narcissists

Unlike their grandiose counterparts, covert narcissists do not broadcast their sense of superiority. Instead, they often appear fragile, sensitive, or even self-deprecating. Beneath that insecurity, however, lies the same need for admiration and control.

Covert narcissists frequently struggle with anxiety, depression, and emotional instability. They may not demand attention outright, but they expect others to attune to their unspoken needs. When those needs are unmet, they often feel victimized and may lash out in passive-aggressive or guilt-inducing ways.

My mother embodied this subtype in many respects. Rather than openly asking for support, she would sigh heavily or make sarcastic remarks, hoping my father would read her mind and respond accordingly. When he did not, she accused him of being emotionally absent or uncaring. Friends and family often rushed to comfort her, unintentionally reinforcing the behavior. This dynamic created a feedback loop: the more dramatic her expressions of distress, the more support she received, even when it came at the cost of genuine communication.

High-Functioning/Exhibitionistic Narcissists

This subtype can be more difficult to recognize, as individuals often appear successful, articulate, and socially polished. High-functioning narcissists are frequently leaders, influencers, or high achievers who present as confident and driven. They may be charming in public, admired for their charisma, and regarded as role models within their careers.

Beneath the surface, however, lies a familiar pattern: a deep need for validation, perfectionism, and emotional detachment. Their ambition is driven less by purpose than by a desire to be seen and praised. Relationships often feel transactional, centered on how others can enhance their image or advance their goals. While they may not create chaos like overt narcissists, they can leave others feeling insignificant, drained, or used.

My father exhibited many characteristics of the high-functioning, exhibitionistic subtype, particularly his emotional detachment and need for perfection. His emotional vacancy often translated into a drive for external validation, as though his self-worth depended on admiration and accomplishment. His perfectionistic tendencies led him to place unrealistically high expectations on himself and others, creating an environment in which nothing ever felt good enough.

Moreover, his interactions were frequently transactional, marked by an implicit expectation of receiving something in return for his attention or affection. This dynamic often left me feeling as though I were merely a means to an end, rather than a person deserving of unconditional love or emotional connection.

Defining Cluster B

To better understand the complex dynamics within families like mine, it's important to define a few more key terms; particularly those associated with personality disorders that fall under Cluster B in the Diagnostic and Statistical Manual of Mental Disorders, Fifth Edition (DSM-5). Borderline Personality Disorder (BPD), which we'll explore in more depth shortly, shares many overlapping features with Narcissistic Personality Disorder (NPD). Both are classified under Cluster B, which includes personality disorders characterized by intense interpersonal conflict, erratic emotional expression, impulsivity, and dramatic, attention-seeking behavior.

Common traits across Cluster B disorders include:

- Insecurity and emotional hypersensitivity
- Externalization of blame and responsibility
- Volatile relationships and poor emotional regulation

These patterns frequently play out in manipulative or self-destructive ways, particularly in the face of stress or relational discord.

According to research by Ma, Fan, Shen, and Wang (2016), Cluster B traits are partially linked to structural and chemical differences in the brain, including a smaller or less active prefrontal cortex, the region involved in executive functioning and impulse control. Trauma and environmental factors also play a significant role in the development of these disorders and may interact with brain maturation over time. For example, emotional neglect, abuse, and inconsistent or poor parenting styles are strongly associated with higher rates of Cluster B pathology (Zhang et al., 2012).

Cluster B personality disorders are characterized by enduring and inflexible behavioral patterns that often present considerable challenges in therapeutic settings. Because of the chronic nature of these traits and the interpersonal turbulence they may cause, many mental health professionals are hesitant to treat individuals with Cluster B diagnoses. These disorders are also frequently stigmatized, even within the mental health field and may sometimes be excluded from insurance coverage.

Nevertheless, it is important to emphasize that meaningful progress is possible. The key predictor of success is not the diagnosis itself but rather the individual's level of insight and motivation to change. When a person is willing to face discomfort, tolerate feedback, and engage earnestly in treatment, they can achieve greater emotional stability and a higher level of functioning.

While genetics and brain structure play a role, trauma is often a central catalyst in the formation of Cluster B traits. In the case of NPD, trauma can take many forms:

- Relational trauma, such as rejection by a loved one or betrayal through infidelity
- Victimization trauma, including bullying, physical assault, or emotional abuse
- Identity-threatening experiences, like job loss or divorce, which destabilize a person's sense of self

These experiences often disrupt an individual's ability to regulate emotions and maintain self-worth, leading to coping mechanisms such as grandiosity, entitlement, control-seeking behaviors, and a diminished capacity for empathy. In response, the person attempts to reclaim power and protect the ego by distorting reality, manipulating others, or refusing accountability.

Both narcissistic personality disorder (NPD) and borderline personality disorder (BPD) have well-established empirical links to childhood trauma, although trauma is not required for diagnosis. Emotional, physical, and sexual abuse as well as exposure to domestic violence are common developmental experiences among individuals with these disorders (Herman et al., 1989). When a child grows up in a chaotic or threatening environment, the psyche may adapt by fragmenting into dissociative compartments as a form of protection. Within these states of psychological distance, survival mechanisms dominate: distrust of others, paranoia, emotional numbing, or manipulative behaviors may emerge as strategies for maintaining a sense of control.

Although these traits are maladaptive in adulthood, their origins lie in self-preservation. For instance, an individual who was routinely betrayed or neglected may learn to anticipate rejection and preemptively sabotage relationships or manipulate others, to ensure emotional safety. Over time, these survival-based adaptations solidify into the defining features of Cluster B personality disorders.

Recognizing Borderline Personality Disorder (BPD)

Among the Cluster B diagnoses, one of the most misunderstood and stigmatized is borderline personality disorder (BPD). While narcissistic traits often dominate discussions of toxic family dynamics, BPD frequently hides in plain sight, shaping relationships through fear, emotional reactivity, and an overwhelming need for attachment. Understanding BPD and the various ways it presents is critical, especially when we consider how it interacts with narcissism within families. These diagnoses frequently coexist or reinforce one another, deepening dysfunction and making emotional boundaries all the more difficult to maintain.

In contrast to narcissistic personality disorder (NPD), BPD is primarily characterized by an intense fear of abandonment and being left behind. It is estimated to affect more than 14 million Americans approximately 1.6 percent of the population, making it likely that most people know someone who struggles with the disorder (Chapman et al., 2022). The profound insecurity associated with BPD can make relationships feel conditional; even minor perceived slights may trigger distorted thinking about others' intentions.

BPD is often marked by *black-and-white* or all-or-nothing thinking. People or situations tend to be viewed as entirely "good" or completely "bad," often based on limited information, such as a single decision someone made or the mood they were in that morning. As a result, individuals with BPD may be impulsive in how they form and dissolve relationships. This emotional intensity can make it difficult for them to maintain long-term friendships. A sideways glance or misunderstood comment may be perceived as rejection, prompting them to withdraw abruptly and without explanation.

Because the thoughts and opinions of others hold such influence, those with BPD often experience an unstable sense of self. They may struggle to identify or express their identity and sometimes mimic others in an effort to fit in. Chronic feelings of emptiness are also common. Whereas NPD is driven by inflated self-assurance, often detached from reality, BPD involves a fragile and fragmented sense of self-worth. Both disorders, however, share distorted perceptions of reality that serve to reinforce internal narratives and further isolate individuals from others.

Individuals with BPD often find it difficult to derive meaning from their lives or to make stable decisions without external validation. Like those with NPD, they exhibit emotional intensity and mood lability, sometimes shifting dramatically several times in a single day. This volatility can lead to misdiagnosis, particularly with bipolar disorder. However, even in cases of *rapid-cycling* bipolar disorder, mood shifts typically occur less frequently than in BPD.

Mood swings in borderline personality disorder (BPD) can shift rapidly—from elevated happiness to rage or tearfulness within hours or even minutes. Anger, in particular, is a frequent and intense emotional expression that often confuses those around the individual. It may appear that the person is overreacting or fixating on trivial details;

however, such reactions typically reflect low distress tolerance and diminished emotional resilience. Minor inconveniences can trigger irritability that persists for hours or days, and the emotional response is frequently disproportionate to the event that provoked it.

The term borderline reflects the disorder's origins in psychoanalytic theory, which positioned it between neurosis and psychosis. Individuals with BPD often display traits of both: high anxiety and a need for control (neuroticism), coupled with perceptual distortions and reality-warping beliefs (psychoticism). They may become suspicious of others' intentions and unconsciously reshape memories or details of events to align with their internal narrative. These behaviors are best understood as maladaptive coping mechanisms developed in response to early psychological trauma.

Childhood trauma is a significant contributing factor in the development of BPD. Repressed anger, paranoia, and extreme sensitivity to rejection can be seen as protective responses once adaptive for survival but no longer functional in adulthood. Paranoia may manifest as persistent questioning of others' motives or as a belief that people are trying to harm or manipulate them, regardless of evidence to the contrary. Attempts to reason with or reframe their perceptions often backfire and may even intensify distress. Because stress tends to amplify these symptoms, individuals with BPD often struggle to cope with even minor external pressures.

As a form of emotional regulation, some individuals with BPD engage in risky or self-destructive behaviors such as reckless driving, binge eating, or impulsive sexual activity. These acts can provide temporary relief from emotional numbness and may generate an adrenaline rush that allows them to "feel alive." Dissociation and emotional detachment are common features of BPD, and such behaviors may serve as a way to momentarily reconnect with the self—both physically and emotionally. In some cases, these actions are also motivated by a desire for attention or connection, which may represent an urgent attempt at emotional survival.

Suicidal threats or gestures are unfortunately not uncommon among individuals with BPD. These expressions are sometimes dismissed by family members or friends, particularly when they occur frequently. Like the parable of "The Boy Who Cried Wolf," repeated threats may lose their perceived urgency yet they always warrant serious attention. In some cases, superficial self-harm results in accidental death, or the emotional pain becomes so unbearable that a suicide attempt is tragically carried out as a desperate effort to regain control.

If you have a friend, partner, or family member who displays symptoms of borderline personality disorder (BPD) or narcissistic personality disorder (NPD), you may find that communication often feels one-sided. The person may dominate conversations or seem emotionally disengaged when it is your turn to speak. Like those with NPD, individuals with BPD frequently engage in self-focused behaviors driven by deep insecurity and a need for emotional survival. Unless the topic directly relates to them, they may struggle to remain attentive or emotionally present.

Many people describe this experience as akin to talking through a glass wall: you can see and hear the other person, but the emotional connection feels distant or entirely absent.

Subtypes of Borderline Personality Disorder

According to psychologist and researcher, Theodore Millon, BPD can be broken into four subtypes. While these types are not mutually exclusive, they offer a useful framework for understanding how the disorder can present differently in each person:

Petulant Type

The petulant subtype of borderline personality disorder (BPD) is often characterized by emotional volatility, passive-aggression, and a pronounced need for control. Individuals with this presentation tend to externalize blame, frequently positioning themselves as victims in situations they have, at least in part, contributed to creating. They may exhibit frequent mood outbursts, simmering resentment, and unpredictable irritability, particularly when their needs are not immediately met. Pessimism, jealousy, and pervasive insecurity often underlie their behavior.

Interpersonal dynamics with individuals of this subtype can feel like walking on eggshells; their affection can quickly turn to hostility without warning. A classic example might be a child caught with cookie crumbs on their lips, yet still insisting that a sibling is to blame. This refusal to take accountability, combined with hypersensitivity to perceived slights or rejection, makes relationships with petulant-borderline individuals especially tense and emotionally exhausting.

Self-Destructive Type

The self-destructive subtype of borderline personality disorder (BPD) is characterized by a pattern of intense emotional pain that is often directed inward. Individuals with this presentation are prone to self-harming behaviors, suicidal ideation, and persistent feelings of emptiness and despair. Their emotional volatility does not always erupt outward; instead, it may manifest as severe self-criticism, hopelessness, and a relentless internal dialogue of worthlessness.

Often deeply depressed and consumed by self-doubt, they may sabotage their own relationships, careers, or physical well-being, sometimes unconsciously as a way of validating their internalized belief that they are undeserving of happiness or stability. Because of the intensity of their symptoms, this subtype is more likely than others to require hospitalization, particularly during crises.

For those close to them, loving someone with this subtype can feel like trying to rescue a drowning person who keeps pushing help away.

Discouraged Type

The discouraged subtype of borderline personality disorder (BPD) often resembles chronic low-grade depression or what was once referred to as quiet BPD. These individuals may not express their distress through overt outbursts, yet their emotional suffering runs just as deep. They tend to be dependent, approval-seeking, and deeply fearful of abandonment. Their self-esteem is fragile and often tied to the validation of others. Outwardly, they may appear shy, passive, or people-pleasing, which can make their struggles more difficult to recognize. Beneath the surface, however, lies profound inner turmoil marked by feelings of inadequacy, resentment, and suppressed rage that may erupt when they feel rejected or ignored. Their emotional pain is typically directed inward, leading to patterns of self-sabotage or withdrawal rather than confrontation.

The discouragement they experience can leave them immobilized trapped in toxic relationships, confined to unfulfilling roles, or silenced by shame.

Impulsive Type

The impulsive subtype of borderline personality disorder (BPD) is characterized by recklessness, thrill-seeking, and a chronic inability to regulate impulses. Individuals with this presentation often struggle with substance abuse, compulsive spending, risky sexual behavior, or disordered eating, all attempts to escape the chaos of their inner world. Beneath their bold and sometimes charismatic exterior lies a profound fear of emptiness, masked by constant motion.

Emotionally, they may seem unpredictable, swinging from elation to despair within hours. They often speak before thinking and act before feeling, later experiencing confusion and regret as the consequences unfold.

Relationships involving this subtype tend to be short-lived or tumultuous, as their intensity can be overwhelming. Though they may appear confident or even magnetic, this façade often conceals deep insecurity and a pervasive fear of being alone. What they crave most is connection, yet their impulsivity frequently drives others away.

While these categories are useful for understanding the various ways BPD can manifest, they are not rigid or mutually exclusive.

Many individuals exhibit traits from more than one subtype. In my mother's case, for example, she demonstrates characteristics of both the petulant and discouraged subtypes: attempts to control people and her environment, emotional instability marked by frequent anger and sadness, a codependent attachment to my father, and an ongoing need to maintain a carefully curated outward image to avoid abandonment. These traits make sense in the context of her enmeshment within a narcissistic relationship.

The Romantic Attraction Between Narcissists and Borderlines

One important dynamic to highlight, now that we have a clearer understanding of these diagnoses, is the magnetic yet volatile relationship between individuals with narcissistic personality disorder (NPD) and borderline personality disorder (BPD). Despite the dysfunction, these two personality types are often drawn to each other in what might be described as a form of functional dysfunction. Their traits can initially appear complementary: the narcissist craves admiration and control, while the borderline individual seeks intense connection and fears abandonment.

This mutual dependency can sustain the relationship longer than it might otherwise last with a more emotionally stable partner. Over time, however, the cycle typically becomes toxic, marked by emotional volatility, resentment, and escalating conflict. Although they may tolerate each other for extended periods, the foundation of the relationship is inherently unstable and often results in deep dissatisfaction and mutual harm.

Assortative Mating

There is a concept in psychology called assortative mating, which refers to the tendency for people to be attracted to others who share similar traits. In many relationships, this similarity can feel exciting at first, finally meeting someone who mirrors one's interests, values, or outlook. However, in relationships between individuals with narcissistic and borderline personality traits, this resemblance can quickly devolve into a power struggle.

For people with Cluster B personality disorders, relationships often become battlegrounds for control. Their shared emotional volatility and rigid interpersonal demands create a dynamic in which each partner views the other as an obstacle whenever expectations are unmet.

Recent research published in the Journal of Personality and Individual Differences explored this phenomenon in narcissistic pairings. The study, conducted by Zajenkowski and Gignac (2021), found that narcissists tend to be attracted to other narcissists. Participants who scored high in narcissism preferred self-focused partners rather than those who were more empathetic or other-oriented—an example of assortative mating in action.

The study surveyed 150 heterosexual couples in Poland and found that individuals with high narcissism scores were more likely to have partners with similarly high scores. Likewise, individuals who scored low in narcissism tended to pair with partners who also scored low. Interestingly, narcissistic individuals rated both themselves and their partners as more intelligent than average, regardless of actual IQ. These inflated perceptions appear to serve the narcissist's need to maintain a grandiose self-image by projecting it onto the partner as well.

This concept also helps explain the dynamics between my own parents, who, as discussed in Part I, both exhibited traits of Cluster B disorders but in different forms.

My father displayed many classic traits of Narcissistic Personality Disorder (NPD):

- A sense of grandiosity and self-importance
- A persistent belief that he knew the "right way" to do everything

- Prioritization of financial gain, manipulation, stealing, and cheating
- Compulsive mistruths expressed for personal benefit
- An excessive need for admiration
- A sense of entitlement
- A consistent lack of empathy, unless it served him in some way

My mother, on the other hand, demonstrated symptoms that more closely aligned with Borderline Personality Disorder (BPD):

- Intense fear of abandonment, both real and imagined, especially involving my father
- A history of limited long-term friendships, often becoming critical and cutting people off
- Lack of respect for others' boundaries and privacy
- Distorted self-image, including self-deprecating jokes about her weight
- Binge eating, compulsive online shopping, and poor impulse control
- Avoidance of healthy coping strategies, like exercise,
- Often "playing sick" to gain sympathy with attempts to garner attention through illness or crisis
- Chronic emotional chaos, unpredictable mood swings, and threats of suicide when abandoned
- Isolating my father from others in her quest for love and attention
- Suspicious ideation (e.g., believing people were following her or listening to her phone calls), and invasive investigations into others' actions and motives

In reviewing her behaviors, it's clear that my mother may also fall under what's called a Borderline Narcissist or Covert/Vulnerable

Narcissist subtype: those who meet criteria for both NPD and BPD. These individuals typically:

- Feel slighted when they are not the focal point
- Need constant reassurance and praise
- Struggle with identity and self-esteem
- Use manipulative behaviors to get their needs met
- Have difficulty empathizing and maintaining long-term relationships
- Fear abandonment and seek control through jealousy and emotional coercion
- Show poor boundaries and are quick to blame others

What's especially telling in these types of relationships is that the romantic partner often takes priority over the children. Children may only become relevant when they serve a purpose for the parent, such as being used to gather information, perform favors, or provide emotional support. This dynamic often leads to profound emotional neglect of the child.

There's also significant overlap in how both NPD and BPD individuals struggle:

- Both have difficulty regulating emotions and tolerating discomfort
- Both expect others to cater to their emotional needs
- Both require attention and affirmation to feel secure
- Both lack awareness of how their actions affect others
- Both often demonstrate rigid, black-and-white thinking, emotional immaturity, and resistance to accountability
- And when triggered, both can spiral into rage or passive-aggressive retaliation

Understanding these patterns is crucial, especially for those raised by such individuals or those who find themselves repeatedly in relationships with similar dynamics. It's not just about how the dysfunction plays out; it's about recognizing that the dysfunction itself often feels functional to those living inside it.

Emotional Immaturity

Throughout this book, I occasionally reference the concept of emotional immaturity, so it's important to define what it truly means objectively and clearly. Emotional immaturity is not simply a matter of being dramatic or difficult; it involves a distinct set of traits that reflect a developmental delay in emotional growth. These traits often include:

- Self-centeredness
- Lack of accountability and a victim mentality
- Avoidant or underdeveloped communication skills
- Impulsivity and emotional reactivity
- Codependence or insecurity in relationships

In essence, emotionally immature individuals appear stuck in an earlier developmental stage, regardless of their chronological age. This immaturity may stem from trauma, neglect, or dysfunctional family dynamics. Under stress, such individuals tend to regress, often behaving in ways that are more childlike than adult.

Consider a young child who becomes overwhelmed by distress. They might cry, throw a tantrum, or lash out until their needs are met. They lack the emotional tools to express themselves calmly or to ask for help effectively. Adults with narcissistic personality disorder (NPD) or borderline personality disorder (BPD) often operate in a similar way, *acting* out their emotional pain rather than verbalizing it. Their inability to manage emotions constructively combined with limited insight into how their behavior affects others leads to frequent outbursts, blame-shifting, and cyclical conflict.

This immaturity, in turn, becomes a barrier to personal growth. Change requires self-awareness, and those who lack it remain locked in maladaptive patterns.

The situation becomes even more layered and volatile when multiple emotionally immature individuals, particularly those with Cluster B traits coexist within the same family. One of the most combustible combinations is a relationship between a person with NPD and someone with BPD. It's a complex interplay of psychological defenses, unmet needs, and manipulative behaviors, all unfolding beneath the surface of everyday life.

In this dynamic, the individual with BPD (or covert narcissism) often radiates a subtle but powerful vulnerability, a kind of emotional chum in the water. This vulnerability is irresistible to the narcissist, who thrives on admiration and control. The BPD partner, in turn, may mold themselves to fit the narcissist's desires in exchange for attention and the illusion of emotional security. What emerges is a game of survival disguised as devotion:

"If I make him dinner every night, toss out my favorite décor, and shape myself into the person he wants, maybe he won't leave me."

Because individuals with BPD often struggle with identity, this kind of emotional shape-shifting does not initially feel like a loss. Over time, however, it breeds deep resentment. Their existence gradually begins to revolve around the narcissist's preferences and emotional demands.

In my own family, my mother often played this accommodating role with my father, but always with an emotional price tag. Even when she gave freely, there was an unspoken ledger. Her generosity came with strings attached, and I learned early on that accepting anything from her meant incurring an invisible debt, one that could never fully be repaid.

These dynamics create a system of emotional wildcards. Each partner keeps their cards close, attempting to read the other before revealing their own intentions. The manipulations become subtle, strategic. For instance:

"Oh, you get upset when I talk to other people? I'll make sure to do it more when you give me the silent treatment, so that you have to talk to me."

This kind of tit-for-tat manipulation illustrates just how central emotional immaturity is in shaping these relationships. It's not merely about dysfunction. It's about two people locked in a psychological tug-of-war, each trying to soothe their wounds by controlling the other. In the process, everyone around them, especially their children, gets pulled into the chaos.

Imbalance of Power

A defining feature of narcissistic relationships is an escalating imbalance of power, carefully crafted through isolation and psychological erosion. One of the narcissist's most effective tools is slowly cutting their partner off from external sources of support. This is rarely done overtly.

Instead, it happens through a series of subtle, insidious suggestions:

> *Little by little, the narcissist chips away at their partner's trust in others. A best friend becomes "toxic." A parent is suddenly "too controlling" or "unsupportive." Over time, the narcissist positions themselves as the sole source of truth, love, and safety. This manipulation deepens the partner's dependency, allowing the narcissist to tighten their grip while facing less outside scrutiny. The quieter the chorus of other voices becomes, the louder the narcissist's voice echoes in the partner's mind.*

This dynamic reminded me vividly of how my mother spoke to my father during their most enmeshed and toxic periods:

"No one's ever there for you like I am. I've been with you through everything. If it weren't for me, you'd be so alone."

Even as a child, I knew this wasn't true. I remember hearing those words and feeling uneasy, confused by why my father couldn't see what she was doing. It was as if he were under a spell, enchanted by the idea that she alone could fill the void inside him. She added, almost mythically:

"Your father used to sleep with his hands clenched tight until he met me. I changed everything."

Somehow, the more she repeated these stories, the more he believed them. They clung to each other in a delusional bond that had little to do with truth and everything to do with control.

For the partner of a narcissist, self-doubt becomes a chronic state. Over time, their internal voice grows quieter, confused and uncertain. The narcissist plants seeds of inadequacy in their partner's mind: that they are not smart enough, capable enough, or worthy enough on their own. Perhaps they have become financially dependent and feel trapped. Perhaps they once had confidence, now buried beneath layers of subtle ridicule and emotional erosion.

"Cooking's never really been your strength, has it?" the narcissist remarks dismissively as their partner tries to prepare a thoughtful meal.

The underlying message is clear: You're lucky to be with someone as amazing as me, given how flawed you are.

Often, the partner enters the relationship with already fragile self-esteem, and the narcissist, sensing this vulnerability exploits it until the illusion of love is built entirely on disempowerment. Each comment, each manipulation, each subtle dismissal becomes a brick in a carefully constructed house of mirrors, where the narcissist's reflection is magnified and the partner's is distorted beyond recognition.

The Four Types of Narcissistic Relationships

When two individuals with pronounced narcissistic traits or broader Cluster B personality features form a relationship, the bond often centers on power, control, and mutual dysfunction. These relationships tend to cycle through manipulation, emotional volatility, and a continual struggle for dominance.

While the specific dynamics may vary, four common types of narcissistic pairings frequently emerge: the toxic, the manipulative, the perfect match, and the rescue relationship. Each reflects its own distinctive pattern of dysfunction.

The Pairings

The Toxic Relationship

This pairing involves two equally abusive and destructive individuals who feed off the chaos they create. They may gaslight, lie to, or exploit one another, yet instead of breaking the cycle, they remain locked in a volatile tug-of-war. Outsiders often grow exhausted by the constant drama and eventually distance themselves from the couple altogether. Despite the turmoil, the partners' mutual dependency on emotional conflict keeps the relationship intact.

The Manipulative Relationship

In this dynamic, one partner holds greater power and engages in most of the harmful behavior, while the other becomes the primary target. The manipulative partner distorts reality, reframes narratives, and makes calculated moves to maintain control. They may, for instance, misrepresent facts to advance their own agenda or minimize the impact of their actions on their partner. The imbalance of power is often concealed beneath layers of charm, guilt-tripping, or manufactured intimacy.

The Perfect Match

In this pairing, two narcissists may appear compatible on the surface, sharing goals, social values, or lifestyle preferences. Yet beneath the polished exterior lies a pattern of ongoing abuse. They might host elegant dinners or maintain an enviable public image, but behind closed doors, jealousy and control dominate. One partner may accuse the other of being "too friendly" with guests, using the situation to assert dominance and reinforce isolation. Ultimately, the relationship thrives on distortion and performance rather than mutual respect or emotional safety.

The Rescue Relationship

This dynamic occurs when one partner "rescues" the other from a prior toxic relationship, only to become equally, if not more, abusive. The rescuer is idealized because they appear to be a savior in contrast to the former partner. For example, John comforts Mary about her unsupportive boyfriend and encourages her to leave. Once she does, John steps in as the new partner, only to reveal similar or even worse manipulative behaviors. The contrast masks the toxicity until the damage is done.

In the case of my parents, their dynamic fell somewhere between the toxic and the perfect match. Both manipulated each other for personal gain while simultaneously aligning on many values, particularly around image and status. My mother clung to the relationship because being with a man was central to her identity. She wanted to appear well cared for and admired as a married woman. She also manipulated those around her often isolating people to maintain control and draw attention to herself, whether by turning my brother and me against each other or by subtly undermining my father's friendships. She often "tested" people through unspoken expectations. If you didn't call after her doctor's appointment, you failed. That failure meant she now held emotional leverage; you owed her. She played the role of the manipulative martyr. If I pleaded with her and my father to stop fighting, she would gaslight me:

"We're not fighting, we're just talking to each other."

Meanwhile, I was covering my ears as they screamed.

My father had his own arsenal of manipulation. After months of ignoring my mother, he would conveniently reappear in her life just as she received an inheritance from her father. He showed up at relatives' deathbeds, making pancakes for the family not out of affection, but for appearances and potential financial gain. He reestablished control over her finances, her appearance, and her movements, and she complied, desperate for his approval. He took things from her home, lied about where he was, and flirted or connected secretly with other women. His verbal abuse was blunt and cruel, shouting "shut up" or "fuck you" whenever his patience ran thin.

Their relationship was a perfect storm of mutual manipulation, image maintenance, and emotional warfare, one that left no room for vulnerability or safety, only performance and control.

Within these types of narcissistic relationships, the following dynamics can be observed:

Subtle Toxicity

As discussed earlier, the toxicity in my family came from both of my parents—just in different forms. It took me years to understand that. As a child, my father's narcissism flew under the radar. Most of my emotional pain was directed toward my mother, whose instability was more overt and easier to recognize. She was dramatic, reactive, and emotionally unpredictable, while my father was quiet, withholding, and covert in his manipulation. Only as I got older did the reasons behind her behavior and their dysfunctional dynamic begin to make sense. They were each destructive in contrasting ways.

When my mother became emotionally overwhelmed, she would engage in triangulation, a common tactic in families affected by personality disorders. This meant inappropriately pulling me into adult matters that pertained to her marriage, using me as a sounding board, or emotionally leaning on me as if I were a peer. She'd tell me details about their relationship, ask me to take sides, or manipulate me into agreeing with her on personal issues. However, once she and my father were "happy" again, she'd deny that any of those conversations had ever happened, leaving me confused and emotionally stranded.

"Don't you think your father should have spoken to me differently? Answer me."

That kind of question, complex and emotionally loaded, was far too much for a child who should have been focused on school, friends, or Nickelodeon. Triangulation can be deeply damaging for children. It robs them of the ability to form their own relationships with each parent and plants distorted narratives that shape their perceptions prematurely. It's not about truth or care; it's about manipulation and influence, and it burdens the child with emotional responsibilities that never belonged to them in the first place.

This kind of emotional confusion can also interfere with a child's development of object constancy, a foundational psychological concept often introduced in Psych 101. Object constancy refers to a child's ability to understand that others exist and care for them even when they are not physically present. For example, if Mom leaves the room, a securely attached child learns she will come back. When that attachment is unstable or interrupted, the child doesn't internalize that sense of safety. If this foundational trust is disrupted, the child may struggle to see others as emotionally reliable, leading to an inability to form secure, empathetic attachments later in life. This is often seen in individuals with NPD and BPD, where emotional permanence is impaired. People are viewed not as complex beings with both good and bad traits, but as either all good or all bad, depending on how safe or threatening they feel in the moment. That fear of abandonment becomes core to how they relate to others seeking control, validation, or distance in response to the instability they experienced early on.

Superficiality of Relations

Both of my parents can be incredibly charming when they want to be. At first glance, they seem warm, engaging, even generous. When you meet them at a dinner party, you might think, *What nice people!* They know how to perform kindness convincingly. But once the guests leave and the door closes, their tone shifts. Suddenly, they're picking apart every attendee: "She didn't bring a gift." "He only talked about himself." "That guy was so boring." Yet if any of those people were to walk back into the room, the act would resume instantly; saccharine offers of help, over-the-top friendliness, all as though the earlier criticisms had never happened. It's a strange kind of duplicity: they don't seem to relate to others as people, but as props in a performance.

I used to think my parents must have lost themselves in each other, that they somehow adopted one another's traits in an attempt to fit or survive within the relationship. Over time, I came to see it differently. It wasn't so much that they gave up a sense of self; it's that there wasn't much self to begin with. Their identities were patchworks of insecurity and performance, stitched together by fear of rejection and fueled by a relentless need for approval. They were like sponges sitting in the same murky dishwater, soaking up each other's dysfunction and saturating the space with it, unable to stay clean or separate.

Watching their relationship unfold felt surreal. It made me question what was real in any connection. Did I also need to perform in my relationships? Was that what love looked like: smiling, nodding, and secretly resenting? I remember wondering how exhausting it must be to pretend so much while harboring so much bitterness. Why spend time with people they clearly didn't like? Eventually, I saw the pattern: it didn't matter who the audience was. The contempt always followed. And because I was their child, someone who couldn't come and go, I became the most convenient target. I wasn't a guest who would leave; I was there to absorb their projections.

Looking back, I believe they treated me as disposable because I had no choice in the matter. When they were angry, I became the emotional dumping ground. When they were happy, I was invisible. There was nothing to gain, in their eyes, from simply being kind to me. Kindness was never offered freely; it always came with strings: expectation of praise, reciprocation, or performance. If they didn't receive that, they withdrew or lashed out. It wasn't about giving for the joy of seeing someone else happy; it was about feeding their egos.

When in conflict with each other, my parents were adversaries. But when it came to invalidating me, they were a united front. They gaslit me in stereo, minimizing and denying my experiences in tandem. To have both parents tell you that your memories and emotions are wrong is profoundly destabilizing. It silences you in ways that breed deep, simmering rage. I carried that rage with me as a child and into my teen years, an anger that was never recognized for what it truly was: a cry for acknowledgment.

Children often express unmet emotional needs through outbursts of rage, not because they are "bad" or "disobedient," but because they feel unheard. Narcissistic parents rarely make that connection. They don't see rage as grief; they see it as defiance. And so, the child is pathologized, labeled, blamed while the roots of their pain go ignored.

The Narcissistic Cycle of Abuse

What happens when both partners in a relationship are attempting to manipulate, dominate, or emotionally control each other, each playing off the other's vulnerabilities? The answer is: escalating chaos. The relationship becomes a psychological battlefield. Over time, as each person learns more about the other's wounds, the weapons become more precise. The emotional cuts go deeper. In toxic pairings, especially between individuals with traits of NPD and BPD, the dysfunction doesn't stabilize; it compounds.

To understand this more clearly, we must examine the Narcissistic Cycle of Abuse, a well-documented and insidious pattern of behavior in many toxic relationships.

The Stages

Idealization & Love Bombing

The cycle often begins with a euphoric rush: the narcissist's charm is magnetic, disarming, and all-consuming. He pulls out your chair, tells you that you're beautiful, and makes you feel as though you're the only person in the room. Being with him makes everything else fade: colors seem brighter, life feels lighter, and you feel chosen in a way you never have before.

This is more than the classic "honeymoon phase," it's love bombing, a stage in which affection and attention are exaggerated and strategically deployed. You are idealized, placed on a pedestal, and made to feel uniquely special. He showers you with compliments, thoughtful gifts, and grand gestures. In therapy sessions, I often heard clients say, "When it was good, it was really good."

But what feels like genuine love is actually a form of control. The goal isn't long-term connection; it's conquest. Narcissists build you up in ways that make you dependent on their validation. That intensity becomes addictive and that's exactly the point.

Devaluation

As quickly as it began, the idealization phase starts to fade. Often without warning, the warmth turns cold. The narcissist begins to notice your "flaws." You leave your clothes out and suddenly that's disgusting. You make a reasonable request, but now you're needy. Small criticisms become daily occurrences. Affection is withdrawn, and you're left wondering what changed.

This is the devaluation phase, and it begins the moment the narcissist no longer sees you as a source of novelty or ego gratification. The pedestal you were once placed on becomes a vantage point from which you're now knocked down.

The shift is confusing and often deeply painful. If you confront the narcissist about their change in behavior, you'll likely be met with deflection, gaslighting, or blame-shifting:

"If you didn't nag me, I wouldn't have to yell." "You used to be fun, now everything is a problem."

There's rarely logic, just emotional punishment. Over time, this dynamic trains you to blame yourself. You internalize the idea that you caused the switch, that if you just behaved differently, the "old him" or "real him" would return.

Breadcrumbing & Hoovering

After devaluation, many narcissists don't fully walk away, they linger. This is where breadcrumbing comes in: sporadic displays of affection, sudden kind words, a thoughtful gesture out of nowhere. It creates just enough hope to keep you hooked. It's the emotional equivalent of bait.

The narcissist uses breadcrumbing to stay in control and prevent you from moving on. It's a tactic that plays on the memory of the initial idealization phase, your emotional "high." You become addicted to the crumbs, hoping they'll lead back to the feast.

If you start to pull away or consider leaving, the narcissist may escalate into Hoovering, named after the vacuum cleaner for its ability to suck you back in. Hoovering can include:

- Emotional pleas: "You're the only one who's ever understood me."
- Manipulative guilt: "If you leave, I don't know what I'll do."
- Promises to change: "I'll go to therapy. I'll do whatever it takes."

Some even enlist mutual friends or family to reinforce the illusion: "He's really hurting.

Maybe you should talk to him." These efforts are rarely sincere. The goal is not reconciliation but reconquest.

Discard

Eventually, when your usefulness to the narcissist runs out, when you stop being a source of validation, admiration, or excitement, you may be abruptly discarded. This often happens without warning, explanation, or closure. You're left confused, hollowed out, and desperate for answers.

The narcissist, meanwhile, moves on quickly. They may already have a new partner; what's often referred to as "new supply." Like a vampire searching for a fresh source of emotional blood, they begin the cycle again with someone else.

For those with BPD traits who become entangled with a narcissist, the discard phase is particularly devastating. The abandonment triggers can be overwhelming. They may desperately try to fix the relationship, revisiting every detail in their mind:

"What did I say wrong? Was it that one text; that one joke?"

Ironically, this desperation often feeds the narcissist's ego even more, leading to further manipulation such as comparing you to the new partner to make you "try harder." Eventually, even this game loses its thrill, and you are left discarded, often at your lowest point.

The Cycle Repeats

The most haunting part of the narcissistic abuse cycle is that it often doesn't end after one rotation. Idealization may reappear weeks or months later: a kind text out of nowhere, a holiday card, a DM just to "check in." This intermittent reinforcement strengthens the psychological grip. You begin to crave that idealization again, forgetting the cost at which it comes.

One of my graduate professors once explained that the neurological reward we receive from the return to idealization is akin to the dopamine rush from gambling or using meth. The brain remembers the high and ignores the devastation. This cyclical trauma creates a kind of emotional addiction. The narcissist becomes both the drug and the withdrawal. You stop seeing the cycle for what it is and instead cling to the hope that this time will be different.

I've seen these dynamics unfold countless times in therapy, and I saw them unfold in my own home growing up. Watching my parents spin through this exact cycle, again and again, was like witnessing a psychological slow-motion car crash that somehow shocked them every time. The more my father pulled away, the more my mother leaned in. The more she begged, the colder he became. They were locked in a pattern they couldn't see and couldn't stop.

Why These Relationships Perpetuate

Romantic attraction often feels mysterious, magnetic, and unexplainable. But as a psychodynamic psychologist, I've come to understand that we are drawn to familiar pain as much as to familiar pleasure. We recreate the emotional dynamics we knew in childhood, not because they were healthy, but because they are recognizable. Our subconscious seeks out what it knows, even if what it knows is trauma.

That's why so many people wake up one day and say, "Oh my God, I married my mother," or, "I became my father." The unconscious drive toward repetition, called repetition compulsion in psychodynamic theory, is an attempt to "master" early wounds by recreating the scenario with a new cast. Instead of mastery, however, we usually find ourselves trapped in a cycle of pain.

What begins as a familiar emotional pattern often morphs into a deeper relational entanglement. Once we are in the relationship, the same psychological templates we developed in childhood: hypervigilance, self-abandonment, emotional caretaking, are activated again. These dynamics don't just shape who we're attracted to; they shape how we show up in the relationship. Over time, this creates fertile ground for codependency, especially when both partners carry unaddressed emotional wounds.

Codependency Manifesting

In relationships where both partners exhibit traits of emotional immaturity, NPD, or BPD, the cycle of abuse becomes mutual, though not necessarily symmetrical. Each person tries to control, manipulate, or "fix" the other as a means of emotional regulation. One partner may crave closeness while the other pushes away. One uses seduction or caretaking; the other uses dominance or withdrawal. This push-pull dynamic creates a volatile rhythm—intensity mistaken for intimacy, volatility mistaken for passion.

The longer the relationship continues, the more both partners become destabilized, and the harder it is to separate identity from dysfunction. Love becomes surveillance. Attention becomes control. At the heart of it all is fear: fear of being left, of being exposed, of being unworthy.

Relationships involving Cluster B personality types, particularly NPD and BPD, often develop deeply entrenched codependent dynamics. The narcissist craves constant validation, admiration, and control, making it difficult for them to leave a relationship unless they've already secured a new source of supply. As a result, they often remain in unhealthy partnerships far longer than they should.

On the other side, individuals with BPD tend to fear abandonment, feel emotionally vulnerable, and seek constant reassurance. Their intense fear of rejection and deep longing for connection often lead them to tolerate mistreatment or instability just to avoid being alone. The mutual neediness and blurred boundaries between the two create a toxic loop: each person relies on the other to meet emotional needs in ways that are unsustainable and ultimately damaging. They remain locked in a cycle not out of love or compatibility, but out of emotional dependency, each fulfilling the other's dysfunction.

Gaslighting: Understanding Its Forms and How It Silences You

This codependent dynamic often paves the way for gaslighting. When a person's self-worth becomes entangled with keeping the relationship intact, they may begin to question their own instincts and perceptions in order to preserve the connection. In emotionally immature or narcissistic partnerships, gaslighting doesn't always appear as overt cruelty. It can be subtle, even disguised as concern, but over time, it erodes a person's ability to trust themselves. The more one partner denies, distorts, or dismisses the other's reality, the more the codependent partner bends out of shape trying to maintain closeness. Their need for attachment overrides their sense of truth. In this way, gaslighting becomes not only a form of manipulation but also a symptom of the power imbalance created by unresolved trauma and emotional enmeshment.

Gaslighting often emerges within isolating and abusive dynamics. Though the term has become something of a cultural buzzword, casually tossed into arguments and memes, when it's real, its impact is profoundly damaging. Gaslighting is not merely disagreement or miscommunication; it's a repeated, intentional pattern of emotional manipulation designed to erode a person's sense of reality, memory, and self-worth.

As Tracy (2021) defines it, gaslighting is "a form of emotional abuse where the abuser manipulates situations repeatedly to trick the victim into distrusting his or her own memory and perceptions." It commonly shows up in four specific forms: withholding, countering, blocking, and trivializing. Recognizing each of these in real time can be crucial for reclaiming clarity and emotional safety.

Forms of Gaslighting

Withholding

Withholding is the refusal to engage, acknowledge, or validate. It's a form of stonewalling whether through silence, deflection, or "playing dumb," that leaves the other person talking into a void.

Example: You finally work up the nerve to bring up something that hurt you. The response? "I don't even know what you're talking about. This is ridiculous. I can't believe we're still on this."

Over time, these reactions wear you down. After enough cycles of trying to communicate and being met with dismissal or silence, you begin to give up. You start to question whether your concerns are valid or if you're just *too much.*

Countering

Countering goes after your memory. Even when you're certain about what happened, the gaslighter finds ways to dispute it, often by referencing your past mistakes or exaggerating your forgetfulness to undermine your credibility.

Example: "You're saying I said that? I never did. Remember when you were so sure you left your wallet in the car and it turned out to be at home? How do we even know your memory is right this time?"

This tactic creates a persistent sense of confusion. You start double-checking your own reality and second-guessing your instincts. Over time, you begin deferring to their version of events just to avoid the mental battle.

This is sometimes referred to as toxic amnesia, particularly when the gaslighter conveniently "forgets" past transgressions:

"I never said that. Why are you making things up again?"

"That's not how I remember it. You always twist things."

Blocking

Blocking is the verbal equivalent of slamming a door in your face. The gaslighter derails the conversation by changing the subject, mocking your sources, or accusing you of being overly influenced by others.

Example: You say, "It hurt me when you talked down to me at dinner." The reply? "Wow, that sounds like something your mother would say," or, "Is that some crap you saw on TikTok?"

Sometimes blocking takes the form of redirecting blame or leveraging social pressure:

"Everyone else agrees with me, I'm not sure what your problem is." "You made me act that way, so really, this is on you."

My mother's go-to line when I brought up difficult feelings was, "I guess I was just the worst mother ever, then." That single sentence was emotionally manipulative and blocked any further communication. It made me feel cruel for even trying to express myself, and eventually, I stopped trying altogether.

Trivializing

Trivializing diminishes your feelings. It frames your emotional experience as exaggerated, irrational, or selfish. This tactic is especially harmful because it targets your sense of worth and your right to feel.

Example: "You're so sensitive. I was just joking." Or, "You're making a big deal out of nothing, like always."

Trivializing can also be layered with guilt:

"Yeah, I didn't pay the rent, but think about everything I've done for you. Can't you just cut me some slack?"

These responses pressure you to drop the issue or feel guilty for being upset in the first place. They turn your boundaries into burdens and leave you feeling as if you're the unreasonable one for having them at all.

The Cumulative Effect of Gaslighting

Each of these tactics, on their own, can leave you confused or momentarily silenced, but repeated over time, they wear away at your confidence, your ability to trust your own mind, and your belief that your emotions are valid. They create a self-erasing effect: You stop speaking up. You start doubting yourself. You lose clarity around what's real.

Gaslighting doesn't just distort conversations, it rewires your self-perception. It teaches you to internalize blame, mistrust your memory, and suppress your needs in the name of keeping the peace.

And that's the point: silence you enough times, and eventually, you stop talking.

While much of this section focuses on how gaslighting shows up in adult romantic relationships, it's important to note that the dynamic takes on an even more insidious form when used against children.

Gaslighting affects children in particularly damaging and developmentally disruptive ways because it interferes with the very foundation of how they learn to understand themselves, relationships, and the world around them. Unlike adults, children don't have fully formed cognitive or emotional tools to challenge distorted narratives, so they tend to internalize them.

For children, experiencing gaslighting undermines their developing sense of reality. Children learn what's true, trustworthy, and emotionally safe by watching how adults respond to them. When a caregiver gaslights them: e.g., saying "That didn't happen" or "You're making that up" in response to something the child experienced, it can make the child doubt their perceptions.

Example: A child sees their parent yelling and throwing things, but later the parent calmly says, "I never yelled. You're imagining things."

Over time, the child may stop trusting their senses and begin dissociating from their experiences, believing others' versions of reality over their own.

The gaslighting teaches them their feelings are invalid or dangerous. If every emotional reaction is met with "You're overreacting," "Stop being dramatic," or "You're too sensitive," children learn that their emotions are wrong or inconvenient. This stunts emotional regulation and can create long-term struggles with identifying and expressing feelings.

Consequence: Many adults who were gaslit as children struggle with emotional repression, people-pleasing, or fear of confrontation, because they were conditioned to believe their emotions would be rejected or weaponized.

Gaslighting also tends to breed chronic self-doubt and shame. Children absorb gaslighting as a reflection of who they are. They might not think, "This person is manipulating me," but instead, "I must be stupid," "I must be crazy," or "Something is wrong with me." This deep-seated shame can evolve into imposter syndrome, low self-worth, and difficulty trusting their instincts well into adulthood.

Further, gaslighting reinforces dependency and obedience over autonomy. When children are told that they're wrong about what they saw, heard, or felt, even when they're right, they begin to rely on the gaslighter for "truth." This makes them easier to control and less likely to rebel or question authority. Children raised this way often become hypervigilant adults who defer to others, seek external validation, or feel anxious when making independent choices.

Lastly, gaslighting can cause long-term mental health issues in several ways. Over time, it may contribute to complex trauma (C-PTSD), anxiety disorders, depression, and dissociative tendencies. Such children often grow up emotionally confused, struggling to trust relationships or even to form a consistent sense of identity.

We'll explore the long-term psychological effects of parent–child dynamics, particularly those shaped by personality disorders, more deeply in a later section.

Other Manipulation Tactics Within Romantic Relationships

DARVO

Another tactic often used in relationships by individuals with Cluster B traits is known as DARVO, an acronym for Deny, Attack, and Reverse Victim and Offender. DARVO is a manipulative defense mechanism that extends gaslighting by flipping the narrative: the perpetrator denies the abuse, attacks the person confronting them, and then positions themselves as the victim.

Example: If you confront someone about harmful behavior, they might respond, "You always paint me as the villain." Even when there's clear evidence of wrongdoing, the focus shifts away from accountability and onto your actions instead. Rather than saying, "I'm sorry I was unfaithful to you," they may say, "You violated my trust by looking through my phone."

In more extreme cases, the manipulator may escalate by threatening legal action without cause or by targeting your most vulnerable insecurities as punishment for speaking up. These behaviors signal a clear lack of rational, empathetic dialogue. No matter how calmly or clearly you present the truth, you're unlikely to receive validation or accountability from this person.

Ultimately, the relief we seek often won't come from the offender. It must come from our own internal healing work.

Traumatic Invalidation

Traumatic invalidation occurs when one's emotions, memories, and lived experiences are consistently dismissed or denied over time. This kind of invalidation can take overt or subtle forms: statements like "That never happened," or "You should look at how you treated me" slowly erode a person's trust in their own reality. According to Dr. Martin Bohus, PhD, and the National Institute for the Clinical Application of Behavioral Medicine ("Treating PTSD," 2023), this type of invalidation can be just as psychologically harmful as the trauma itself.

Over time, these experiences create a pervasive sense of personal insignificance. You start to wonder why someone who's supposed to love you would repeatedly deny your experience. The only conclusion that seems to make sense is that you must be the problem. If you had value, you reason, you would be treated with care. This line of thinking becomes a dangerous cognitive loop, feeding low self-esteem, guilt, and emotional confusion.

There's also the fear that if you continue to "complain" or express discomfort, the person invalidating you might abandon you altogether. So instead, you begin to overexplain your feelings to others, hoping that if you just explain it right, they'll finally understand. This leads to emotional exhaustion. Or worse, to questioning your own experiences entirely: "Maybe it wasn't that bad. Maybe I exaggerated." But often, the question shouldn't be whether your version of reality is flawed, it should be, Why is the person I care about denying what happened?

I had to return to this question over and over. My father isn't just the kind man who cooks for sick relatives and says he "tried his best." He's also the man who cheated; on his taxes, on my mother, on our family's emotional trust. Both of those realities can coexist. It's not black and white.

When you've endured traumatic invalidation, you may continue the cycle by invalidating yourself. Even long after the relationship or traumatic experience ends, you find yourself minimizing your emotions, brushing off your pain. It's a form of self-protection at first, but eventually it becomes self-sabotage. This often leads people to stay in or repeat harmful relationships or to avoid therapy altogether because they assume no one will believe them, or that they don't deserve help in the first place.

It's common to lose trust in someone who repeatedly questions your truth. Emotional intimacy erodes, replaced by surface-level interactions. You stop confiding in them, knowing that any vulnerability might be twisted, ignored, or used against you. And without trust, whether in a marriage or a parent–child relationship, the bond slowly disintegrates.

Traumatic invalidation can also take the form of verbal and emotional abuse: belittling, blaming, or outright neglect. It can be culturally reinforced, especially in environments where vulnerability is seen as weakness or where therapy is stigmatized. Being told you're "lying," "exaggerating," or "too sensitive" only deepens the wound.

I often heard things like, "You're just an unhappy person. Focus on other things," whenever I tried to express that something had hurt me. I was left with unanswered questions, a sense of defectiveness, and a persistent ache of not being heard. That kind of invalidation shakes your identity and self-worth at the core. Traumatic invalidation is often linked to the development of personality disorders, disordered eating, and even suicidality or self-injurious behavior.

It's important to understand that traumatic invalidation exists on a spectrum. It can be blunt or deeply covert and often, the subtle kind is more insidious because it causes us to doubt every perception we have. A teenager says they're sick, and the parent replies, "You're fine; go to school." Or the child expresses self-loathing and is met with, "Don't talk like that. You're beautiful." While these statements might seem benign or even kind, they can inadvertently strip the child of agency and emotional accuracy.

Traumatic invalidation is harmful not because a single statement is overtly cruel, but because repeated patterns of emotional dismissal;

especially when subtle, undermine a person's sense of reality, autonomy, and emotional trust in themselves. Let's break down these two examples:

"You're fine, go to school."

On the surface, this may sound like a typical parental nudge, but when a child expresses physical discomfort and is told they're "fine," several toxic messages are delivered at once:

- Your body is not to be trusted.
- It is I, not you, who determines how you feel.
- Your needs inconvenience me.

Over time, this erodes the child's internal compass. They learn to override their physical and emotional boundaries, which can later manifest as dissociation, poor self-care, or chronic self-doubt.

Let's now focus on the second example: "Don't talk like that. You're beautiful." This may sound like a compliment, but when offered in response to a vulnerable expression of self-loathing or low self-worth, it becomes emotionally dismissive. Here's why:

- It skips over the emotional content of what the child said (the pain, shame, or need for connection).
- It shames vulnerability by essentially saying, "That feeling is wrong and shouldn't exist."
- It substitutes reality with idealism, giving a feel-good response in place of emotional attunement or authenticity.

The child doesn't feel seen or heard. Instead of feeling soothed, they may feel misunderstood or silenced, especially if this pattern repeats over time. These statements undermine the child's trust in their own perception of reality. Subtle invalidation confuses the child because it often comes disguised as love or encouragement. This can cause internal fragmentation:

- "Why do I feel hurt when they're saying something nice?"
- "Maybe I'm just being too emotional."
- "Maybe my feelings really are wrong."

Sometimes you're told to calm down, hide your anger, or treat elders with respect, even when that respect isn't mutual. The message becomes clear: "Your feelings are less valid than the feelings of others." Unless we consciously challenge that idea, we internalize it.

You don't need to have been in physical danger to have experienced trauma. You don't need to have everything figured out to trust your experience. It's valid, even if it took you years to realize what it was; even if others had it worse, or if you're doing "okay" now.

The Narcissist as a Parent

When a narcissist or someone with borderline personality disorder becomes a parent, the experience can differ dramatically from that of the average person. While most parents feel a deep sense of sacrifice, joy, and fulfillment in nurturing a newborn, the narcissist often remains unchanged. The arrival of a child doesn't mark a shift in priorities or values; it's simply one more addition to their world. The child doesn't become central to their life; they merely take up space in it.

For the child, this can feel like being an afterthought; an accessory rather than an integral part of the family. The narcissist sees the child as a means to an end: to project an image of success, maintain a façade of normalcy, or secure someone to care for them in old age. In many ways, the child is never seen as a separate individual with unique needs, desires, or identity, but rather as an extension of the parent's own ego.

For me, I often felt that my role in the family was to hold my parents' marriage together. Their relationship was fragile, and without an external focal point like me it might have crumbled under the weight of its own dysfunction. I served as the bridge in their emotional tug-of-war, a tool through which they expressed frustrations and resentments that had nowhere else to go.

Subtypes of the Narcissistic Parent

Just as narcissistic personality disorder (NPD) includes different subtypes, narcissistic parents can also be categorized in distinct ways based on how their behaviors affect their children and family dynamics. These classifications go beyond clinical definitions and reflect real-world patterns observed in families impacted by narcissism.

Below are some of the most common and recognizable types of narcissistic parents, each with its own style of control, emotional manipulation, and unmet needs.

Cerebral Narcissistic Parent

This type of parent presents themselves as intellectually superior—always the smartest person in the room. Their need to be seen as all-knowing fosters doubt and insecurity in their child, undermining the child's independence and confidence. Cerebral narcissists may manipulate facts, dismiss others' knowledge, or refuse to admit when they're wrong.

I remember giving my father directions in an area I knew well. He refused to listen, insisted he was right, and ultimately got lost. Rather than admit his mistake, he silently corrected his route and pretended nothing had happened. Moments like these taught me that logic didn't matter only his ego did. Over time, this parenting style fosters emotional dependence and stifles a child's ability to trust their own judgment.

Malignant Narcissistic Parent

The malignant narcissist is the most harmful and toxic variation. This parent can be cruel, controlling, and intentionally hurtful, often using fear or humiliation to maintain dominance. Their behavior isn't merely self-centered, it's vindictive. They may mock their child in public or punish them simply for expressing emotion.

Living under this kind of parenting means constantly walking on eggshells. The child learns to suppress their feelings to avoid ridicule, rejection, or punishment. The emotional damage can be severe, leading to anxiety, shame, and chronic hypervigilance.

Antagonistic or Competitive Narcissistic Parent

This parent views their child as a rival. Rather than celebrating the child's successes, they feel threatened and often try to outshine them. If a child wins a spelling bee, the parent might hijack the moment to brag about their own childhood achievements. The child's milestones are minimized, dismissed, or overshadowed.

Over time, this dynamic teaches the child that their worth depends on how well they serve the parent's ego. The result is often low self-esteem, perfectionism, and a persistent feeling of never being "enough" unless they are outperforming others or themselves.

Key Parenting Dynamics

There are several common dynamics that emerge between narcissistic parents and their children, often leaving lasting emotional scars. Let's revisit some key points from Part I to further explore these dynamics:

Competition

Competition is a frequent and insidious feature of both narcissistic and borderline parenting. These individuals often feel threatened by their child's independence, success, or even emotional experiences. If a child accomplishes something noteworthy, the parent will often find a way to insert themselves into the narrative: *"Well, she gets that from me,"* or *"I sacrificed so much so they could do that,"* turning the child's moment into a reflection of their own perceived greatness. And if the child is struggling, the parent may co-opt the pain entirely: *"You think you're upset? You have no idea what I've been through."*

The spotlight always shifts in their favor. It's not about the truth of the moment; it's about preserving their self-image. This dynamic makes it nearly impossible for the child to fully internalize success as their own. Instead of feeling competent and self-driven, they may carry the lingering belief: *I can't succeed unless this person approves, helps, or controls the process.*

Another common pattern is the narcissistic parent's refusal to update their mental image of the child. Even after years of growth, achievement, or healing, they continue to relate to their child as the version they held the most control over; the insecure teen, the struggling student, the socially awkward kid. Why? Because that version is the least threatening. The old image keeps the parent dominant and the child dependent.

This process is profoundly invalidating. Even when you've worked hard to evolve, built a career, a family, a meaningful life, your parent still treats you as if you're the powerless, voiceless child from decades ago. For me, this created an eerie sense of being invisible in my own family. I felt unknown at every stage of life: child, adolescent, adult. And perhaps worse, I felt that my parents had no interest in truly knowing me. Their perception was fixed, and I had no say in the matter.

Smear Campaigns and Family Denial

Another destructive dynamic that often occurs between a narcissistic parent and their child is the smear campaign, a subtle but persistent strategy of manipulation and isolation.

Looking back, I can now see how frequently this happened in my own family. My mother would often narrate my supposed wrongdoings to my father and brother, painting herself as the victim and me as difficult. The pattern was always the same: she would present her side of the story, secure their validation, and then one of them would come to me with a lecture. "Why can't you just behave?" they'd ask. "Just listen to your mother. She means well."

I can't recall a single time anyone paused to ask what I was feeling, or whether there might be another side to the story. It was as if my voice didn't matter, and my mother's narrative carried absolute authority. Her voice was the loudest and most persuasive in the family, and everyone seemed to fall in line.

What makes this kind of family system so resistant to growth is that its members often bond through denial. They co-sign each other's versions of reality not because those versions are truthful, but because they're familiar and convenient. This mutual reinforcement creates a closed loop where nothing ever evolves; there is no room for challenge, no push toward introspection, no motivation for change.

Ironically, it's often the targeted child, the one who is blamed, misunderstood, or scapegoated, who begins the healing journey. Because the family system offers them no true support, they are forced to look elsewhere. Healing, in this context, becomes an act of individuation, a way of breaking free from a narrative that never fit and constructing a new sense of self outside the confines of dysfunction. While painful, this process is also liberating. It is where true growth begins.

Disregard for Feelings

As discussed earlier in the context of traumatic invalidation, one of the most insidious aspects of growing up with a parent who has traits of narcissistic or borderline personality disorder is their chronic disregard for your emotional reality. Your feelings are not only minimized, they're often used against you. Gaslighting, projection, and emotional exploitation become common tactics in the relationship. Such parents may accuse their children of being selfish, dramatic, or ungrateful, when in fact they are projecting their own behaviors and insecurities outward. This leaves the child in a constant state of confusion, often asking, Is it me? Am I the problem?

Projection is particularly disorienting. For example, if the parent accuses you of caring only about your own needs, chances are it's because they are guilty of that exact behavior. These accusations often stem from the parent's unresolved issues, and in turn, the child becomes the scapegoat for the parent's emotional shortcomings.

Many emotionally immature parents also attempt to resolve their own unrealized dreams or failures through their children. The child is not raised to explore their own identity, but rather to fulfill the parent's unmet ambitions. The implicit (and sometimes explicit) message is: You exist to make me feel better about myself. As a result, the child's desires and sense of self are stunted. Personal growth is only encouraged when it benefits the parent's narrative, image, or emotional needs. This dynamic often carries into adulthood, making it difficult for the grown child to separate their identity from the parent's expectations.

This chronic disregard for feelings frequently leads to conflict and emotional exhaustion. Even mundane decisions, like where to go for lunch, become emotionally charged and unnecessarily complex. Everything must revolve around the parent's preferences, mood, or ego. Any pushback is met with guilt, resistance, or escalation. The parent–child dynamic is built on the assumption that the child should yield.

For me, birthdays became a symbolic representation of this pattern. Even when they were acknowledged, they were rarely about me. The details of whatever we ended up doing reflected what my parents wanted. It was their version of a celebration, and I was expected to express gratitude for it. As a child, I internalized this pattern: my wants were not only secondary, they were invisible. Birthdays, those few days when you're supposed to feel seen, only underscored how deeply unseen I truly was.

Manipulation and Self-Doubt

Parents who fall under the Cluster B spectrum, particularly those with narcissistic or borderline tendencies, are often frighteningly skilled at detecting emotional vulnerabilities and exploiting them. Their manipulation is rarely loud or overt; it comes in subtle, cutting remarks that strike like daggers, disguised as concern or insight. They know just where your insecurities lie, and they plant doubt there, watering it slowly over time.

For instance, they might say, "I know you must feel so bad that your friends didn't invite you to the party. I bet you're worried they don't like you anymore. That must be scary." On the surface, it sounds like empathy, but it's laced with poison. The goal isn't to comfort you; it's to deepen your insecurity and keep you emotionally off-balance. This kind of manipulation creates an environment where you begin to question everything about yourself and the people around you. It chips away at your self-trust.

Over time, these experiences train us to conceal our vulnerability. We stop sharing how we feel, not because we don't want connection, but because we've learned that honesty is dangerous. Our words have been twisted and used against us too many times. We become emotionally guarded, believing that even our most innocent disclosures could be weaponized.

This pattern doesn't just stay in childhood. It lingers. We carry it into our friendships, romantic relationships, and professional interactions. We hesitate before opening up. We overthink simple conversations. We begin to wonder if we're too sensitive, too needy, or just fundamentally flawed.

In reality, what we've internalized is not our own brokenness, but the emotional instability and manipulation of a parent who could not tolerate the presence of a separate, feeling person. And so, we silenced ourselves to survive.

Scapegoating

Scapegoating is another common defense mechanism used by narcissistic or emotionally immature parents to deflect responsibility and assign blame. If something goes wrong, it's never their fault; it's the child's. The scapegoated child becomes the family's emotional dumping ground, bearing the brunt of the frustrations, disappointments, and guilt that the parent refuses to own. Often, the more outspoken or emotionally aware child is cast into this role. If you question the family narrative or speak the truth, you become the problem.

Scapegoated children often learn to apologize for their very existence. They come to believe that keeping the peace requires total compliance, silence, and self-erasure.

In my case, if I had a negative reaction to the Israel trip I went on with my father, it was spun into, "Well, you invited yourself." If I expressed hurt about being left out of family events, I was "too sensitive." There was no space to examine whether the parents' choices might have contributed to those feelings. The idea that they could be wrong was never on the table. Instead, the spotlight was always redirected to me, as if my hurt were the real offense.

Over time, scapegoated children often develop into highly empathic adults. Many take on caretaking roles in their relationships or become outspoken advocates for justice because they have spent a lifetime learning to decipher pain, especially their own. But they are also frequently labeled as "rebellious" or "difficult," often by the very family members whose dysfunction they are exposing.

For me, it was clear early on that I was the only one who consistently named the truth when something felt off. And I also learned, just as quickly, that I would never be rewarded for doing so. My voice was seen as a threat, not a contribution.

Triangulation and Parentification

Both triangulation and parentification are forms of emotional enmeshment that involve pulling a child into roles or dynamics that are inappropriate for their developmental stage. They place the burden of adult conflict or responsibility onto a child who is neither equipped nor meant to carry it.

Triangulation occurs when a parent draws a child into the middle of their relationship conflicts, often to avoid direct communication or to manipulate outcomes. During my parents' divorce, my mother consistently put me in the role of emotional intermediary. Even when I said I didn't want to know about the details of their sexual relationship, she told me anyway. When she wanted updates about how often my father was seeing his girlfriend, she used me to gather the intel. She'd insist that I pass along messages after my father explicitly asked her not to contact him. I became the courier of her pain, enlisted to carry feelings and tasks that were never mine to hold.

What she needed was to communicate directly with my father, or to accept his boundaries and grieve. Instead, she leaned on me to fill the emotional void he left behind. It didn't matter whether I was willing or not, I was used either way.

Parentification, while similar in its distortion of roles, is more focused on the child being forced to take on emotional or practical responsibilities that belong to the parent. This can include caring for siblings, offering emotional support, giving life advice, or even having to create their own sense of safety because the parent is too overwhelmed or self-absorbed to provide it.

Whether I set boundaries or not, my mother continued to force-feed me her emotions and punish me for my father's actions, as though they were mine. I was made to serve as her confidant and therapist, giving advice on her marriage from the time I was a young child well into adulthood. What made it even more confusing was that, despite constantly seeking my input, she seemed to hold very little respect for me. I often wondered, Why are you asking for my guidance when you don't even seem to value my perspective?

That contradiction, being simultaneously leaned on and dismissed, was one of the most destabilizing aspects of our relationship. It sent the message that I was important only when I served a function. My emotional value was transactional, and never quite enough.

Playing the Victim

A common trait among Cluster B parents is the chronic adoption of the victim role, often wielded as a manipulative tool to elicit guilt and compliance. You might hear statements like, "No one ever supports me. I do everything for everyone and no one does anything for me." These expressions aren't mere venting, they're strategic. They blur boundaries, shift blame, and create an atmosphere where saying "no" feels like betrayal.

One example I remember vividly was when my mother said, in a sharp, entitled tone: "You never have me over for a barbecue, but you're always having people to the house for those ribs you make. I guess I'm not as important as they are."

This wasn't remotely true. I invited her all the time, but with a narcissist, it is never enough. Their sense of deprivation is perpetual. Any attention you give to others becomes an act of rejection toward them. If I took her out to dinner last week, well, that was last week. Today is a new day and a new offense.

This compulsive victimhood also explained why my mother had such conflicts with my paternal grandmother. If my grandmother was sick or needed attention, my mother would bristle. She couldn't tolerate anyone else occupying the spotlight of suffering. Victimhood had become the core of her identity. It provided her with attention, absolved her from taking responsibility, and allowed her to stay rooted in self-pity. And society, especially those unwilling to look deeper, often rewarded her for it.

Acting Out

When they don't get what they want, narcissistic or borderline parents often act out. Instead of engaging in healthy dialogue, they rely on behavior, silent treatments, outbursts, disappearances to express displeasure or assert control.

My mother, for instance, would go quiet and pretend she didn't hear you if something uncomfortable came up. She'd default to passive aggression. My father would retreat to his office for hours, saying nothing, or go on long walks and not return until after dark. These behaviors were not just avoidance, they were punishment.

When you try to address irrational or hurtful actions, they pivot. Instead of reflecting, they bring up your past mistakes, often from childhood, comparing your adult boundaries to things you did when you were ten. It's not about resolution; it's about distraction and deflection.

I remember telling my mother how hurt I was when she and my grandfather had dinner near my home and didn't tell me. "You ate at the place right next to where I live and passed my door to get there. That hurt me," I said.

She didn't acknowledge the feeling. Instead, she snapped, "You eat out in places all the time and don't invite me, so what?"

She missed the point entirely. This wasn't about a random dinner out. It was about my grandfather, a man who rarely left the house anymore and a dinner I wasn't told about, despite her habit of narrating every mundane detail of her day. The omission felt deliberate. But when I expressed my hurt, she became angry. My feelings made her uncomfortable, so she acted out, redirecting the discomfort back onto me. I never received any validation, just backlash.

And if either of my parents felt disobeyed, the response was theatrical. My mother would cry. My father would yell. Conflicts were never resolved; they were diverted, always ending with me being the one who had to soothe them.

Types of Neglect

Neglect isn't always loud or violent. It doesn't always come with bruises or shouting. Sometimes it's silent, subtle, and just as damaging. Broadly, there are two kinds of parental neglect: active and passive.

Active neglect is more overt and often easier to identify. It includes moments when a child is directly denied affection or dismissed for expressing emotion. A parent turning away when a child asks for a hug, mocking them for crying, or punishing them for being "too sensitive" are all examples. It's the deliberate shutdown of a child's emotional or physical needs, saying things like "You're being ridiculous" or "Stop crying, or I'll give you something to cry about." These behaviors teach a child that their feelings are not only unwelcome but unacceptable.

Passive neglect, on the other hand, is quieter and often goes unnoticed, even by the people experiencing it. It can look like a family that never talks about their feelings, parents who are emotionally unavailable, or caregivers who never make the effort to truly know or understand their child. No one's yelling. No one's hitting. And yet the child is left emotionally starving. On the surface, no obvious harm appears to be taking place, but the message lands all the same: You are not worth the time, attention, or effort it takes to know you.

Both forms of neglect deliver the same core wound, you don't matter, just through different routes. Both shape how we show up in the world as adults.

Think about the child who learns not to ask for help because no one ever came. The teen who keeps their feelings bottled up because emotional expression was always dismissed. The adult who feels like a burden every time they need comfort or connection. These are the quiet aftershocks of neglect, carried into relationships, workplaces, and even self-perception.

Neglect isn't just something that happened. It's something we learned. And until we name it, we continue to live as if it were normal.

The Narcissistic Family Tree

In narcissistic family systems, there's often a well-defined, if unspoken, hierarchy. At the center is the narcissist, surrounded by supporting roles that maintain the system.

Key Roles

The Orbiting Spouse

One key role is the Orbiting Spouse: typically the partner who enables the narcissist, either through willful ignorance or a desperate desire to keep the peace. They don't question the dysfunction. In some cases, they've been manipulated or charmed into compliance themselves.

The Golden Child and The Scapegoat

Then come the children, most often divided into the *golden child* and the *scapegoat*. The golden child is favored, idealized, and used to reflect the narcissist's perfection back to them.

The scapegoat, by contrast, is the one who absorbs blame, carries the shame, and speaks the truth, which is exactly why they are punished.

The Flying Monkeys

And finally, there are the Flying Monkeys discussed earlier: friends, extended family, or even therapists who unwittingly (or knowingly) support the narcissist's version of reality. They silence, excuse, or minimize the harm, preserving their own relationship with the narcissist at the expense of the truth.

In my family, my parents took turns playing the roles of the narcissist and the orbiting spouse. Depending on the situation, one would call out the other's dysfunction, but never when it involved the impact on their children. If I came to my father upset about my mother, he'd minimize the issue and offer excuses. If I spoke to my mother about my father's hurtful behavior, she'd go quiet or become distracted.

I could never go to either of them and say, "This hurt me." There was no repair. No accountability. No safe space for the truth.

Family Tree Dynamics

Preferential Treatment

Within the family tree, there are many important dynamics that play out between each of the aforementioned roles. The Golden Child and Black Sheep dynamic is a common pattern in families with Cluster B parents. Often, if a mother has two children, she will identify one, frequently the male, as her favorite. More accurately, however, the favored child is usually the one most eager to please her and easiest to manipulate. Independent thinkers, by contrast, typically become the least favorable, as discussed earlier. They are often scapegoated and blamed for the family's dysfunction.

A Cluster B parent may actively pit siblings against each other, creating conflict and competition through gossip, secrets, or calculated comparisons. The favored child, sometimes unknowingly, becomes a defender of the parent, reinforcing the division. They waltz in like a knight in shining armor, often echoing the parent's defense without prompting: "Don't talk to Mom like that, after all she does for you." This further isolates the scapegoated child.

I remember one Easter when I was five or six; my parents gave me a stuffed rabbit I named Carol. They repeatedly emphasized how lucky I was because my brother didn't get one. For context, he was twelve years older than me, seventeen at the time, and well past the age of stuffed animals. I didn't understand then why they insisted on making that distinction so many times. Looking back, it feels like a deliberate attempt to make me feel special at his expense.

Other times, I'd overhear my mother on the phone whispering to him or slipping him checks for his kids in secret. Why the secrecy?

Why not treat your children equally and openly? This covert favoritism ensured that there would always be tension between us, a wedge that my mother seemed to intentionally drive deeper.

Setup to Fail

Another hallmark of personality-disordered parenting is the chronic moving of goalposts. No matter how hard you try, it's never enough. I could complete two of the three tasks asked of me, but the focus would always fall on the one I didn't do, as if my other efforts never happened.

This kind of dynamic breeds perfectionism. As children and teens, we internalize the belief that if we just do more, be more, try harder, we might finally win approval. But that finish line keeps moving. There's always someone doing better, being more thoughtful, achieving more at least in the eyes of the parent.

Comparisons are often used as weapons. "Peggy's kids always get her such thoughtful gifts for her birthday…" These comments are designed to motivate through shame. The result is not motivation but self-loathing, jealousy, and a deep sense of inadequacy. Over time, this constant devaluation can erode a child's self-trust and self-worth, leaving them feeling incompetent, unworthy, and emotionally unsafe even in their own skin.

Betrayal Blindness

When survival depends on the very person causing harm, the mind sometimes chooses blindness over truth. Betrayal blindness refers to the unconscious denial or minimization of abuse, neglect, or emotional abandonment, especially when the perpetrator is a caregiver. Children depend on their parents not just for food and shelter, but for emotional development and a sense of safety. Acknowledging that the person meant to protect you is harming you creates overwhelming inner conflict, and so the mind shields itself rationalizing, suppressing, or denying reality in order to preserve some form of psychological stability.

I didn't have the vocabulary for any of this growing up, but I felt it in my body. I woke up every day with dread. I feared expressing myself to my parents because my feelings were always perceived as "starting an argument." I wasn't trying to be difficult; I just wanted peace, understanding, connection. But that wasn't available in my home. For a long time, I couldn't admit to myself that what I was experiencing was abuse. I remember thinking, *Neglect and mistreatment only happen in other people's homes, not mine.* That was the denial. That was betrayal blindness.

Trauma Bonding

Closely related is the concept of trauma bonding, a powerful emotional tie that forms through cycles of abuse. Even when the relationship is harmful, the child keeps seeking love, hoping for change, convinced that this time might be different.

This hope reinforces the parent's power. Meanwhile, the child is often labeled as overly sensitive, dramatic, or difficult simply for wanting emotional connection. But the biological drive to bond with one's parent is strong. When that bond becomes entangled with pain, confusion, and unmet needs, it distorts a child's understanding of what love is supposed to feel like.

I know that I clung to the idea that my parents would eventually see me, hear me, care for me in the ways I needed. I explained away hurtful behaviors, minimized their impact, and held out for moments of connection that rarely came. The hope kept me tethered, even when it was harming me.

Poor Coping Skills

Children raised by Cluster B parents often carry chronic stress into adulthood. We may struggle with emotional regulation, impulsivity, or unhealthy coping mechanisms. Depression, guilt, and shame are common, and many of us isolate ourselves to avoid further invalidation.

It makes sense. If our earliest experiences of closeness were painful or unsafe, why would we trust others now? Our parents become the lens through which we view the world. And if they were manipulative, hypercritical, or emotionally unavailable, we may assume that everyone else will be too.

For me, solitude became a refuge. I felt safer on my own. Negative reinforcement taught me that being around people often meant feeling rejected or inadequate. Alone, I didn't have to perform. I didn't have to explain myself. I had control.

I noticed poor coping patterns early. If I had multiple assignments for school, I'd become overwhelmed almost instantly. Instead of tackling them one by one, I'd spiral into frustration and anger. I convinced myself I wasn't capable, even when I was. That belief disabled me more than the tasks themselves ever could.

Conditional Love

Eventually, I grew exhausted from wearing a mask, the role self I had created to navigate life with emotionally immature parents. This persona aligned with what they wanted me to be: agreeable, self-sacrificing, always striving to earn approval.

Occasionally, I'd be rewarded with scraps of praise when I fully stepped into the role. But even those moments felt hollow. The love I received was always conditional, based on compliance, performance, or usefulness. It never felt like love for me.

In families like mine, love is often transactional. We're taught to believe we are only worthy when we serve a purpose. That conditioning is hard to shake. It trains us to seek value through giving our time, our energy, our selves, until we're left depleted.

This mindset robs us of presence. We're too busy anticipating the next hoop we have to jump through to simply be. It keeps us focused on survival, not fulfillment on pleasing others, not honoring ourselves.

The Influence on the Offspring: Romantic Relationships

One way the aftermath of narcissistic parental abuse can manifest is through a phenomenon known as limerence. Coined by psychologist Dorothy Tennov in the 1970s, limerence goes beyond ordinary attraction; it's a deep yearning for emotional union and the desire to be truly "seen" by a romantic partner. For those who grew up emotionally neglected or invalidated, this yearning can morph into an obsessive need to secure emotional intimacy, often with partners who mirror the inaccessibility of early caregivers.

Limerence is characterized by fantasies about the other person, preoccupation with their responses, and an intense desire for reciprocation. Unconsciously, the object of our affection becomes a stand-in for unmet childhood needs. This obsessive focus offers a temporary balm for the emotional void left by emotionally unavailable parents.

When we lack secure attachment in childhood, we often develop anxious or insecure attachment styles, driven by a persistent fear of rejection or invisibility. Limerence, then, becomes a mechanism to soothe abandonment wounds and create a false sense of stability and belonging. Individuals with traits of NPD or BPD, often carrying their own intergenerational trauma, may also engage in these obsessive emotional fixations.

I witnessed this firsthand between my parents. My mother yearned for my father's validation to an obsessive degree. Her entire sense of worth seemed contingent upon his attention. Through the lens of limerence, her fixation can be traced back to rejection by her own father: an emotional wound she unconsciously tried to mend through her marriage. In psychology, we call this reconstructing: trying to heal a childhood wound by replaying it in adult relationships. Her internal narrative seemed to be, If he loves me, then I will finally be whole.

Often, we idealize our partners, projecting onto them the nurturing and acceptance we never received. We may convince ourselves we've found "the one," even if reality says otherwise. The goal isn't sustainable connection, it's emotional relief. We choose comfort in the moment over confronting long-term uncertainty. Importantly, limerence is not exclusive to those with personality disorders; it can affect anyone navigating the fallout of unmet emotional needs.

The Challenge of Healthy Connection

When love and validation are offered to someone who's never known them, it can feel foreign, even threatening. Accepting care requires vulnerability, awareness, and immense bravery, especially when early experiences have conditioned us to expect rejection or betrayal.

Survivors of emotional neglect often develop people-pleasing behaviors, hide their true feelings, or become hypersensitive to perceived disapproval. Healthy boundaries may be difficult to establish, especially when they were never modeled in childhood. Instead of welcoming connection, we might fixate on others' flaws or pull away, driven by an ingrained belief that others are ultimately unreliable.

These tendencies are protective, but they also prevent intimacy. As we heal, it's common to feel overwhelmed. But that overwhelm is not a sign of failure, it is a kind of emotional birth, signaling growth.

Dr. Gabor Maté, a physician renowned for his work on trauma, reframes trauma not as the event itself but as what happens inside of us as a result. This distinction empowers us. If trauma is internal, then healing can be too. Instead of being permanently wounded by the past, we can examine the emotional meaning of our experiences, learn what they reveal about our unmet needs, and begin to nurture ourselves in ways our caregivers couldn't.

Yet many of us get stuck trying to change our parents or fix the past. This is known as the fallacy of change, the belief that we can alter someone else simply because we want them to be different. With narcissistic caregivers, this is often a losing battle.

I once heard that the parent–child relationship is like the intertwined roots of neighboring trees, forever connected and mutually shaped.

That's what makes going no-contact with a parent so profoundly painful. Even when we know it's the right choice, our biology rebels. We may stop loving them, but more often, we stop loving ourselves.

When a parent refuses to repair a ruptured relationship, the impact on our self-concept can be profound. We internalize their neglect, believing that *we* must be unworthy. Trust in ourselves is not innate; it's built through repeated validation. Without it, we begin to unravel.

Workaholism as Avoidance

I became a workaholic before I even knew the word. In school, I never felt I had studied enough. As an adult, I built a private therapy practice and saw ten clients back-to-back without a break. Even a free hour would send me into a spiral: *Why am I not busy? Am I failing?* Stillness felt dangerous.

My addiction wasn't just to achievement, it was to distraction. I equated productivity with self-worth, believing that constant motion protected me from emotional pain. I became hypercompetitive, overprepared, and burnt out.

Trauma survivors often overfunction in this way. They fill their days with endless tasks, neglecting hunger, rest, and even basic self-care. Some compulsively socialize or chase financial control. Others become hypervigilant about safety, obsessively locking doors or scanning rooms. Regardless of the form, the goal is the same: to create control in order to avoid feeling vulnerable.

An Obsession with Justice

Over time, I noticed how deeply I resonated with themes of justice, especially in my work with clients. If someone shared a story of being bullied or ignored, it struck a raw nerve. I've always rooted for the underdog, and I now understand why: it mirrored my own unmet need for acknowledgment.

Watching peers receive love and validation from their parents while I struggled with emotional abandonment felt deeply unfair. That sense of injustice lingered, even among loving friends or partners. In response, I became an advocate for the silenced, offering what I had longed for: recognition, validation, and the belief that their pain mattered.

Anxiety as Adaptation

When children ask for help and are ignored, anxiety becomes adaptive. The world feels unsafe, so we attempt to protect ourselves by anticipating every possible threat. The invisible child becomes the overthinking adult.

We try to stay ten steps ahead of everything. When plans change, we panic, not just out of inconvenience, but because we feel unprotected. I spent years living with chest pain, stomachaches, and heat rashes, believing they were just part of life. I had no idea they were symptoms of chronic fear.

Emotional Stunting

Childhood trauma often leads to emotional dysregulation, reactivity to facial expressions, emotional shutdown during conflict, explosive anger, or a total inability to express feelings. We may feel empty, detached, or emotionally frozen in relationships.

Caretakers with personality disorders often teach us to suppress our emotions. Reactive abuse, when someone provokes you until you explode and then blames you for your reaction, is common. I was told I was "too angry," but my outbursts were often reactions to feeling ignored.

Hearing "You're such an angry person" from your parents when you're actually just hurting is profoundly disorienting. It creates a false identity rooted in shame. Over time, we begin to believe we're broken.

Many children of narcissists feel alien, as if they don't belong in their family or even in the world. We might feel disconnected from our culture, our peers, or even our achievements.

Success doesn't translate to fulfillment, because deep down, we still feel inadequate. Emotional connection feels elusive, and asking for help becomes incredibly difficult.

The Aftermath of Trauma

After trauma, we often shift into one of three modes: hyperarousal (everything feels urgent), hypoarousal (we feel frozen), or emotional numbing (we pretend we're fine). In all three, we're disconnected from ourselves. We may reread the same page three times and absorb nothing, scroll through our phones for hours, or fake smiles in social settings. It's exhausting.

Complex trauma also affects the body. Living with emotionally volatile caregivers puts the nervous system in a constant state of alarm. This can manifest as digestive issues, hormonal imbalances, acne, sleep disturbances, hair thinning, immune system dysfunction, and even chronic illnesses such as lupus or Crohn's disease.

We may experience racing hearts, eczema, joint pain, or fibromyalgia. Cortisol floods our bodies, increasing the risk of disease and weight fluctuations. Trauma also drives soothing behaviors such as binge eating or obsessive habits, ways to create predictability and comfort where there is none.

Loss of Voice: Invisibility as a Survival Strategy

When we experience overstimulation, whether from stress, anxiety, or the accumulated toll of complex trauma, we often retreat inward. In the absence of safety, silence becomes a survival strategy. For many trauma survivors, this pattern becomes so automatic that we don't even notice it.

In social situations, I frequently defaulted to being the observer, the one who listened quietly, nodded politely, and rarely interrupted. Part of it stemmed from the belief that no one really cared what I had to say. The other part was avoidance: speaking up often required being aggressive or confrontational just to be heard, which felt foreign and unsafe.

On the rare occasions when I did chime in, my voice was so soft or tentative that I'd get steamrolled by the loudest person in the room. Each of these moments seemed to confirm my invisibility, feeding a cycle of learned helplessness: "Why bother?" It was simply too much effort to be acknowledged.

And yet, this silence came at a cost. I began to notice that when someone genuinely wanted to listen, I sometimes missed the opportunity entirely. My default belief, that I wouldn't be heard, created a kind of confirmation bias that filtered out evidence to the contrary. Even when safety was present, I couldn't always recognize it.

There's a common notion that narcissists and empaths are two sides of the same coin, both shaped by childhood trauma but responding in opposite ways. Narcissists externalize pain, disown vulnerability, and demand attention to protect their fragile egos. Empaths, on the other hand, internalize pain, striving to soothe others so that no one suffers as they once did. It's not that empaths are inherently more virtuous; they've simply chosen the opposite survival strategy. Narcissists replicate the harm, while empaths work to repair it. Both are shaped by similar wounds. One seeks power, the other seeks healing.

Isolation and the Strain of Social Interpretation

For many survivors, isolation is not just a preference, it's emotional self-preservation. After a long week of masking, monitoring, and managing our internal state, the idea of a Friday-night dinner party feels exhausting, not energizing.

Our brains are working overtime. While others engage in casual back-and-forth, trauma survivors are often performing a set of mental gymnastics: scanning for tone, watching facial expressions, analyzing pauses and phrasing, and silently asking, *"Is this safe?"*

We don't just hear what's said; we also try to decode what's not said. Because for us, misreading a situation in the past meant punishment: criticism, rejection, judgment, or abandonment. In response, we developed hypervigilance: a protective instinct to decode every social cue as a potential threat.

This is why even a benign comment can feel like a veiled insult. It's not hypersensitivity; it's an adaptive response to chronic invalidation. When you've been repeatedly hurt by those close to you, the brain learns: *assume the worst, stay safe*. We preemptively push people away so they can't hurt us later. We misinterpret silence as rejection, sarcasm as disdain, and neutrality as threat.

As Freud is (perhaps apocryphally) quoted, *"Sometimes a cigar is just a cigar."* But for trauma survivors, that phrase can feel absurd. We were conditioned to believe there's always a subtext, because there often was. Learning to take things at face value becomes part of the healing journey, not the starting point.

This constant filtering takes its toll. We may feel misunderstood, annoyed, or deeply hurt by others, often without ever expressing it. To those around us, we may seem distant or oversensitive. But beneath that is a nervous system that has never known safety, trying desperately to interpret a world it still doesn't fully trust.

Attachment Styles as Related to Traumatic Experience

As I moved through adulthood, particularly in the aftermath of severing ties with my family, I found myself grappling with relationship patterns that felt deeply rooted yet difficult to explain. It wasn't until I learned about attachment theory that the pieces began to fall into place. My connections with others, the ways I sought closeness, pushed people away, or feared abandonment, were not random. They were echoes of my earliest relational environment, shaped by caregivers who were unpredictable, inconsistent, and often emotionally unsafe.

DR. ASHLEY QUIROZ, PSY.D.

Disorganized Attachment: The Fear of Safety

In families marked by personality-disordered dynamics, it's not unusual for children to develop a disorganized attachment style. The very people who are supposed to provide safety and security become the source of fear and confusion. This conflicting foundation creates deep challenges in forming secure, trusting relationships later in life.

Disorganized attachment often develops in response to caregivers who are unpredictable, inconsistent, or emotionally unavailable. These caregivers might oscillate between being nurturing and neglectful, affectionate and distant. As a result, the child becomes unsure of what to expect, and the natural sense of trust that should evolve in childhood is shattered. This type of attachment is sometimes referred to as fearful-avoidant, because individuals with this style both crave love and fear it simultaneously.

People with disorganized attachment often long to be seen, loved, and accepted by others, but may sabotage those very connections when they receive the affection they desire. Anxiety can rise in these situations, as they are left feeling uncomfortable with the closeness they both crave and fear. From the outside, it may appear as though they are self-sabotaging—pushing others away just when they start to get close.

For those with disorganized attachment, relationships can feel like a battle between aloofness and clinginess. At times, they may become emotionally distant, avoiding intimacy out of fear of getting hurt again. Other times, they may become excessively needy or anxious, constantly looking for reassurance that they won't be abandoned. Even when their partner shows love, it may not feel like the right kind of love, often triggering anxiety or frustration.

This cycle of push-pull behavior can be difficult to break. The person may unconsciously express dissatisfaction with their partner's affection, not because they don't want it, but because they're terrified that the love they're receiving won't last, or that they are unworthy of it.

They may not even realize that they are trapping themselves in a cycle of fear and mistrust.

The root of the issue is often a lack of trust, not just in others, but in themselves. A person with disorganized attachment may have learned to doubt their own needs and feelings, creating a mental and emotional lock on their ability to fully connect with others. As a result, they may unintentionally push people away or fill the emotional voids of others without seeking to have their own needs met in return. This behavior can mirror the unhealthy dynamics experienced in their family of origin, where emotional neglect or inconsistent care created patterns of self-reliance and isolation.

If not carefully examined, individuals with disorganized attachment may replicate these patterns in adult relationships, unknowingly filling the void for others until they are no longer needed, and finding themselves alone yet again.

Looking back, my relationship with both of my parents, especially during and after the divorce, was a case study in chaos. One moment they wanted to pull me close; the next, I was scapegoated or ignored. Their unpredictable emotional states kept me in a near-constant state of vigilance. I never knew whether I was going to be the confidant, the therapist, the punching bag, or the ghost in the room.

This environment cultivated what I later came to recognize as disorganized attachment, a pattern in which I yearned for emotional intimacy but panicked when it became real. I wanted to be seen and loved, but when someone got too close, I questioned their sincerity or found reasons to back away. I became skilled at identifying red flags, but I was also quick to interpret connection as danger. Vulnerability felt like handing someone a weapon they might use against me later, because that's how it had worked in my family.

There were times in relationships when I found myself either overly aloof or frantically needing reassurance, unsure of how to stay grounded in the middle. I was often the one who offered emotional labor, helped others heal, and then watched them leave once they no longer "needed" me, a painful reenactment of my role at home. Love, as I understood it, came with conditions, instability, and an expiration date.

Anxious Attachment: The Clingy and Uncertain

In contrast to disorganized attachment, anxious attachment typically develops from experiences of emotional abuse or neglect in childhood. This attachment style is primarily characterized by an overwhelming fear of rejection and abandonment, coupled with a deep need to be emotionally connected to others for security. Individuals with anxious attachment may display behaviors that are seen as "clingy" or dependent on others for validation, constantly seeking reassurance in relationships.

Anxious attachment often arises when a child's parent is emotionally unavailable or inconsistent, making it difficult for the child to interpret the parent's behaviors or intentions. Much like disorganized attachment, the parent's unpredictability creates a sense of instability for the child, who learns to feel unsafe in relationships. The absence of clear, consistent emotional support means that the child's needs are left unmet, leaving them to seek validation elsewhere.

Additionally, anxious attachment can stem from a lack of boundaries within the parent–child relationship. A parent who lacks emotional boundaries not only fails to help the child process their own emotions but may also demonstrate emotional instability themselves. In these environments, children may internalize the belief that they are responsible for their parent's emotional responses, leading them to blame themselves when relationships falter or when they experience emotional turmoil.

In adulthood, anxious attachment can manifest in romantic relationships as jealousy or clinginess. For example, if a partner spends time with others, the anxiously attached individual may feel threatened, even if the absence is brief. There is often a deep-rooted fear that the partner will leave, and reassurance may be needed frequently to soothe this fear. However, the effectiveness of such reassurance is often short-lived, requiring more and more validation as time goes on. This need for constant reassurance and emotional check-ins can create a cycle of insatiable demands for affirmation, driven by an underlying fear that the relationship is unstable or that the partner's affection will fade.

I also carried patterns more closely aligned with anxious attachment, especially in friendships and romantic relationships. The emotional neglect I experienced, particularly my mother's inability to regulate her emotions or model stability, left me constantly scanning for signs of rejection. Her attention came in waves, often interwoven with her own need for validation. As a child, I was never quite sure where I stood with her, and that ambiguity trained me to read micro-signals in others' behaviors obsessively.

In adulthood, this translated into a deep need for external reassurance. I feared being too much or not enough and constantly sought confirmation that everything was okay. If someone I cared about was quiet or distant, I often assumed I had done something wrong. I had internalized the belief that if a relationship was unstable, it was probably my fault.

I became someone who overextended myself; emotionally, logistically, financially, to keep connections intact. I often prioritized other people's needs while ignoring my own, hoping my selflessness would earn security in return. But reassurance, when given, never quite stuck. The hole had no bottom. I didn't know how to feel safe inside myself, because my earliest examples of love were tethered to emotional volatility and enmeshment.

Avoidant Attachment: The Distant and Self-Protective

The final attachment style commonly linked to generational trauma is avoidant attachment. This pattern often forms when a caregiver consistently fails to meet a child's basic needs, responds with neglect, or communicates, explicitly or implicitly, that the child's needs are a burden. In such environments, the child learns to rely solely on themselves, internalizing the message that dependence is unsafe or shameful.

As adults, individuals with avoidant attachment may tend to minimize their emotional needs and maintain emotional distance from others. Relationships are often approached cautiously, and interactions may remain on the surface level. There's a deep-rooted discomfort with vulnerability, stemming from early experiences of rejection or inconsistency. Because caregivers were not trustworthy or emotionally available, trust in others becomes difficult to develop.

When someone with an avoidant attachment style senses others trying to get close, particularly in romantic relationships, they may feel claustrophobic or emotionally smothered, even if their partner is behaving appropriately. To protect themselves, they may construct internal walls, limiting emotional access to their inner world. They often project an image of being self-sufficient or "low maintenance," avoiding asking for support to prevent feeling rejected, dismissed, or dependent.

This guardedness can lead to concealing vulnerable aspects of the self: such as pain, emotional struggles, or unhealthy coping mechanisms like addiction or self-harm. Expressing emotions may feel foreign, uncomfortable, or even shameful. As a result, these individuals may appear emotionally unavailable or detached, though beneath the surface they often carry deep wounds related to not feeling safe or worthy of care.

Reflecting on my own attachment patterns, I recognize a strong undercurrent of avoidant attachment that surfaced whenever I felt too exposed. When my needs were ignored or shamed in childhood, when I was told I was too sensitive, too needy, or simply too much, I learned to bury them. I learned that self-sufficiency was safer than asking for help. In relationships, this made it difficult to trust others with my inner world.

I often came across as "independent," as the one who didn't need anything and could handle it all. That image was mostly armor. Inside, I struggled with the belief that if I let people see the messier parts of me: my sadness, my anger, my trauma; they'd run. Or worse, they'd confirm the fear I carried all along: that I wasn't worth sticking around for.

Avoidant behaviors gave me a sense of control. I kept things superficial or intellectualized connection to avoid feeling vulnerable. I didn't want to risk asking for something I wouldn't get. When I was hurting, I often isolated, afraid that my pain would be used against me, as it had been before. If I acted as though I didn't need anything, maybe I couldn't be disappointed.

The truth is, I saw all three of these styles in myself. They showed up in different ways depending on the relationship and how safe I felt. What I once thought were just "quirks" or "personality traits" were, in fact, adaptations; deeply wired responses to unpredictability, emotional abandonment, and trauma.

Understanding these patterns didn't magically fix everything, but it gave me a language to describe what I'd been feeling for years. It helped me recognize that my fear of intimacy, my craving for reassurance, and my tendency to shut down were all logical responses to illogical, unsafe beginnings.

This knowledge didn't just help me relate more compassionately to others. It helped me relate more compassionately to myself.

Rupture and Repair

But knowing the why doesn't always soften the ache, especially when, in my lived experience, conflict rarely ended in closeness. More often, it ended in silence or denial.

When we've endured complex trauma, especially the kind that leaves emotional needs perpetually unmet, conflict doesn't just feel uncomfortable; it feels catastrophic. A disagreement can seem like an immediate threat to the relationship's survival. For many people who haven't experienced emotional abuse or neglect, there's an inherent expectation that conflict is something you work through, and that resolution leads to greater understanding. But for trauma survivors, a rupture can feel like abandonment in motion, a signal that we were right to be on guard all along.

This is where the concept of rupture and repair becomes so critical. In healthy relationships, a rupture: a missed cue, a harsh word, a broken promise, doesn't have to mean the end. It can, in fact, become a bridge toward deeper connection *if* the other person is willing to meet us in the aftermath. Repair means acknowledging harm, taking accountability, and choosing to move forward *together*. It's not about assigning blame. It's about effort, empathy, and emotional presence.

If a parent never attempts to repair the hurt they've caused, whether or not they meant it, or agree with our feelings, the child internalizes that pain. They learn that their emotions are burdensome and adapt by becoming avoidant or anxious in their relationships. I know this because I lived it.

My family system operated under the unspoken rule that nothing was to be questioned, especially not if it made my parents look bad or required them to reflect. When my mother supported my brother in hiding the purchase of his new house from me, the betrayal wasn't just in the secrecy; it was in the aftermath: the silence, the lack of effort to make it right, and the expectation that I move on as if nothing had happened. There was no repair, only refutation. I was told, implicitly and explicitly, that my feelings were inconvenient. That sadness, hurt, or anger were acceptable only if they didn't challenge the image of my parents as loving and well-intentioned.

Even as an adult, my grief was framed as ingratitude. In our home, enabling behavior wasn't just common, it was a survival strategy. My parents often acted like co-conspirators, defending each other's worst tendencies. My father would say, "Your mother means well, and she loves you so much," even after she had berated or belittled me to the point of tears. That phrase: "means well," became a justification for everything, as though intention alone could absolve harm.

Narcissistic parents often enable one another in their avoidance of accountability, circling the wagons to protect the family narrative rather than the family members themselves. It was like watching Bonnie and

Clyde: united until they turned on each other, and then it was every man for himself.

What I never saw was two adults who knew how to repair. What I learned instead was how to accommodate, appease, or disappear. I had no model for staying in connection through a rupture, only for surviving one by minimizing myself.

And really, that's the damage. If we've never witnessed the survival, let alone the strengthening, of a relationship after conflict, how are we supposed to believe it's even possible?

Over time, I had to learn that rupture isn't the problem. The lack of repair is what wounds us. The unspoken issues, the unresolved tension, the unwillingness to meet each other in the mess, these are what fracture relationships and leave trauma in their wake. When we are left to carry the pain alone, the message becomes clear: "You weren't worth fixing it for."

In closed family systems, where transparency is treated like treason and emotions are policed, secrecy and silence become the air you breathe. When you're the one who tries to break that silence: to name what's happening, to stop playing your assigned role, you become the problem. You're the scapegoat. But I know now that being the one who breaks the pattern isn't the problem. It's the first act of healing.

The Lasting Scars of Eggshell Parenting: Trauma, Dissociation, and Emotional Confusion

"Eggshell parenting" refers to a style marked by emotional volatility, inconsistency, and an unstable household climate; forcing children to constantly tiptoe around their parent's moods. These children often feel like they're 'walking on eggshells,' unsure of when calm might turn to chaos. This instability doesn't stem from the child's behavior, but from the parent's internal emotional world, which spills into daily interactions unpredictably. An agitating phone call, for example, may result in unjustified scolding for the child. The home becomes less a sanctuary and more an emotional minefield.

In contrast to the chaos at home, I developed a deep affection for the seasons—one of the few things in life I found predictable. Fall always followed summer; winter always came next. Their reliable rhythm grounded me, offering a kind of emotional constancy I never received from my parents. Unlike the emotional weather inside my house, where I could be a "miracle baby" one day and a burden the next, the seasons never lied to me. That predictability became its own kind of safety.

When we grow up in emotionally unpredictable or neglectful households, our developing brains adapt to this chronic instability in order to survive. We learn to attune to our parents' changing moods, modulate our behavior to avoid outbursts, and ignore our own emotions in favor of managing theirs. Over time, this creates profound disruptions in our sense of identity, emotional regulation, and physical connection to ourselves.

One of the most damaging patterns in such households is what psychologist Gregory Bateson called the "double bind." Imagine being praised for your kindness one moment, only to be scolded moments later for being too "needy" or "attention-seeking." This emotional whiplash is at the heart of the double bind: a situation in which a child receives contradictory messages and is punished regardless of their response. If they speak up, they're too sensitive; if they stay quiet, they're cold or ungrateful. The child internalizes the belief that they are inherently wrong no matter what they do.

As a child, I would often cry out in moments of helplessness. My mother would sometimes comfort me and sometimes walk out of the room entirely. Her responses felt random, as though I were being trained by an inconsistent reward system. This created immense anxiety. It also taught me to silence myself, because expressing needs or feelings didn't lead to reliable outcomes.

In a landmark 2011 study, researchers Stepp, Whalen, Pilkonis, Hipwell, and Levine examined the parenting behaviors of mothers with borderline personality disorder. They found that these mothers were often "disengaged, inconsistent, insensitive, intrusive, and self-focused." They tended to oscillate between idealizing and devaluing their children, mirroring the push–pull dynamics of their own internal emotional struggles. Their children often developed disorganized attachment styles, problems with emotional regulation, and dissociative symptoms. I remember feeling like a ghost of myself around my parents, always performing, always scanning for danger.

Emotional inconsistency also breeds what I call emotional impermanence. Because love, attention, and approval were given and taken away so arbitrarily, I never fully trusted that they would stay. Even today, when someone expresses affection, a part of me braces for it to vanish. This anxiety creates a compulsive need for reassurance and a deep difficulty in trusting the permanence of positive feelings.

In response to these chaotic conditions, many children develop a heightened sensitivity, not just emotionally but physiologically. Our nervous systems exist in a near-constant state of hypervigilance. The amygdala becomes overactive; cortisol levels remain chronically elevated. Over time, we may start to lose touch with our internal bodily signals, a phenomenon known as disrupted interoception. We don't know when we're hungry, tired, angry, or in pain, because we've learned to override these signals in order to survive.

I now understand that the reason I sometimes forget to eat, fail to register that I'm tired, or feel disconnected from pain is not laziness or neglect, it's the long-term outcome of being trained to ignore my body. When the body is treated as irrelevant in childhood, the adult self becomes disconnected from it. We become strangers to our own needs.

Being highly sensitive doesn't mean we're broken. It often means we have a finely tuned nervous system. Research shows that highly sensitive individuals may have lower baseline serotonin or greater sensitivity to dopamine. This can make us more emotionally responsive to our environment, both positively and negatively. In a nurturing home, this sensitivity might flourish; in a toxic one, it becomes a wound.

Another hallmark of this kind of upbringing is dissociation. Dissociation can be dramatic, such as memory loss or out-of-body experiences, but more often, it's subtle. It might look like zoning out during a conversation, feeling emotionally numb during joyful events, or struggling to recall details from entire periods of your life. It is the psyche's way of escaping an environment it cannot physically leave.

As a child, I remember staring at a wall while chaos unfolded around me, my mind floating elsewhere. I was in the room, but not really there. This blanking out, this shutting down, was not a flaw in me; it was a brilliant adaptation. My nervous system knew it was unsafe to be present.

Even now, in moments of intense conflict or emotional stress, I often feel my mind leave. I can be staring someone in the eye and not register what they're saying. These dissociative patterns are often misunderstood as inattention or coldness. In truth, they are survival responses, hardwired into us through years of emotional unpredictability.

Understanding these patterns: double binds, emotional impermanence, dissociation, and disrupted interoception, gives us the language to describe what was once just a fog of confusion. It allows us to break the cycle, to stop apologizing for being "too much" or "too sensitive," and to begin recognizing that our pain has always had a source, and that we were never crazy for feeling it.

Narcissistic Trauma's Impact on the Growing Brain

Research shows that trauma, especially chronic emotional abuse, can physically alter the brain. The hippocampus, responsible for memory, can shrink, while the amygdala, our internal threat detector, becomes overactive. This leads to a state of constant hypervigilance: racing thoughts, shallow breathing, muscle tension, and a hair-trigger startle response. Our bodies act as if danger is always imminent.

Chronic stress wears down the limbic system, which governs emotional regulation. Over time, this can manifest as dissociation, anxiety, difficulty concentrating, memory impairment, and mood instability. Cortisol, the body's primary stress hormone, floods the system, weakening memory and leaving us feeling foggy or disconnected. This biological wear and tear increases the risk of chronic illness, fatigue, and burnout.

Oxidative Stress

When people think of stress, they often picture sleepless nights or anxious thoughts spiraling out of control. But there's another kind of stress: one that doesn't just live in the mind but burrows deep into the cells of the body. It's called oxidative stress, and for those of us raised in environments shaped by emotional volatility and chronic invalidation, it can quietly wreak havoc for years before we even realize it's there. This form of stress is especially common in narcissistic family systems.

Oxidative stress is a biological imbalance that occurs when the production of free radicals, unstable molecules that can damage cells, outpaces the body's ability to neutralize them with antioxidants. Think of it as a slow-burning internal fire, one that scorches tissues and accelerates cellular aging. While oxidative stress is a normal part of metabolism and even useful in small amounts, chronic exposure causes inflammation, damages DNA, and has been linked to everything from heart disease and diabetes to depression and autoimmune disorders.

Children of narcissistic parents often grow up in a state of chronic emotional vigilance. You're always scanning the environment for danger: Did I disappoint them? Will they explode this time? Is this silence the calm before another storm? This constant activation of the stress-response system, known as toxic stress, keeps the body flooded with cortisol and adrenaline far beyond what's healthy or necessary.

Over time, that flood becomes corrosive. Stress hormones trigger a cascade of oxidative processes, increasing the production of free radicals. The body, already drained from prolonged tension, struggles to maintain its antioxidant defenses. This leads to persistent oxidative stress, embedding psychological trauma deep into physical form.

Eriksen et al. (2022) found a link between childhood maltreatment and increased oxidative stress. In simple terms, adults who experienced neglect or abuse as children showed more damage to the basic building blocks of DNA and RNA; changes also associated with a higher risk of developing mood disorders. In essence, neglect and abuse don't just affect us emotionally; they leave measurable imprints on a cellular level.

Interpreting and Relating to our Environment after Trauma

Understanding the deeper consequences of trauma means moving beyond surface symptoms and recognizing how it changes the way we interpret reality itself: physiologically, emotionally, and socially. Trauma isn't just stored in our minds; it becomes embedded in our nervous systems. This is where concepts such as neuroception and *polyvagal theory* become essential in explaining why survivors often feel unsafe, disconnected, or dysregulated, even in seemingly nonthreatening environments.

An extension of the mind–body connection is a physiological process known as neuroception, a term coined by Stephen Porges (2004), which refers to the brain's unconscious ability to evaluate environmental cues and determine whether we are safe. Sometimes, even when our conscious mind does not detect a threat, our body perceives one through this mechanism and launches us into a fight-or-flight response.

So, what are the sensory indicators that help us determine what is safe? For individuals with trauma histories, these internal warning systems often become distorted. Some develop hypersensitivity, where everyday stimuli feel threatening and it becomes difficult to distinguish between what warrants panic and what is benign. Others may experience desensitization, becoming emotionally numb or repeatedly exposing themselves to harm, touching the metaphorical hot stove over and over without registering pain.

Survivors of narcissistic abuse or those living with complex PTSD often experience chronic activation of neuroception, putting their nervous systems into a state of constant alert. This can manifest as generalized anxiety and an inability to relax, even in safe environments. Many of my patients express this through statements such as "I don't know how to relax" or "I don't know how I feel." They live in a state of persistent tension, which interferes with their ability to recognize when it is safe to let their guard down. As a result, it becomes difficult to form healthy attachments or connect with others. Our willingness to engage socially is largely shaped by a sense of *safe neuroception*. When that internal signaling system is broken or overactive, we may misread environments and people, often interpreting safety as threat, or vice versa.

These polyvagal-informed practices include:

- Vocal toning or humming, which stimulate the vagus nerve and support relaxation
- Self-soothing techniques, such as gentle massage or pressure-point work
- Conscious breathwork, especially diaphragmatic breathing to slow the heart rate and signal safety to the body

In essence, trauma can skew the data our body uses to assess the world. Yet with consistent therapeutic support, healthy new relationships, and the integration of regulatory practices, we can retrain both mind and body toward more adaptive patterns.

If trauma can be transmitted across generations, so too can healing. The first step, however, is awareness. Without conscious attention to how trauma manifests in our bodies and minds, these patterns may linger, silently shaping how we live, relate, and interpret the world around us.

Introspective Questions

If you're unsure whether your parent fits some of the patterns described in this chapter, consider reflecting on the following questions:

- Does my parent often talk about themselves more than they listen to or ask about me?
- Do they tend to make themselves the center of attention or treat their needs as more important than mine?
- Is guilt used, subtly or overtly, as a tool for control or manipulation?
- Does my parent rely on me to meet their emotional needs, either explicitly or implicitly?
- Have I ever been pulled into their relationship conflicts, made to take sides, or act as their confidant?
- Do I feel anxious, suffocated, or emotionally trapped when I anticipate being around them?
- Am I afraid to set boundaries with them, or do I feel it's unsafe or futile to do so?
- Were my feelings truly welcomed and validated in childhood, or were they ignored, minimized, or punished?
- What did love look like in my family growing up, and did it feel safe, or conditional?

If many of these questions resonate with you, it may be time to explore what you truly need to feel emotionally safe and supported. Acknowledging these dynamics can be the first step toward understanding your experience more clearly, and making empowered choices about how to navigate, redefine, or protect this relationship moving forward.

PART III

FINDING WELLNESS

Much of our healing begins with grief. Not just the grief that follows a loss, but the kind that creeps in when we begin to realize what we never had. We grieve the parent who never showed up for us emotionally. We grieve the childhood stage we didn't get to savor because we were too busy surviving. We grieve the image of the life we once imagined, the one we were sure we'd grow into but never did.

This kind of grief deserves our attention. It asks us to pause and feel it, not rush past or bury it. I often think of grief as a physical presence; something we carry with us, whether or not we're ready to acknowledge it. Our minds may encourage distraction or denial, but unprocessed grief doesn't dissolve; it lingers until we're willing to sit with it.

For years, I convinced myself that my family didn't struggle with mental illness. That was something that happened to other people, not us. I internalized this belief over time, likely because of my parents' consistent denial. Whenever I tried to point out patterns I thought were dysfunctional, I was met with dismissal, even ridicule. That led me to second-guess myself for a long time.

Looking back now, it's striking how many of my family members were visibly impacted by untreated mental health issues, directly or indirectly, and yet no one ever named it. We weren't that family. At least, that's what my parents projected. On the outside, they appeared polished; living in upscale condos, dining at fine restaurants, exuding class and composure. But behind closed doors, they threw objects, hurled insults, and descended into chaos that more closely resembled a daytime talk show meltdown than anything approaching stability or maturity.

The poor communication, the volatility, the silence, all of it left a mark. The day-in, day-out dysfunction frayed my nervous system like an old rope stretched too thin.

If secret-keeping is part of your family legacy, you may not feel safe asking questions or even expressing your feelings. You may not have recognized how toxic the dynamic was, particularly if it was well-hidden, and instead may have turned the blame inward: for noticing, for being different, for trying to name what others refused to see.

One way this shows up is through a chronic sense of survival mode. You might get through the day on a kind of emotional autopilot. You're not thinking about whether something brings you joy; you're just focused on getting through it. Even simple choices, like what to eat for lunch, can feel exhausting. There's no capacity for pleasure, just the grinding need to check off the next task. We exist, but we're not really living.

The good news is that these effects are not permanent. They are malleable. With therapy, reflection, and crucially, distance from those who caused the harm, healing becomes possible.

Research consistently shows that, although this may not be our first choice, separating from the narcissistic parent or partner is often essential. Otherwise, it's like disturbing a wound every time it starts to heal.

The Silent Epidemic: Understanding the Rise of Estrangement

It used to be rare to hear someone say they were estranged from a parent or sibling. It carried a quiet shame, an implication that someone had failed morally, emotionally, or socially. If family was everything, then choosing distance felt like admitting to a kind of brokenness.

And yet, more and more people are making that choice. Not impulsively or spitefully, but deliberately, after years, sometimes decades, of trying to improve the relationship.

Estrangement is no longer a whispered secret; it has become a growing phenomenon.

According to a Cornell University study, more than 25 percent of Americans are currently estranged from a member of their family

(Pillemer, 2020). Adult children are walking away from parents. Siblings are going years without speaking. Grandchildren are growing up without knowing their grandparents. And while the reasons are complex, they most often stem from long-standing patterns of emotional abuse, neglect, boundary violations, or fundamental value misalignment.

I used to think estrangement was a tragedy. Now I understand it can also be an act of self-preservation. We're living in a cultural moment that's beginning to question inherited roles.

Where once there was blind loyalty, now there is permission to ask: *Does this relationship serve my well-being?*

The rise of mental health awareness, especially surrounding trauma, narcissism, and attachment wounding, has illuminated what was once invisible. Words like "gaslighting," "enmeshment," and "emotional neglect" have entered the mainstream, providing language and validation for experiences many of us always felt but could never quite explain. With that language comes clarity, and often, heartache.

Estrangement doesn't always stem from abuse in the traditional sense. Sometimes it's death by a thousand cuts: years of being dismissed, erased, manipulated, or held to impossible expectations. Sometimes it's the unbearable weight of being assigned a role: scapegoat, golden child, caretaker, that erases who you actually are.

The truth is, family estrangement is often the result of a deep and prolonged effort to stay connected. It is a final boundary drawn after every other boundary has been crossed. One of the hardest parts of estrangement is that it is rarely honored as grief. When a parent dies, people bring casseroles and cards. When you go no-contact, they bring judgment. They ask questions meant to indict: "Have you tried reaching out?" "What if they die tomorrow?" "But she's your mother."

The world sympathizes with aging parents who are rejected by their children, but rarely with children who feel they had no choice but to walk away. The onus to explain always falls on the one who leaves. And often, the explanations don't make sense to outsiders because these wounds were never loud. They were quiet, cumulative. The kind that doesn't leave visible scars, but the kind that often cuts the deepest.

Estrangement is not just personal; it's generational. Many in our parents' generation were taught to suppress, tolerate, endure. Love was conditional. Emotions were shameful. Respect meant silence. So when a child sets boundaries, it can feel like betrayal to those who equate love with self-sacrifice.

But we are not just living our own stories; we are living the aftermath of theirs. The unhealed trauma, the unspoken pain, the silent deals made in childhood homes where the rules were clear: don't speak, don't feel, don't need.

When we walk away, it's not because we are weak or unkind. It's because we are trying not to perpetuate what broke us. Estrangement forces you to redefine what family means. It teaches you that love can come from unlikely places: chosen friends, mentors, community. It shows you that peace is sometimes more valuable than proximity. It invites you to parent yourself and to offer yourself the love, protection, and recognition you never received.

It's not a happy ending, but it's an honest one; and sometimes, honesty is the beginning of healing.

There's a word I once stumbled across that stopped me in my tracks: metanoia. In its original Greek, it means "a transformative change of heart." It signifies not just a surface-level shift but a deep inner turning, a reorientation of one's entire being.

Estrangement, while often perceived as a relational breakdown, can also serve as a profound psychological turning point. In clinical terms, metanoia is a concept rooted in Jungian psychology, describing a spontaneous restructuring of the personality that follows a period of inner crisis. Rather than signaling dysfunction, metanoia reflects the psyche's attempt to recalibrate and heal from longstanding maladaptive patterns.

For individuals who sever ties with emotionally abusive or personality-disordered parents, the process of estrangement may trigger a metanoic response: a radical shift in identity, self-perception, and relational expectations. It marks the transition from externalized validation to internalized self-trust, and from survival-based coping mechanisms (e.g., people-pleasing, emotional suppression, hypervigilance) to a more integrated and autonomous sense of self.

In my own experience, the decision to end contact with my parents initially felt destabilizing. However, what emerged in the aftermath was not collapse but reorganization. Estrangement acted as a psychological rupture that made space for new internal frameworks to develop, ones no longer dependent on the dysfunction I had normalized throughout my upbringing.

This reorganization didn't occur instantaneously. It unfolded slowly, through grief, reflection, and the reexamination of ingrained familial narratives. Over time, I came to understand that estrangement, while painful, catalyzed the process of individuation, a core tenet of psychological development. Metanoia thus became not only a clinical concept but a lived reality: a process through which I dismantled the internalized roles assigned by my family system and began constructing a more authentic identity, grounded in agency, self-awareness, and emotional clarity.

It's not just about cutting ties; it's about building new ones. Creating boundaries is not an act of rejection; it's an act of design. The blueprint for your life is no longer inherited; it's authored. Estrangement doesn't mean you stop loving someone. It means you stop allowing that love to destroy you. It's not easy, simple, or without consequence. For many of us, it's the first time we've chosen ourselves and that choice is radical, especially in a culture that tells you family is forever, no matter the cost.

Maybe the more important question is this: *What kind of family do we want to be part of?* One built on duty, silence, and survival, or one built on mutual respect, empathy, and truth?

Estrangement is not the failure of a relationship; it's the result of trying to preserve your dignity in a relationship that has already failed you. We don't always get the families we deserve, but we can learn how to become the people we needed. In that becoming, we build something better, not in spite of the pain, but through it.

The Gray Rock Method: A Tool for Managing Narcissistic Abuse

When faced with ongoing manipulation or abuse, many people turn to the Gray Rock Method as a way of coping. This strategy involves making yourself as unremarkable and uninteresting as possible, effectively discouraging emotional vampires from engaging with you. These individuals thrive on chaos, and by withholding emotional or dramatic material, you deprive them of what they crave.

In my own experience, I used to share more about my life with my mother, but I eventually realized that providing minimal information was often the safest approach. I learned this the hard way: personal stories I had trusted her with would be relayed to others, often distorted to fit her narrative. No matter how many times I asked for privacy, the breach continued. It hurt endlessly, yet I couldn't break the cycle.

When I began using the Gray Rock Method, I noticed a significant reduction in criticism and judgment. I learned to redirect conversations, focusing them on my parents and their activities, which often left me off the hook for sharing anything about myself. This approach disappointed my mother, who had grown used to juicy gossip or emotional drama, but I began to recognize that keeping the exchange bland and uneventful was the only way to protect myself.

The Gray Rock Method can also involve withdrawing attention from the manipulative person altogether. For example, when my mother would theatrically lament my father's departure, years after the fact, I would remain silent. At first, her emotions flared in anger, desperate for a response. But eventually, the lack of positive reinforcement for her theatrics led to a decrease in these behaviors; at least around me. Over time, my conversations with my parents became shorter, more vague, and emotionally neutral. Eventually, I came to the painful realization that I couldn't maintain relationships where I wasn't emotionally invested. It was simply too exhausting: either my feelings were weaponized against me, or I was forced into inauthenticity neither of which was sustainable.

As I reflected on my relationship with my parents, I realized that I had once tried to approach them from an emotional perspective. I would open up, pouring my heart out in the hope of creating mutual understanding, but my parents didn't function that way. They struggled to emotionally connect or empathize, which made my attempts feel like speaking a foreign language. This realization shifted my focus toward my own healing, independent of them. The Gray Rock Method became a functional way to protect myself, and I let go of the false hope that our relationship could ever be something it wasn't. A deep connection simply wasn't possible as far as they were concerned.

Dual Awareness: Reconnecting Mind and Body

Trauma often creates a deep rift between the mind and body as a coping mechanism. It's as if our consciousness partitions itself, protecting us from the unbearable weight of past wounds. Yet to truly heal, it's crucial to rebuild the connection between our internal and external worlds, between our body and our mind. One powerful way to do this is through a process called Dual Awareness.

Dual Awareness is a technique used in trauma therapy that helps us rebuild this vital mind–body connection. The "dual" aspect of the process involves simultaneously noticing the safety cues in your environment while tuning in to any uncomfortable emotions or physical sensations in your body. This practice allows us to build tolerance for distress and gradually recondition our sense of threat. By learning to hold both of these awarenesses at once, we begin to reshape our relationship with discomfort and danger.

For example, you might begin by focusing on something stable and unchanging in your environment, like the green grass outside your window. The unshifting nature of the grass can offer a sense of safety. After grounding yourself in this, you would then bring your awareness to your body; perhaps noticing the flexing of your hands or the rise and fall of your chest as you breathe. You might even bring up a pleasant memory, allow that feeling to settle, and then shift your attention back to the sounds around you.

There's no one-size-fits-all approach to Dual Awareness. It can evolve based on your needs and preferences, but the essential goal remains the same: to create new associations in your mind that allow you to engage more fully with your body and your environment. This practice helps you feel more at ease within yourself and with the world around you.

For much of my life, I was disconnected from my body. It started early, growing up in a home where feeling safe enough to let go was nearly impossible. I avoided situations where I would have to relax, like nap time in school. I couldn't close my eyes and be vulnerable as a small child. I had to be aware and observant. I watched the other children around me with fascination as they effortlessly gave in to the moment, falling asleep without fear.

As a teenager, this hypervigilance took on physical manifestations. I was hypercritical of myself, struggling with weight, or hugging my purse in my lap as a protective shield whenever I could. I didn't realize at the time that these behaviors were symptoms of deeper issues. I was always on edge, subconsciously preparing for something terrible to happen. There was no space for living, only for surviving. I felt unworthy of being seen, convinced that others were always more important than I was. I learned to stay alert, never knowing when my words or actions might invite criticism, punishment, or just the familiar feeling of invisibility.

Survival mode disconnects us from our bodies, pushing us into a more cognitively oriented space. Our minds become consumed with worry and fear, creating loops of anxiety that prevent us from being present in the moment. But by developing Dual Awareness, we begin to reconnect with ourselves; physically and mentally, like awakening for the first time. We stop merely surviving and start living again.

Grounding: Reconnecting with the Present Moment

Much like Dual Awareness, the therapeutic technique of grounding helps us stay connected to the present moment, even when our trauma pulls us toward the past or the future. Grounding uses our environment to help us regain balance, reminding us that we can return to the here and now, a place of safety and stability.

For those with complex trauma, the past and future can feel like unbreakable loops, constantly pulling us away from the present. Grounding offers a vital counterbalance. However, it requires a sense of safety; without that safety, the instinct to dissociate can remain strong.

Grounding techniques typically involve engaging our five senses. This allows us to anchor ourselves to the physical world around us and reconnect with our bodies. One common grounding exercise is to stand barefoot on the earth, noticing the sensation of the ground beneath your feet. You might also focus on your surroundings; what you see, hear, smell, taste, and feel. Each of these sensory experiences brings you back into the present.

Another grounding technique involves tapping. By lightly tapping your fingertips on pressure points such as your temples or forehead, you can create a calming rhythm that helps to center your mind. This rhythmic motion provides a safe and soothing stimulus, helping your mind focus on something grounding instead of getting lost in intrusive thoughts, flashbacks, or overwhelming emotions.

These grounding techniques work by narrowing your focus, blocking out mental noise, and redirecting your attention to something safe and immediate. They help interrupt the pattern of rumination that can amplify anxiety and fear, guiding you back to the present moment and fostering a sense of calm.

Self-Care: Nourishing the Soul

Those who have gone through narcissistic abuse often carry an invisible weight: the guilt of tending to their own needs. Self-care can feel selfish, indulgent, even dangerous, especially when love was conditioned on how useful you were to others. In homes where your worth was tied to sacrifice, the simple act of resting, eating well, or saying "no" can trigger a deep, unspoken fear: *What if I stop earning love and start losing it?*

For a long time, I felt that fear.

Over the years, I've learned that one of the most effective tools for managing complicated grief and loss; especially the unique ache that comes with estranged or distorted parental relationships isn't revenge, rumination, or repression. It's self-care.

This means nurturing my soul; whether that's exploring a curiosity, speaking to myself compassionately, or getting lost in a new novel. I used to think self-care was just bubble baths and face masks; however, I now understand it as something far deeper: a radical act of repair, of reclaiming the relationship I have with myself.

When I say self-care, I don't just mean the kind that comes in pretty packaging or with Instagrammable aesthetics. I'm talking about radical, soul-level care. The kind that conveys: *You matter. You're allowed to exist on your own terms now.*

Sometimes that meant creating a calming routine; other times, it meant traveling to places I had dreamed of. I had finally given myself permission to experience joy. I stopped postponing the good things in life, realizing no one else was going to deliver them. I had to give them to myself.

Physical self-care, in particular, was a foreign concept during my childhood. Growing up in an environment that lacked healthy habits, I never learned the value of caring for my body. As I began to prioritize it, I saw the benefits unfold. Physical well-being became key to my overall functioning and vitality. The dissociation that stemmed from my upbringing had left me disconnected from my body, but by learning to tune in and strengthen it, I began to rebuild my sense of self-worth.

Strength training, of all things, became a turning point. There was something sacred in it. In a world where so many things felt unpredictable, this gave me control. One rep at a time, I felt my body growing resilient. My muscles became quiet proof that I was rebuilding from the inside out. I wasn't just lifting weights, I was lifting myself out of patterns of self-abandonment.

Even food, once an afterthought, became a form of love. I began eating not to cope or restrict, but to nourish. There is an element of mindfulness in what I now choose. Each healthy, balanced choice to fuel my body became a declaration: *I matter.* And slowly, that message started to sink in.

This wasn't about perfection or routine for its own sake. It was about reconnecting to a truth I hadn't been told as a child: that my well-being wasn't optional, that tending to myself; mind, body, and spirit, was not selfish, but essential.

One important aspect of self-care for the offspring of those with NPD or BPD is providing oneself with loving discipline. This entails respecting ourselves, honoring our word to ourselves when we've set a goal, and maintaining boundaries even when it's difficult. This practice becomes necessary in the reparenting process.

Over time, this evolved into a feedback loop. The more I invested in self-care, the more it returned to me in strength, in stability, in peace. What once felt foreign became second nature; what once seemed indulgent became necessary. Over time, this practice became a positive feedback loop: the more I devoted myself to self-care, the more it nurtured me in return.

Examining Ambition and Burnout

Burnout isn't just a result of working too hard. It's often the cumulative impact of working too hard for too long to prove your worth.

People with childhood trauma often carry invisible contracts; unspoken beliefs that they must constantly earn their right to exist. When love or attention was conditional growing up, we learned to overcompensate. We became master achievers, expert caretakers, and relentless perfectionists, not because we're selfish or obsessed with success, but because we're scared. Scared that if we stop performing, we'll stop mattering.

I didn't burn out because I lacked strength. I burned out because I never felt like I was enough without being strong.

The connection between trauma and burnout is well documented. Survivors often struggle to regulate distress, so they pour themselves into achievement as a form of control. Add in societal expectations, particularly for women, to be endlessly competent and emotionally available, and it becomes a perfect storm. We work twice as hard to prove ourselves, then twice as hard to sustain it, all while denying ourselves rest or recognition.

I began to see the signs: mounting anxiety with no clear trigger, chronic fatigue paired with insomnia, and an inner critic so loud it drowned out every accomplishment. On the outside, I had a polished life: a strong résumé, a well-curated image, a career I had poured myself into. But underneath it all was a worn-out version of me, holding everything up on bruised and trembling shoulders.

Healing began when I stopped trying to earn my existence. I still care deeply about my work. I still chase goals. But now, my ambition is rooted in self-respect, not self-erasure. I've begun to see success as something I create *with* myself, not *at* the expense of myself.

Ambition is no longer about proving my value; it's about aligning with my values. I've learned to rest without guilt and to say no without shame. To recognize that boundaries are not barriers; they're bridges back to myself. My ambition still burns, but it no longer consumes me.

If you, too, find yourself constantly overworking, overgiving, overproving, I urge you to pause. Ask yourself: What am I really chasing? Whose voice is driving me? What would it feel like to let that go?

Because here's the truth: you are not a machine. You are not your productivity. Your rest is not laziness. Your joy is not indulgent. Your worth was never meant to be earned. It already exists.

Breath Work: Regulating Our Nervous System

At first, I dismissed breathwork as overly simplistic or ineffective. I'd tried it briefly before, only to invalidate it. But I now realize that my resistance was rooted in a fear of tuning in to myself. I was terrified of what I might find in the stillness, afraid of my own body and the emotions I had been avoiding.

I didn't realize how often I was holding my breath until I started paying attention to it.

For years, I lived in a state of subtle to significant tension: shoulders tight, jaw clenched, breathing shallow. It was my body's way of staying on alert, a habit formed long ago in a home where the emotional weather could change at any moment. I didn't know I was stuck in fight-or-flight; I just thought it was normal to feel that way all the time. That's where breathwork came in.

As a therapist working with pain management, I came to understand how breathwork could also be used as a powerful tool in healing trauma. Through focused breathing, I learned to regulate my heart rate and emotions, effectively using my breath as a remote control to manage my responses. No longer was I a prisoner to my body's reactions; I regained control, finding peace in the rhythm of my own breath.

It began simply by noticing my breath. In through the nose, out through the mouth in a slower, deeper, fuller rhythm. What I found was astonishing: the more I breathed with intention, the more my body softened. My mind quieted. My heart stopped racing. I had never realized that something so basic and accessible could be a gateway to safety, clarity, and even healing.

Breathwork can take many forms, from box breathing, a visual method that guides your inhales and exhales, to the traditional 4-7-8 breathing technique, in which you inhale for four seconds, hold for seven, and exhale for eight. Controlled breathing, especially practices like diaphragmatic breathing or box breathing, activates the parasympathetic nervous system, which helps reduce anxiety, lower cortisol levels, and improve focus and emotional regulation.

The key to effective breathwork is ensuring that the exhalation is longer than the inhalation, which activates the relaxation response in the nervous system. As I trained myself to breathe more deeply from my diaphragm, instead of relying on my usual shallow chest breaths, I saw a significant reduction in anxiety and panic.Breath is the one bodily function that is both automatic and voluntary. That means it's a bridge, a direct link between the unconscious (where trauma lives) and the conscious (where healing happens). When we consciously slow and deepen our breathing, we send a signal to the nervous system: *It's okay to relax. You're safe now.*

For many years, I believed that the impact my parents had on me was strictly emotional. But as I began researching the mind-body connection, I realized that my chronic exhaustion, inflammation, and even skin conditions weren't just random. They were physical echoes of the stress I had endured, deep inside my cells.

Naming this experience gave me a new kind of clarity: my body was carrying a story I hadn't yet told. By using breathwork to address oxidative stress and its role in trauma, I began to treat myself differently, not just emotionally, but biologically. I learned to support my nervous system, to feed myself with care, and to stop running the constant race for approval. Because healing isn't just about changing how we think; it's about healing how we live in our bodies.

In one 2017 study published in Frontiers in Psychology (Ma et al., 2017), participants who practiced slow, deep breathing for just a few minutes a day experienced measurable reductions in stress and improvements in mood and well-being.

Breathwork also became a spiritual experience for me. A form of communion with myself. It didn't require equipment, money, or a therapist. Just a willingness to pause, tune in, and exhale. It's hard to underestimate the power of that. After years of feeling voiceless, even breath became a form of reclaiming space: each inhale a declaration: *I deserve to be here*; each exhale a release: *I no longer need to carry what wasn't mine.*

In breath, I found a home inside myself.

Meditative Moments: Cultivating Stillness

For much of my life, I equated silence with threat. In a house filled with tension, quiet often preceded a storm. So I learned to fill the space; to talk fast, move faster, stay busy. Stillness felt unfamiliar, even threatening.

But as I stepped deeper into healing, I began to see the quiet not as a void but as an invitation. Alongside grounding practices like breathwork and somatic awareness, I started cultivating meditative moments—not with incense or mantras, but with intention. I would soften my pace, slow my speech, and allow myself to simply *be*. It wasn't about perfection; it was about presence.

Sometimes I would sit in the soft light of early morning, letting the hum of the world wash over me. Other times I'd lie back and let music flood my senses, not as background noise, but as something to feel. I began to notice textures in sound I had never paid attention to before: the grain of a voice, the quiver of a violin, the breath between piano keys. These moments weren't just peaceful; they were portals back to myself.

What surprised me most was the power of witnessing my thoughts without obeying them. Not every impulse needed a reaction. Not every emotion required a plan. I could simply let them float by like clouds across a still sky. Learning to pause, really pause, felt radical. I stopped bracing against discomfort and started sitting with it. And in that sitting, I began to find strength.

Where I once believed that distress needed to be fixed immediately or avoided entirely, I began to understand that emotions are waves: they rise, they crest, they pass. I wasn't drowning; I just hadn't learned to float.

This was one of the most liberating shifts of my healing journey: realizing that I am not at the mercy of my thoughts or feelings. I can be their observer instead of their captive. I can choose the rhythm of my inner world.

In stillness, I discovered safety. In quiet, I found clarity. In learning to sit with myself, I finally began to *hear* myself.

Choosing Our Responses: Empowerment Through Awareness

This brings me to the idea of choosing our responses. Viktor Frankl, a Holocaust survivor, psychiatrist, and author, said, "Between stimulus and response, there is space. In that space, we have the power to choose our response. In our response lies our growth and our freedom." I return to this often when I think about the way my life is unfolding. What do I want my life to look like, and how might I be unknowingly standing in my own way because of past experiences?

For example, do I make assumptions about others based on my past experiences rather than seeing them for who they truly are? Frankl's words help me understand that we can choose how we respond, regardless of the circumstances. Sometimes, even choosing not to engage or respond can be the most powerful reaction.

Frankl's insight resonates with a similar concept from Japanese writer and anime scriptwriter Kinoko Nasu, who said, "An entire sea of water cannot sink a ship unless it gets inside the ship." This speaks to our power to determine how much hardship, negativity, or suffering we allow to impact us. We have the choice to compartmentalize or protect ourselves through our own consciousness. We may not control the chaos around us, but we can choose whether we let it flood our inner lives.

I think of this concept when I'm faced with negative situations or environments. It aligns with the therapeutic principle of creating a "Teflon mind," a term coined by Marsha Linehan, creator of Dialectical Behavior Therapy. Essentially, it means allowing external events to slide off us without letting them infiltrate our inner world. Just like water off a duck's back, we can choose how much energy we invest in things outside our control.

To me, this is what empowerment really looks like, not loud declarations or constant striving, but the quiet discipline of choosing how we show up, again and again. Even when it's hard. Especially when it's hard.

Development of Self-Awareness: The Art of Conscious Living

Building self-awareness has been both emboldening and humbling. It's easy to overlook its importance because it rarely makes a dramatic entrance. It shows up quietly, in the pause before a reaction, in the way we speak to ourselves when no one else is listening, in the questions we dare to ask about our own motives.

At its core, self-awareness is the art of paying attention, really paying attention, to our thoughts, behaviors, and patterns without flinching. It means looking in the mirror not just to admire or criticize, but to understand. To ask: *Where did this reaction come from? What am I feeling underneath this anger, this silence, this urgency to be perfect or pleasing or invisible?*

It's not always easy. Sometimes self-awareness stings, but it's also the only real path to freedom. Without it, we live on autopilot, reliving the same cycles, reacting from old scripts, mistaking triggers for truth.

The biggest transformation I've experienced through cultivating self-awareness is learning to live more consciously. Rather than simply surviving the day or rushing from task to task, I've begun to notice my environment, my emotions, the tiny shifts in my body when something doesn't feel quite right. I've traded numbness for presence.

Even when discomfort arises, I try not to run. I try to stay, observe, and reflect. What is this teaching me? Why am I clenching my jaw right now? Why did that comment bother me so much? What does this situation remind me of?

There's no perfection in this practice; just a deepening. I still struggle at times with old habits rooted in trauma: overworking, second-guessing myself, overexplaining. Instead of punishing myself for falling into those patterns, I notice them with compassion. I name them. And then I decide: *Is this helping me grow, or is it keeping me stuck?*

This is where mindfulness meets accountability. The more self-aware I become, the less I live in emotional reactivity. I can separate fact from feeling, pause before acting, and choose responses that align with who I want to be, not just who I was taught to be.

Self-awareness is also where I've found the courage to celebrate my growth. It's easy to focus on what still needs fixing, but it's just as important to honor how far I've come. To say: *I handled that better than I would have last year. I'm proud of how I showed up. I'm healing.*

This practice of mindfulness allows me to differentiate between my emotions and the facts at hand, preventing me from misinterpreting my surroundings or acting impulsively. It helps me live with integrity and purpose, guided by intentional choices rather than reactive patterns.

Despite still grappling with perfectionism at times, I shine a light on those tendencies and make conscious decisions. I ask myself: *Will this bring me closer to what I want, or further from it?*

Living with this level of consciousness isn't about becoming a new person. It's about becoming more yourself beneath the noise, the survival strategies, and the self-doubt. It's about waking up to your life while you're still living it. And that, to me, is the truest kind of freedom.

Learning as a Tool: The Power of Curiosity

When trauma leaves you fragmented and questioning your own reality, learning can serve as a lifeline. In my experience with healing, I began to embrace learning as a tool for growth. This wasn't about formal education but rather about cultivating curiosity without the pressure of grades or external expectations. It became a way to deepen my understanding of the world and of myself.

Learning something new, even something small, each day became its own form of therapy. It expanded my sense of agency. It gave me vocabulary for my pain and tools for change. It helped me articulate my truth, and in doing so, I began to feel safer sharing myself with others. I was no longer just reacting to life; I was actively shaping it.

Reading philosophy and psychology offered a profound sense of belonging. I was no longer alone in my questions about the world or myself. Socrates' relentless inquiry, Confucius's pursuit of virtue, and bell hooks's meditations on love and justice all served as companions in my internal dialogue. Through them, I found echoes of my own thoughts, ones I had long buried or feared were too strange or heavy to say aloud.

Alchemy and Stoicism, in particular, left a lasting mark. Alchemy gave me a powerful metaphor for healing: the transformation of base metals into gold. This ancient science was less about actual gold and more about the inner transformation that occurs when we pass through life's fires and emerge wiser. It taught me that difficulty was not a detour from growth—it was the growth. The emotional "heat" I endured through loss, estrangement, and grief was not meaningless; it was a crucible.

Stoicism, by contrast, offered structure and clarity. It reminded me that while I couldn't control other people's behavior, my parents' inability to acknowledge my pain, my brother's judgment, the silence that replaced once-close relationships, I could control my response. I began to focus on what was mine to carry and put down what wasn't. One of the most powerful Stoic teachings I embraced was *equanimity* the ability to maintain emotional balance in the face of chaos. This idea mirrored Buddhist inner stillness, offering a way to maintain stability.

These teachings became more than intellectual interests; they were companions in solitude. They helped me metabolize my experiences, turning pain into perspective and confusion into clarity. They taught me that wisdom isn't just found in surviving hardship; it's found in making meaning of it.

Through this process, I started to invest in myself, not only in terms of emotional growth but also in reclaiming a sense of self-worth that had been long eroded by trauma. Every book I read, every new idea I entertained, felt like an act of self-affirmation.

Curiosity reminded me that we are all works in progress; unfinished, evolving, and full of potential. And maybe that's the most powerful thing of all: the permission to remain a student of life, always expanding, always becoming.

Spirituality: A Journey of Self-Discovery Through Astrology

The deeper I delved into philosophy and self-inquiry, the more curious I became about what else might illuminate my inner world. I had long been drawn to questions that didn't have clear answers, questions that science couldn't fully satisfy and traditional religion had never quite answered for me. That's when I turned to something I had quietly been intrigued by since childhood: astrology.

At first, I approached it with measured skepticism, unsure whether I was searching for meaning or simply craving connection. But there was also wonder; an openness to see whether this ancient practice might reflect truths I hadn't yet unearthed. Since I couldn't control how things unfolded with my parents or change their behavior, I decided to focus on understanding myself.

"When one is lost, seek information," I told myself.

Astrology wasn't new to me. My grandfather used to pull out his worn astrology books during family gatherings, pointing out quirks of each sign that made us laugh and nod in eerie agreement. "Leos crave attention," he'd say, or "Cancers have long limbs and tender hearts." Even as a child, I felt there was something mystical in those pages; some invisible thread connecting our personalities, our paths, and perhaps even our pain. While I never embraced organized religion, astrology offered a way to explore something bigger than myself without dogma. It felt intuitive and wide open.

I made an appointment with an astrologer. I remember the setting clearly: a narrow stone path flanked by shops selling sage bundles, salt lamps, and crystals that glittered like fragments of frozen stardust. His office smelled of incense and old wood, its walls adorned with oil paintings, mandalas, and symbols of the cosmos. It felt like stepping into a sacred space between the seen and the unseen. Buddhist- and Hermetic-inspired décor covered the walls. He greeted me warmly, printed out my birth chart, and studied it with the intensity of someone reading a secret text. After slowly tracing his fingertips along the lines of the paper, he looked up.

"You experienced emotional abandonment as a child," he said.

The words hit me harder than I anticipated. They rang out like a bell; not in a dramatic, theatrical way, but in a truth-cutting way. This was a sentence I had long felt but had never heard aloud. Until that moment, I hadn't fully understood that abandonment doesn't always look like someone leaving. It can be quieter. It can be being looked at but never truly seen. It can mean that others fail to meet your emotional needs, don't value your presence, break promises without apology, or dismiss your needs without a second thought. His words cracked open something inside me that had been waiting to be acknowledged. Hearing that sentiment from him felt validating.

He went on: "You've struggled with a deep sense of inferiority, and yet you keep showing up. You need to see yourself clearly now. You are not your past. Stop waiting for them to validate your worth. Prove them wrong, or better yet, prove yourself right."

That reading was more than a prediction; it was a mirror. Whether astrology is real in the scientific sense didn't matter to me in that moment. What mattered was how deeply it resonated. It was the first time someone had connected the dots between my inner chaos and outer choices in such a visceral way. It was therapy, myth, and self-confrontation rolled into one. It helped me name the grief I carried, not just for what had happened, but for what never did.

That session didn't magically solve everything, but it did something important: it gave me permission to stop waiting for someone else, especially my parents, to change. It handed the pen back to me. I could write a new story, one not dictated by pain but by possibility.

That day, I made a promise to myself: I would move forward, no longer shackled to old wounds or haunted by the echo of those unspoken apologies. I would seek meaning not from those who hurt me, but from the power I had to heal. Whether written in the stars or found in the void, that insight gave me something rare: the reminder that what I went through was real, and the courage to begin again.

Non-Attachment: Embracing Freedom Through Letting Go

As I continued to write, to reflect, and to validate my own story, I began to notice that the power I had once given away; hoping for recognition, waiting for apologies, chasing closure; slowly returned to me. I was no longer writing for justice, revenge, or approval. I was writing for freedom. That freedom deepened when I began to explore the concept of non-attachment.

Buddhism teaches that suffering arises not from pain itself but from our attachment to how things should be. Non-attachment doesn't mean we stop caring or disengage from life, but it does mean loosening our grip on outcomes, identities, and expectations. It means allowing life to unfold without needing to control or define every part of it.

Attachment had kept me tangled in sadness, not just the sadness of what had happened, but of what never happened. I had spent so long hoping my parents would change, clinging to the idea that one day they'd see me clearly. But this hope, disguised as love, had become a quiet form of suffering. It kept me rooted in the past and blinded me to the present.

Non-attachment helped me focus less on what my parents should have done or how they should have treated me. Instead, I turned my focus inward, learning to reparent myself and release the ego. It meant understanding that I could still love my parents and also acknowledge their limitations, or that I could move forward without dragging my pain behind me.

Letting go of the desire for my parents to change wasn't easy, but it was necessary. Forgiveness, in my case, didn't mean reestablishing contact or expecting an apology; it meant releasing the emotional hold their actions had over me. By taking away the meaning I had assigned to their behavior, their actions no longer had power over me. They simply were.

This shift allowed me to stop focusing on what they hadn't done and focus instead on my own peace.

Much of this peace came from gratitude for small things. I began to savor the quiet moments: the way the morning light cast rainbows on the wall, or the smell of the crackling fire on a Friday night; like soft reminders that life was still unfolding and that I was still here.

They reminded me that healing doesn't always come in waves. It can arrive in flickers, in subtle shifts, in the quiet beauty of the everyday. These moments didn't erase the pain of the past, but they helped me believe in the possibility of joy again. Not as a distant destination, but as something I could glimpse right here, right now.

Finding Your Voice: From Silence to Empowerment

There was a time when I made myself small to make others comfortable or to avoid conflict. I stayed quiet to keep the peace, confused silence for strength, and mistook being agreeable for being loved. But beneath that quiet lived a pulse of truth, waiting to be unearthed.

Finding my voice wasn't a single moment, it was a slow, bold unraveling. I started speaking up in rooms where I used to shrink. I said "no" without justifying. I asked for what I needed instead of hoping someone would guess correctly. It felt unnatural at first, like wearing shoes that didn't quite fit.

Some people responded positively, while others faded from my life. But I kept going, because the more I honored my truth, the less space I had for relationships that required me to abandon it.

The turning point wasn't in being heard, it was in realizing I was worth listening to. My voice, once buried under years of people-pleasing and fear, became my compass. I no longer needed to scream to be seen; I only needed to stand in my truth. In doing so, I found not just my voice, but my power.

The people who mattered respected my boundaries, and this brought a shift in both my professional and personal relationships. I realized that my long-standing lack of self-belief had allowed others to follow suit. That realization made change necessary.

A big part of finding my voice came through singing with my husband. It had been years since I'd done that with anyone. He demonstrated a warmth I wasn't used to; an unconditional positive regard toward me. He didn't let me hide the way I was used to doing with most others.

We began a new tradition: cozying up on the couch with his acoustic guitar, singing our favorite songs together. Initially, I was petrified. Singing in front of him, someone I think so highly of, felt like complete exposure, and I made countless excuses not to do it. He gently nudged me to sing anyway. I needed that push from someone if I was going to excavate myself from the shell that had formed over the years.

Although we were just singing at home for ourselves, it felt like a huge step. For so long, my voice had been suppressed. With his encouragement, I found the nerve to let it out again. Singing became a form of self-love a chance to nurture myself, something I'd neglected in the past.

One of the most transformative ways I reclaimed my voice was also through writing. Putting my story on the page gave me the distance I needed to revisit old memories with new eyes; less reactive, more reflective. As I shaped this narrative, I began to untangle the pain from the past and view it with greater clarity and compassion. In doing so, I gave myself something I had been seeking for years: acknowledgment. Writing became a form of self-witnessing, offering the validation my parents never could. Slowly, I came to understand that the validation I needed didn't have to come from them. It had to come from me.

DR. ASHLEY QUIROZ, PSY.D.

The Gift of Living: Healing Through Simplicity and Self-Compassion

Healing is not an event; it is a journey back to the essence of who we are. It's a return to simplicity: slowing down, breathing deeply, and embracing the finery of the present moment. It's the quiet rebellion of letting go of complexity and surrendering to stillness. It is, perhaps most profoundly, a reawakening to patience: patience with the world, patience with others, but above all, patience with ourselves.

True healing doesn't come from grand gestures or dramatic transformations. It emerges through consistency; the gentle rhythm of small, intentional actions that nurture us day by day. It thrives in stillness, in the pauses we take to reconnect with our own hearts and souls, without distraction or expectation. It is an act of radical acceptance: accepting others as they are and, most importantly, accepting ourselves, flaws and all.

In sharing my story, my hope is that you find an invitation to explore your own. In doing so, may you find the courage to free yourself from the shackles of what has held you back in the past. We must remember that healing can be achieved even without hearing I'm sorry from anyone. Your own acknowledgment and validation are the most powerful affirmations you'll ever receive. Forgive yourself for setting boundaries, for saying goodbye when needed, and for following your intuition. Grant yourself the grace to learn, to evolve, and to be who you were always meant to be.

Your parents may have given you life, but it is in your hands, and yours alone, to give yourself the gift of truly living.

I will carry my parents in my heart each day, holding their memory in a space where love and grief intertwine. I will love them from afar. I will mourn the connection that could have been, and yet I will find peace in the love I have for those who truly see me: my husband, our friends, and the creatures who fill our home with joy.

I will not be perfect, but I will live with authenticity and honor my values, knowing they are mine to uphold. I will practice empathy without expectation, giving freely, but always with the understanding that it must flow from a well full within myself. When the shadow of spite creeps in, I will choose to serve, to lift others, and to extend love where it's needed most.

I will not dwell on what could have been. Instead, I will care for myself with the tenderness I once longed for. I will nourish the parts of me that were once ignored, and I will embrace the fullness of my being with open arms.

In the end, healing is the gift we give ourselves. The gift of living fully, unencumbered by the past and rooted in the love that we, and only we, can cultivate within.

I will love with depth. I will grow with grace.

And I will sing.

Legal Disclaimer

This memoir contains the author's personal memories, perceptions, and subjective impressions. It is a work of personal recollection, and, as such, certain events are described as the author remembers them; memory is inherently fallible and may be incomplete, inaccurate, or affected by the passage of time. For purposes of privacy, confidentiality, and narrative coherence, the author has altered, combined, or omitted names, identifying details, timelines, locations, and events.

The views, opinions, and interpretations expressed herein are solely those of the author and are not presented as verifiable statements of fact regarding any individual's character, conduct, motives, or behavior. Any resemblance to real persons, living or deceased, is based on the author's subjective experience and is not intended, nor should it be construed, as factual representation or assertion about those individuals.

The author expressly disclaims any intention to defame, harm, disparage, or misrepresent any person, entity, or group. No statements in this work should be interpreted as allegations of wrongdoing or factual claims about any identifiable individual. Additionally, nothing in this memoir is intended to constitute medical, psychological, therapeutic, or professional advice. Any references to health, trauma, treatment, or healing reflect the author's personal experiences and should not be relied upon as guidance or instruction; readers should seek the advice of qualified professionals for any such concerns.

Bibliography

Bateson, G., Jackson, D. D., Haley, J., & Weakland, J. (1956). Toward a theory of schizophrenia. *Behavioral Science, 1*(4), 251-264.

Blow, C. M. (2012, September 20). I know why the caged bird shrieks. *Campaign Stops.* https://archive.nytimes.com/campaignstops.blogs.nytimes.com/2012/09/19/blow-i-know- why-the-caged-bird-shrieks/

Bramley, E. V. (2023, April 12). The trauma doctor: Gabor Maté on happiness, hope, and how to heal our deepest wounds. *The Guardian.* https://www.theguardian.com/lifeandstyle/2023/apr/12/the-trauma-doctor-gabor-mate-on-happiness-hope-and-how-to-heal-our-deepest-wounds

Campbell, S. (2019). *But it's your family...* Morgan James Publishing.

Cattane, N., Rossi, R., Lanfredi, M., & Cattaneo, A. (2017). Borderline personality disorder and childhood trauma: Exploring the affected biological systems and mechanisms. *BMC Psychiatry, 17*(1), 221. https://doi.org/10.1186/s12888-017-1383-2

Chapman, J., Jamil, R. T., & Fleisher, C. (2022). Borderline personality disorder. *National Library of Medicine; StatPearls Publishing.* https://www.ncbi.nlm.nih.gov/books/NBK430883/

Eriksen, J. K. D., Coello, K., Stanislaus, S., Kjærstad, H. L., Sletved, K. S. O., McIntyre, R. S., Faurholt-Jepsen, M., Miskowiak, K. K., Poulsen, H. E., Kessing, L. V., & Vinberg, M. (2022). Associations between childhood maltreatment and oxidative nucleoside damage in affective disorders. *European Psychiatry, 65*(1), e46. https://doi.org/10.1192/j.eurpsy.2022.2300

Herman, J. L., Perry, J. C., & van der Kolk, B. A. (1989). Childhood trauma in borderline personality disorder. *American Journal of Psychiatry, 146*(4), 490–495. https://doi.org/10.1176/ajp.146.4.490

Jung, C. G. (1968). *Psychology and alchemy* (2nd ed., R. F. C. Hull, Trans.). In H. Read, M. Fordham, G. Adler, & W. McGuire (Eds.), *The collected works of C. G. Jung* (Vol. 12). Princeton University Press. (Original work published 1953)

Levy, K. N. (2012). Subtypes, dimensions, levels, and mental states in narcissism and narcissistic personality disorder. *Journal of Clinical Psychology, 68*(8), 886 897. https://doi.org/10.1002/jclp.21893

Ma, G., Fan, H., Shen, C., & Wang, W. (2016). Genetic and neuroimaging features of personality disorders: State of the art. *Neuroscience Bulletin, 32*(3), 286–306. https://doi.org/10.1007/s12264-016-0027-8

Ma, X., Yue, Z., Gong, Z., Zhang, H., Duan, N., Shi, Y., Wei, G., & Li, Y. (2017). The effect of diaphragmatic breathing on attention, negative affect, and stress in healthy adults. *Frontiers in Psychology, 8*, 874. https://doi.org/10.3389/fpsyg.2017.00874

Macfie, J., & Swan, S. A. (2009). Representation of the caregiver-child relationship and of the self, and emotion regulation in the narratives of young children whose mothers have borderline personality disorder. *Development and Psychopathology, 21*(4), 993–1011.

Pillemer, K. (2020). *Fault lines: Fractured families and how to mend them.* Avery.

Porges, S. W. (2004). Neuroception: A subconscious system for detecting threats and safety. *Zero to Three, 24*(5), 19–24.

Porges, S. W. (2011). *The polyvagal theory: Neurophysiological foundations of emotions, attachment, communication, and self-regulation.* W. W. Norton & Company.

Russ, E., Shedler, J., Bradley, R., & Westen, D. (2008). Refining the construct of narcissistic personality disorder: Diagnostic criteria and subtypes. *The American Journal of Psychiatry, 165*(11), 1473–1481. https://doi.org/10.1176/appi.ajp.2008.07030376

Stepp, S. D., Whalen, D. J., Pilkonis, P. A., Hipwell, A. E., & Levine, M. D. (2012). Children of mothers with borderline personality disorder: Identifying parenting behaviors as potential targets for intervention. *Personality Disorders, 3*(1), 76–91. https://doi.org/10.1037/a0023081

Treating PTSD and Traumatic Invalidation. (2023, October 6). *NICABM.* https://www.nicabm.com/traumatic-invalidation/

Tracy, N. (2021, December 17). Gaslighting definition, techniques, and being gaslighted. *HealthyPlace.* Retrieved April 22, 2024, from https://www.healthyplace.com/abuse/emotional-psychological-abuse/gaslighting-definition-techniques-and-being-gaslighted

Unpacking "Traumatic Invalidation." (n.d.). *The Shiftless Wanderer*. Retrieved April 22, 2024, from https://theshiftlesswanderer.com/blog/unpacking-traumatic-invalidation

Zajenkowski, M., & Gignac, G. E. (2021, April). Narcissism and intelligence among couples: Why are narcissistic women perceived as intelligent by their romantic partners? *Journal of Personality and Individual Differences, 172*, 110579. https://doi.org/10.1016/j.paid.2020.110579

Zhang, T., Chow, A., Wang, L., Dai, Y., & Xiao, Z. (2012). The role of childhood traumatic experience in personality disorders in China. *Comprehensive Psychiatry, 53*(6), 829–836. https://doi.org/10.1016/j.comppsych.2011.10.004

www.ingramcontent.com/pod-product-compliance
Lightning Source LLC
Chambersburg PA
CBHW020455030426
42337CB00011B/121